American
Talk

Other Books by Robert Hendrickson

Human Words

The Literary Life and Other Curiosities

More Cunning Than Man

The Grand Emporiums

Lewd Food

The Ocean Almanac

American Talk

The Words and Ways of American Dialects

Robert Hendrickson

VIKING

VIKING
Viking Penguin Inc., 40 West 23rd Street,
New York, New York 10010, U.S.A.
Penguin Books Ltd, Harmondsworth,
Middlesex, England
Penguin Books Australia Ltd, Ringwood,
Victoria, Australia
Penguin Books Canada Limited, 2801 John Street,
Markham, Ontario, Canada L3R 1B4
Penguin Books (N.Z.) Ltd, 182–190 Wairau Road,
Auckland 10, New Zealand

First published in 1986 by Viking Penguin Inc.
Published simultaneously in Canada

Grateful acknowledgment is made for permission to reproduce
the maps of Appalachia and Gullah Country.
Copyright © 1977, 1985 by The New York Times Company.
Reprinted by permission.

LIBRARY OF CONGRESS CATALOGING IN PUBLICATION DATA
Hendrickson, Robert, 1933–
American talk.
1. English language—Dialects—United States.
2. Americanisms.   3. English language—Spoken English—
United States.   I. Title.
PE2841.H38   1986   427′.973   86–40119
ISBN 0–670–81330–3

Printed in the United States of America by
R.R. Donnelley & Sons Company, Harrisonburg, Virginia
Set in Baskerville
Designed by Ann Gold

For my daughter, Lauren Starre

I hear America singing, the varied carols I hear,
. . . their strong melodious songs.
—Walt Whitman
Leaves of Grass

Contents

Preface

✦

Though our best scholars have studied American dialects systematically for about a century now, there has, to my knowledge, never been a full-length book on the subject for the general reader. My effort owes much to the dedicated dialectologists who have produced a large body of brilliant technical studies in a relatively infant field; this debt is acknowledged throughout these pages, but I have depended to a large extent on my own ear and what I've heard in extensive travels through the country during the past ten years. If my ear disputes those of the eminent scholars, or does not confirm their findings, I have at least noted this, though I am fully aware that I am more likely to be wrong than they. I would like to thank individually all the many people, specialists and laymen, who have helped me in the several years it took to complete this book, but space doesn't permit that pleasure. Special thanks must be given, however, to my editors, Barbara Burn and Tracy Brown, for their many valuable suggestions; to my wife, Marilyn, for all the help and understanding she has given; and to Joseph Hallstein, good friend, scholar, and seasoned world traveler, whose researches in the Sea Islands provided the basis for the Gullah pages of this work. I am also indebted to a national resource most writers on this subject haven't mined—the work of many fine newspaper columnists familiar with American regional speech, including, among others, Mike Royko in Chicago, Jimmy Breslin in New York, Lord Ashley Cooper (Frank

Gilbreth) in Charleston, and Russell Baker, who handles all dialects as well as he does everything else.

Some seventy years ago Teddy Roosevelt pronounced that we had "room for but one language here" and shouldn't be "dwellers in a polyglot boarding house," sentiments shared by many Americans before him, including Ben Franklin and Thomas Jefferson. But the fact is that, almost from the beginning, the language of the nation has been a various language of tongues beyond number, mixing in the melting pot and turning out a great feast of dialects that have enriched American English. There is no sign that this will cease at any time in the near future, and no reason to fear the process. Dialects, like languages themselves, are simply different ways people have of speaking, and by better understanding our own American dialects we can better understand our fellow Americans who speak them. I hope, in this age of violent misunderstanding, that this work will help in some small way to make such empathy possible—and that the reader will enjoy this semantic journey into all the byways of America.

—Robert Hendrickson
Far Rockaway, NY

American
Talk

1 Ever' Body Says Words Different: American as She Is Spoke

✦

Midway through *The Grapes of Wrath* John Steinbeck has young Ivy remark: "Ever' body says words different. Arkansas folks says 'em different, and Oklahomy folks says 'em different. And we seen a lady from Massachusetts an' she said 'em different-est of all. Couldn't hardly make out what she was sayin'." Steinbeck seemed confident that our rich, vibrant, often poetic regional American talk would continue to thrive, but thirty-five years later, in 1974, another master of dialogue, with an ear second to none, warned that American dialects might not even endure. After a leisurely trip through the country, Erskine Caldwell reported in *Afternoon in Mid-America* that not only do too many Americans take their "point of view of events" from the morning and evening news—American speech patterns are also beginning to sound like standardized network talk. "Radio and television are wiping out regional speech differences," Caldwell wrote. "There is a danger in Big Brother, in having one voice that speaks for everybody."

Years after he wrote *The Grapes of Wrath*, John Steinbeck, too, expressed a fear that American dialects were dying, reporting his observations in *Travels with Charley* (1962), an account of his attempt to rediscover America in a camper with his French poodle, Charley, as his only traveling companion: "One of my purposes was to listen," Steinbeck wrote, "to hear speech, accent, speech rhythms, overtones and emphasis. For speech is so much more than words and sentences. I did listen everywhere. It seemed to me that regional speech is in the process of disappearing, not gone but going. Forty years of radio and twenty years of television must have this impact. Communications must destroy localness, by a slow, inevitable process. I can remember a time when I could almost pinpoint a man's place of origin by his speech. That is growing more difficult now and will in some foreseeable future become impossible. . . . No region can hold out for long against the highway, the high-tension line, and the national television."

American dialects *are* holding on, though, hanging in there, as younger people might express it in their dialect; as Steinbeck's own Ma Joad says about her kind of hardy people, the traveler through these States senses that our dialects are "goin' on— changin' a little maybe, but goin' right on"; they "ain't gonna die out." While there is certainly cause for concern, it isn't likely that regional speech will become as uniformly flat and tasteless as commercial white bread in the foreseeable future. Local dialects are doubtless changing and some are becoming more alike, in the opinion of many authorities besides Steinbeck and Caldwell, but then these dialects have never been worlds apart, and anyone who travels widely in America can attest that they are still very much with us. There are speech experts who still claim, in fact, that they can pinpoint any American to within a hundred miles or so of where he lives by the way he talks. Recently, University of Pennsylvania Professor of Linguistics William Labov testified at the trial of a Pan American Airways cargo handler charged with telephoning bomb threats to Pan American offices in Los Angeles. The threats had been recorded and the Long Island native was identified by a clerk in the office as the caller. Dialectologist Labov, however, testified that the caller's accent could be traced to an area within a seventy-five-mile radius of Boston and that the defendant had a metropolitan New York accent. The judge acquitted the defendant on the spot. Such identifications must be made by experts, however, often in the laboratory, by electronically dissecting tape recordings of a person's accent and analyzing them. Even in the case referred to, the clerk misidentified the caller, and a prosecutor later observed, "Maybe anyone with an Eastern accent would've sounded like the bomb threat caller to us because we're from the West Coast and can't really tell one Eastern accent from another."

There are very few dialect detectives as proficient as Professor

Henry Higgins, who in George Bernard Shaw's *Pygmalion* immediately pinpointed the origins of a Cockney flower girl by her accent and vocabulary. One graduate-school professor at a large university asked his class to describe several unidentified voices recorded on tape. The only voice described as "rustic and uncultivated" by the students was that of the professor. The late Raven I. McDavid, Jr., a noted linguist and past president of the American Dialect Society, observed that few people can identify even the race of a speaker by pronunciation and voice quality alone. "In experiments in Chicago," he wrote, "middle-class Middle Westerners consistently identified the voice of an educated urban white Southerner as that of an uneducated rural Negro, and many identified as Negro the voice of an educated white Chicagoan. Similar experiments in New York have yielded similar results. And many white Southerners can testify to personal difficulties arising from this confusion in the minds of Northerners. In Ithaca, New York, I could not get to see any apartment advertised as vacant until I paid a personal visit; over the telephone I was always told that the apartment had just then been rented."

An associate of McDavid's has observed that if iron-willed tyrants like Mussolini and Franco and their goon squads weren't able to eliminate dialects, it seems likely that it will take more than "television network pronunciation," which is a standardization of the speech of white Middle Westerners (often still called by the "prescientific" term "General American dialect"), to wipe out regional speech differences in America. Mussolini, as many Italians remember, tried abolishing all regional societies, reasoning (wrongly) that his people would surrender their dialects and use the national language exclusively. "El Caudillo," Francisco Franco, refused to let Basque and Catalán be taught in those regions of Spain, but the dialects remain long after his death. And there is no evidence that the Breton dialect of Brittany is dying, though France forbids the teaching of Breton there and postal authorities return all letters addressed in Breton with the stamp: *Adresse en Breton interdite* (Address in Breton forbidden).

While some American dialects are being watered down by standardized network speech and the spread of literacy and education, not to mention the movies and vast improvements in transportation and travel, none has yet been lost, and recent investigations indicate that some of our regional dialects may well evolve into different dialects, with many of their old characteristics and many new ones, developments owing to the influence of important new changes.

In the four centuries that English has been spoken in the United States, it has undergone an infinite variety of changes that show no sign of ending. Today these changes are strongly influenced by the babble of new accents heard throughout the land. Walk the streets of any of our cosmopolitan cities such as Miami and you will hear what British author and traveler Jan Morris called "tongues beyond number—a dozen kinds of Spanish for a start, a dozen kinds of American English, too, slithery Creole of Haiti, rustic dialects of Barbados or the Caymans, vibrant Rio Portuguese or British Honduran English, which seems to be a sort of Swedish-accented Australian." Morris, who has been called the "Flaubert of the jet age," heard the ominous cry "Rungway, rungway!" directed at her while driving through a poor section of Miami and thought people were cursing her—until she suddenly realized she was driving down a one-way street the wrong way. Many Americans have had similar dialect interpretation experiences and I would guess that I have heard not dozens but *hundreds* of accents on and under New York streets, where it is often impossible *not* to eavesdrop. Thanks to integration, Black English is heard in places where blacks never ventured before, Latinization proceeds at a rapid pace from New York to Texas and California, the times and the nature of the language they are a-changing as new ingredients pour into a melting pot still brewing the contributions of the tens of millions of immigrants who have arrived here since the first boatload on the *Mayflower*.

Within another century, American dialects may be so different that they will be barely recognizable in some areas, considering the great hegira to these shores that has been occurring since the Immigration Act of 1965 opened up the large-scale immigration from the Third World that President John Kennedy had encouraged. Today fully two-thirds of all immigrants *in the world* come to the United States, and these new arrivals are truly representative of the entire world, not only Europe, as they had mostly been throughout American history. Though some objections are heard that are similar to *Atlantic* editor Thomas Bailey Aldrich's poem "Unguarded Gates"—"Accents of menace alien to our air, /

Voices that once the Tower of Babel knew!"—written in the late nineteenth century, most Americans agree with Walt Whitman that "These states are the amplest poem, / Here is not merely a nation but a teeming nation of nations," or with Herman Melville's judgment that "We are not a nation so much as a world." Into the melting pot pour Hmong tribesmen from Laos, Vietnamese, Cambodians, Chinese, Koreans, Filipinos, Mexicans, Cubans, Dominicans, Jamaicans, Haitians, Soviet Jews, Indians, and scores of other nationalities. The enormous migration is already altering the makeup of American life and language. The United States, a country that constantly reinvents itself, seems to be doing so at a faster rate than at any time in its history. In our big cities today there are reports of black schoolgirls jumping rope while chanting numbers in Chinese; custom license plates abound in dozens of foreign languages; expressions like *Ciao!* or *See you mañana* issue from the mouths of children who have never studied Italian or Spanish; graffiti can be seen in exotic languages like Farsi. At a cost of close to $400 million annually, bilingual school programs are conducted in some eighty tongues ranging from Amharic to Tongan and the Yapese of Micronesia. In Los Angeles courtrooms today, interpreters are provided for eighty different languages, and last year one judge threw a case out of court because a police officer read the defendant his rights in the Chinese Tai-shan Cantonese dialect rather than the Cantonese dialect that the suspect understood.

From America's Little Odessas, Little Havanas, Little Saigons, Koreatowns, and all the other foreign-language bastions across the country are bound to come new words and accents that will couple with American English and contribute to its new forms, however subtly. There are many indications that this is happening now. A new dialect called "Spanglish" has already developed (see Chapter 10). Sociolinguist Roger Shuy of Georgetown University believes that "an extensive modification of vowel sounds is now taking place in the Northeast *that presages a vowel shift as dramatic as the vowel shifts of the Middle Ages,*" a period when Chaucerian English evolved into Shakespearean English. Others say that changes in American pronunciation and vocabulary will be as striking as the changes that evolved between Shakespeare's day and the twentieth century. (Shakespeare's line "Daw, you have begecked me! I yuke to pingle with you and york you till you ghost!" offers a good example of the vocabulary differences, translating as: "Fool, you have cheated me! I itch to fight with you and smash you until you die!") Such theories are corroborated by William Labov's scientific analysis of urban speech at the University of Pennsylvania Linguistics Laboratory, which indicates that the urban dialects of Northeastern cities are definitely not withering away on the vine or being diluted by the great leveler, network standard speech, as are some traditional rural dialects. "Nothing could be farther from the case," Labov wrote in a recent paper. "The New York City dialect is moving further along its evolutionary path with undiminished vigor; and this is true for any number of metropolitan dialects."

The changes in question probably originated after World War II, are evolving most rapidly among the white lower-middle classes, and are thought in this case to be a negative reaction, the reflection of a new localism in the face of recent waves of immigration to American cities from Asia, Latin America, and the American rural South, the local accents becoming intensified as a way of reinforcing local identity and a sense of belonging. In New York City, for example, Labov says the short *a* often picks up a long *e* before it. *Cab* is thus rapidly pronounced KEE-ab, and *bag* is BEE-ag. Those who have adopted this peculiar change in New York, however, do not use it in all words, the short *a* in *cat, pack, bat,* and *bang,* among other words, being pronounced in the standard way. As we'll see, many such pronunciation changes are causing American Northeastern urban accents to become stronger and more divergent from each other, and similar changes appear to be taking place in Middle Western and Southern cities, too.

As we change, our speech changes. No one seems to be able to get a collar on the rough slippery beast of American dialect, much less catch and cage the shifty chameleon as it slouches down Route 66, toward Bethlehem, Pennsylvania, and every other city, town, and hamlet in the States, manuring and seeding the American language as it has for twenty generations, making it "a new thing under the sun," as Steinbeck wrote to a friend toward the end of his life, a new thing "with an ease and a flow and a tone and a rhythm unique in all the world." It is no wonder that American dialect study can be no paradigm of scholarship. But that holds true for the dialect study of any living language, despite all our tape recorders, computers, and linguistic laboratories. Brave scholars do their best with the beast, yet they can only be infinitely patient with our infinite changing variety.

There is no general accord on the definition, but a dialect can be broadly defined as "one of the varieties of a language arising from local peculiarities of pronunciation, grammar, vocabulary, and idiom." The word is first recorded in 1577, deriving from the Latin *dialectus* (way of speaking). It is often forgotten that dialects frequently become languages—Italian, Spanish, Portuguese, French, and Rumanian, for example, began life as regional dialects of Latin. There are some 2,796 languages (from the Latin *lingua,* tongue) on our planet, these divided into 60 families and having some 8,000 dialects or language variants, ranging from the Xhosa, or click-clack dialect of the South African Khoi-Khoin tribe —which is full of harsh staccato clicks, clacks, and kissing sounds (like *tsk-tsks*)—to dat beloved Brooklynese of ours, unique in other ways. (Boers in South Africa called the Khoi-Khoin people *Hottentots* because their speech sounded to Dutch ears like so much *hateran en tateren,* stuttering and stammering, while Brooklynites have been called much worse, as noted in Chapter 3.) Dialects appear to be more widely distributed through nature than previously thought. Only recently have scientists discovered that different groups or pods of killer whales have their own ways of speaking, retaining individual dialects unchanged over long periods, possibly even for life—though there is no evidence that there are "Yawl leviathans" from the South Pole and "Youse whales" from the North.

In other countries there may be such critters as "proper, standard dialect"; in England, for example, proper standard speech is that used by educated Londoners, variously called London English, BBC English, the King's English, the Oxford Accent, Southern English Standard, and most commonly, Received Standard; while in France the correct speech is that spoken in prestigious Paris and approved by the Académie Française. The French Minister of Culture has, in fact, recently published a booklet of English words banned from official French communications—*disk jockey* must be *animateur,* etc.—as well as another pamphlet listing hundreds of English colloquialisms that are now actionable. Some forty French companies have been sued for using English words in ads, including a firm that called its new product *le fast drink*!

But in our own growing democracy there is no national support for any standardized speech, neither the General American that is used by radio and television announcers, nor, as is discussed later at some length, the so-called Harvard Accent of Boston. Americans are quite aware that we speak in different ways from one another, even if only subtly so, but for the most part traditions of democratic individualism and strong local cultural traditions have staved off any attempt by dictionary worshipers to foster a standard language or a national academy that would determine correct word usages and pronunciations. If someone says *greezy* for *greasy,* as both educated and uneducated people do in southern Illinois, they are no better than the educated and uneducated speakers who pronounce *greasy* as *greecey* in the northern part of that state. Perhaps the only possible "perfect" pronunciation of American English is defined by Walt Whitman in his *American Primer:* "The subtle charm of the beautiful pronunciation is not in dictionaries, grammars, marks of accent, formulas of a language, or in any laws or rules. The charm of the beautiful pronunciation of all words of all tongues, is in perfect flexible vocal organs and in *a developed harmonious soul.* All words spoken from these have deeper, sweeter sounds, new meanings, impossible on any less terms."

Yet there will always be those who insist *to hell with your harmonious soul, mine alone is the subtle charm of the beautiful pronunciation!* The acidulous British traveler Mrs. Frances Trollope remarked in her *Domestic Manners of the Americans* (1832): "I very seldom, during my whole stay in the country, heard a sentence elegantly turned and correctly pronounced from the lips of an American. There is something either in the expression or the accent that jars the feelings and shocks the taste." This has more or less been the opinion of English writers ranging from Oscar Wilde, who wrote, "We and the Americans have much in common, but there is always the language barrier," to George Bernard Shaw, who observed that "England and America are two countries separated by the same language." Signs have indeed been noted reading "American Spoken Here" in the land where *Z* is *zed.* On the other hand, many English people enjoy and value *United States talk,* a phrase that still has some currency in their country as "plain and forceful speech." The brilliant and always game etymologist Eric Partridge explained it with the example: "Call a spade a bloody 'shovel,' not a 'garden implement,' none of your English la-di-da!" It was an Englishman who pointed out to me that the American pronunciation of *schedule,* with an *sk (skedule)* rather than an *sh* is (like many American pronunciations) probably more British than the British pronunciation *(shedule)*—or at least much older and "traditional." The prevailing British pronunciation appears to have been widely adopted only in the second quarter of the nineteenth century. The word itself derives from the Latin *scedula* and apparently entered the language early in the fifteenth century.

One British traveler, with a snobbery bordering on self-destructiveness, complained more than a century ago that American was not "pure enough Anglo-Saxon English." The American language, with its numerous native terms or Americanisms (from 14,000 to 100,000 of them, according to various estimates) deriving from local conditions and the infusion of so many foreign tongues, would obviously differ from Received Standard British English on that score alone, not to mention the effect of these tongues on American *pronunciation.* Perhaps a hundred languages are spoken in the United States in addition to English. The top six, according to the 1970 Census, are German (6 million speakers), Italian (4 million), French (2.5 million), Polish (2.5 million), Yiddish (1.5 million), and Scandinavian languages (1.2 million). Of Native American languages Navaho is spoken by more people (100,000) than any other, with Ojibwa, or Chippewa, next (30,000) and Sioux, or Dakota, third (20,000). Indian languages alone have contributed a great number of words to our vocabulary, and obviously these and other Americanisms have become part of the true universal English language, just as have words from the scores of languages that influenced British English over a much longer period of time (see "Under the Influence: English Words from Other Languages," page 25). In truth, no such thing as Anglo-Saxon English exists anymore, if it ever did. There are well over a million Latin scientific names for animals used by English-speaking people, a million for insects, a million for flowers. That alone totals over 3 million English words with a foreign base. It seems clear that only a small portion of the 8 to 10 million English words (including technical terms and slang) were native-born in the British Isles.

Those snippy remarks of Mrs. Trollope and friends might have been expected of Britishers at the time, but Americans themselves have frequently been guilty of such parochialism. Walt Whitman had such people in mind when he wrote, in *By Blue Ontario's Shore:* "Who are you indeed who would talk or sing to America? / Have you studied out the land, its idioms and men?" Raven I. McDavid, Jr., told of how his stodgy college professors, literally interpreting the pronunciations indicated in the *Merriam-Webster Collegiate Dictionary,* fifth edition, criticized his educated South Carolinian pronunciation of the word "American"; McDavid pointed out that there are at least five regional pronunciations, one as good as the other, these including the second syllable with the vowel of *hurry;* with the vowel of *hat;* with the vowel of *hit;* with the vowel of *hate;* and with the vowel of *put.* There is no all-American pronunciation of "American."

Similarly, provincial Americans voted against what H. L. Mencken sarcastically called "the caressing rayon voice" of Wendell Willkie because the Hoosier pronounced "American" as Am*ur*rican; chose Herbert Hoover over Alfred E. Smith because Smith said r*add*io; got Henry Wallace in trouble south of the Potomac in 1946 for using the term *the common man,* which is regarded there as a term of contempt, and frequently remarked during the administration of Lyndon B. Johnson—Old Cornpone, as he was more charitably and gently called—that "the foreign policy of the United States should not be conducted in a Texan accent." Spokanians voted against John F. Kennedy because he pronounced their city's name *Spokane* (to rhyme with *cane*) instead of *Spoke-ann.* Geraldine Ferraro's New York accent may well have cost her more votes in her bid for the vice presidency than her sex. On the other hand, dialects can often help a political candidate; Davy Crockett was only the first Congressman on the campaign trail who trotted out his backwoods accent (and coonskin hat, which he used solely for campaigning) to show how "down home" he was. When it comes to dialects in the United States, it always seems that someone else is speaking them. What *we* speak is standard English, people frequently tell field investigators: "Ah reckon we-uns doan got none a them die-lects roun' hyar. Yawl trah down th' holler thereabouts whar they-all tawk kinda funny."

American as she is variously spoke may be a bit sloppy or informal, but it isn't a bit snippy, to paraphrase English actor George Arliss on the chief fault of American as opposed to British English. But then, even the BBC (known familiarly as the Beeb to British-

Pronunciations By Region

These pronunciations contrast the various ways certain words are spoken in different regions of the U.S., all of which will be covered at some length in these pages. Sometimes there are alternate pronunciations in a region (*horse* can also be pronounced *hôs* in eastern New England, for example, and *ask* can be pronounced with a broad *a*), but these pronunciations are the most common in the areas.

WORD	EASTERN NEW ENGLAND	NORTH CENTRAL	NEW YORK CITY	MIDDLE ATLANTIC	MOUNTAIN	SOUTHERN	CENTRAL MIDLAND	NORTHWEST	SOUTHWEST
ask	ask	ask	ask	ask	ask	ask	ask	ask	ask
due	do͞o	do͞o	do͞o	do͞o	do͞o	dyo͞o	do͞o	do͞o	do͞o
log	log	lôg	log	lôg	lôg	lôg	lôg	lôg	lôg
orange	orinj	ôrinj	orinj	orinj	ôrinj	ôrinj	ôrinj	ôrinj	ôrinj
horse	hôs	hôrs	hôs	hôrs	hôrs	hôs	hôrs	hôrs	hôrs
greasy	grēsē	grēsē	grēzē	grēsē	grēsē	grēzi	grēsē	grēsē	grēsē

Pronunciation Key

a = as in *map, add*   ī = as in *ice, write*
e = as in *end, pet*   o = as in *odd, hot*
ē = as in *even, free*   ô = as in *order, jaw*
i = as in *it, give*   o͞o = as in *fool, pool*

ers) has become a bit sloppier and less snippy over the years. No longer does the BBC wish to be regarded as the exemplar of spoken English. Some trace the beginnings of the change to 1937, when the BBC ceased publishing lists of words, "properly pronounced," in its magazine *Radio Times*. George Bernard Shaw, chairman of the Beeb's Advisory Committee on Spoken English, had quipped at the time: "If the announcer can produce the impression that he is a gentleman, he may pronounce as he pleases." Others believe that the BBC "changed from leader to disciple" in 1975, when "its radio and television announcers were instructed to give in to popular demand and start pronouncing Indira Gandhi's name as GAN-dy instead of GAHN-dy, which was a blow to both the broad *a* and tradition." Still others agree with one crusty Englishman that "the BBC has never been the same since it stopped requiring its radio announcers to wear a black tie and dinner jacket whilst reading the evening news."

In his *A Course in Modern Linguistics* (1958) Charles Hockett makes a good point about British English past, one that amplifies Shaw's quip and which also explains the enchantment of some Americans with dialects like "network General American" or the so-called Harvard accent.

"We often find," Hockett writes, "that the speech of the privileged classes is more uniform from one locality to another than is that of the less fortunate: educated British English is much the same in London, in Manchester and in Southampton, but the local dialects in and near those three cities show great divergence. . . . Standards of correctness derive largely from the natural habits of the privileged classes and are promulgated mainly for the guidance thereof. Adherence to the rules becomes one symbol of class membership. In a stratified society with little vertical mobility—that is, one in which the son of a farmer is predestined to become a farmer himself, and knows it—the special connotation of correctness does not arise: the privileged class has its usages and the lower classes have theirs, and that is that. But when there is the belief that humble origin is no necessary barrier to social advancement, the doctrine of correctness comes into the picture, with its whole panoply of rationalizations and justifications. The acquisition of 'correct' habits of speech . . . becomes one of the rungs in the ladder of success. The doctrine may then survive long after the sccial structure which gave rise to it has been altered. This seems to be largely what happened in the United States."

In this regard it is interesting to note that William Labov found in his study "The Effect of Social Mobility on Linguistic Behavior" (1966) that American speakers "with a past history of upward mobility are most apt to resemble the *next higher* socioeconomic group" in their vocabulary and pronunciation "than the one with which they are commonly associated." Onward and upward with the Broad *A* & Co.!

Anyway, the Beeb has in some respects become more democratic than the American networks with their standard pronunciation guides, broadcasting schools, and former ironclad requirement that national newscasters shed their regional accents for the "colorless cracked-twig sound" of General American in the name of uniformity, consistency, and convenience. One well-known television newscaster had to rid himself of all traces of his Western drawl before he could rise to prominence, and many electronic journalists (or "anchor-person eunuchoids," as they have been called) often seem to be imitating the most famous among them: some years back, everybody tried to sound like David Brinkley; then Walter Cronkite gave the broadcasting world a good case of "Cronkitis." Yet the networks have recently begun to hire reporters with regional accents, while local advertisers help preserve regional speech by promoting their messages in local dialects over the airwaves for an intimate down-home "I'm your neighbor" approach. As for the great majority of Americans, not many pay much attention to the standard speech practiced by the networks or any other would-be homogenizer of the language; from Harlem to Hooterville, they go on speaking their own way, especially when relaxed and unguarded. Some have their standard "television network" American English in reserve for whenever the occasion requires it, but their local dialect is their language of the heart, the one they live and love and die in and bang their funnybones and stub their toes on.

One dialect is distinguished from another by pronunciation, vocabulary, and grammar (including word construction, syntax, and slang). Besides regional or geographical dialects, dialectologists recognize social or class accents, including Black English (see Chapter 6) and blue-collar speech; most regional dialects include two or three such social dialects. Little or no work has been done on the dialects of age and sex groups; old people, for example, often use words and pronunciations outmoded in a region, and women tend to use words like *lovely* and *darling* more than men, who are generally more blasphemous and employ fewer modifiers and more slang. One study shows that where women more often say *trousers, china,* and *houseguests,* men say *pants, dishes,* and *visitors.* Young people, on the other hand, are even more imitative than TV newscasters in aping the speech of the more successful among them, such as popular singers, who, in turn, have been tremendously influenced by Southern white or black speech patterns. Certain features of pronunciations are "becoming endemic" to speakers between the ages of sixteen and twenty-five throughout America, in all regions, according to Professor James Hartman of the University of Kansas. These include the pronunciation of vowels in words like *now, cow, no,* and *crow* as if they were the same (pronounced *neh-oh, keh-oh, neh-oh,* and *kreh-oh*); and weakening of vowels before the letter *l—sale* thus sounding like *sell, really* like *rilly,* and *feel* like *fill.*

Word pronunciation (see "Pronunciations by Region" chart on page 11) is, of course, a much better guide to identifying American regional accents than vocabulary or grammar; for that matter, there are almost no significant grammatical differences from region to region. Investigators have demonstrated repeatedly that many words and phrases associated with one region are actually found in several. More important, vocabulary is the most fluid aspect of dialects; while pronunciation and syntax is learned early in life and rarely completely forgotten, people learn new words and forget old ones throughout their lives, and for the most part their vocabularies are always expanding. Nevertheless, perhaps because it is the most interesting, least technical part of dialect study, regional vocabulary seems to have received more attention than any other aspect.

The different regional names for objects is among the most entertaining aspects of dialectology. Collectors have found, for example, that the famed *hero sandwich* of New York, named for its heroic size (not for Charles Lindbergh or any other hero), has at least *eleven* different names in other regions. In New Orleans, similar huge sandwiches on split loaves of French (not Italian) bread are *poor boys (po boys)* because they were first given to New Orleans beggars in the late nineteenth century. Heroes are called *hoagies* in Philadelphia and thereabouts, *submarines* in Pittsburgh, *grinders* in Boston (you need a good set of grinders to chew them), *torpedoes* in Los Angeles, *Cuban sandwiches* in Miami, *wedgies* in Rhode Island, *Garibaldis* (after the Italian liberator) in Wisconsin, and *bombers* and *rockets* in other places.

In my own travels, I have found basic differences in common food names over distances of less than one hundred miles. In New York City, for example, small red-skinned potatoes, the first of the season, are generally called *new potatoes.* Travel less than a hundred miles east, out to Long Island's North Fork, and these become *salad potatoes,* probably because they are used in potato salad. The signs pitching "Lobster and Salt Potato—Only $6.95" along the Boston Post Road in Connecticut, less than fifty miles away across Long Island Sound, puzzled me until I learned that the red-skinned potatoes are so called because they are cooked in salted water.

There are at least four different American definitions and five different pronunciations of *bayou,* which means a sluggish stream in Louisiana, a deep ravine or watercourse in Texas, "a stretch of still water off to the side of a river" in the North Country, and a lake or pond in Oklahoma and other states. Besides its standard pronunciation, it is called a *BAH-oh* in Texas, a *BY-oh* in Tennessee, a *BY-oo* in Arkansas, and a *BY-uh* in Wisconsin.

Other discombobulating twists in the way Americans talk include the various words used regionally for the kiddie seesaw, which can be, among other terms, a *teeter board,* a *tinter,* a *tippity bounce,* a *cock horse,* a *dandle,* a *hicky horse,* a *tilting board,* and a *teeter totter.* A sofa, similarly, can be a *couch,* a *settee,* a *davenport,* an *ottoman,* a *settle,* and a *daybed,* while the living room where it sits can be the *big room,* the *front room,* the *parlor,* and the *chamber.*

Is it pronounced *sliding pond* or *sliding pon*? That also depends on where you come from in America. Many experts believe that the metal slides found in most playgrounds were first named *sliding ponds* because they reminded people of how they used to slide on the ice of ponds before playground *slides* were invented sometime in the nineteenth century. By this reasoning *sliding pon* is simply a shortening of *sliding pond.* But some *sliding pon* advocates claim that *pon* here is the corruption of any number of foreign words that were brought to the States by immigrants and thus could be applicable. A third guess is that *sliding pon* comes from "sliding upon." Other American terms for *sliding pond* include *sliding board, sliding pot,* and even *chutey-chute* (from the British *chute,* which is almost obsolete today). Strangely enough, no major American dictionary lists *sliding pond* or *sliding pon,* including *The Dictionary of Americanisms* and *The Dictionary of American Slang,* though the terms have been commonly used in the metropolitan New York area at least since early in this century and have certainly spread throughout the country by now in both oral and written language.

The candy flecks, usually chocolate, that ice-cream cones are dipped into are called *sprinkles* in New York, but *jimmies,* for some unknown reason, in New England; in other locales they are called *nonpareils, sparkles, dots, shots,* and even *ants. Soda* in New York is *pop* in the Midwest, *tonic* in Boston, and *dope* in the South. American kids playing hide-and-go-seek often shout *Olly-olly-oxen-free* or *Home-free-all* when beating the "It" to base, but *Olly-olly-income-free* is a variation, Ohio kids shout *Bee-bee-bumble-bee—everybody in free,* and Montana kids for some reason, or no reason, shout *King's X!*

Regional pronunciations sometimes result in new words or expressions. For example, *If I had my druthers,* meaning "If I were free to choose," is whimsically based on *I'd ruther,* an American dialect form of *I'd rather.*

In the state of Washington a *skid row* is a *skid road;* in Salt Lake City you praise the *lard* and put the *Lord* in the refrigerator, while in the Bay Area of California etcetera is *essetera,* a realtor is a *realator,* hierarchy is *high arky,* and temperature is *tempature.*

A heavy rain, for another example, is called a *dam-buster* in Alabama, a *hay-rotter* in Virginia, a *leak-finder* in Wisconsin, a *million-dollar rain* (beneficial to crops) and *ditch-worker* in Illinois, a *pond-filler* in Missouri, a *tree-bender* in Massachusetts, a *sewer-clogger* in Michigan, a *mud-sender* in California, a *gully-maker* in Ohio, a *gutter-washer* in Georgia, a *stump-washer* in South Carolina, and a *gully-washer* in thirty-three states. Other terms include a *goose-drowner,* a *toad-strangler,* and a *duck-drencher.* There are also at least 175 different ways in which people describe heavy rains, from *It's raining cats and dogs* (national) to *It's raining pitchforks and angleworms* (Michigan), *It's raining pitchforks and barn shovels* (Maine), and *It's raining pitchforks and bull-yearlings* (Texas, of course).

Over 100,000 regional expressions like these will be listed in the monumental *Dictionary of American Regional English (DARE),* which Harvard's Belknap Press expects to publish in four volumes during the late 1980s. *DARE,* the first volume (A–C) of which appeared this year, is being prepared by a staff of twelve University of Wisconsin editors headed by English Professor Emeritus Frederic Cassidy, seventy-seven, who has so far spent twenty years working on the first comprehensive dictionary of American regionalisms, though the dictionary was conceived by scholars almost a century ago. *DARE* field workers interviewed 2,752 native Americans in 1,002 communities and combined their results with regional word lists compiled by the American Dialect Society since 1889, folk expressions from some 200 regional novels, newspapers, and diaries, and many other printed sources. Professor Cassidy, a past president of the society, and his crew have turned up regional gems like *chow chompers, plaster pearls, snappers,* and *china clippers* for false teeth. They have discovered that though *baby carriage* is used nationally, a Midwestern and Western synonym is *baby buggy,* while in the Mid-Atlantic states *baby coach* is a popular variation. Even manners are expressed in regional terms. People mostly say *Gesundheit* when someone sneezes in the Northeast and upper Middle West and West, but in the Southeast and Southwest

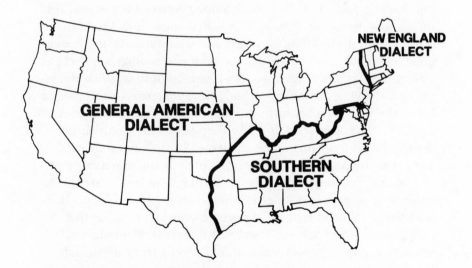

The Three Main American Dialects

people usually say *Scat.* Similarly, most Americans say *Turn out the light* when they desire darkness or lower electric bills, but Southerners say *Cut off the light,* Northerners sometimes say *Shut off the lights,* the expression *Outen the light* is heard in Pennsylvania Dutch country, and the charming *Douse the glim* was once heard in several areas. Among Professor Cassidy's favorites are *He has beans up his nose,* Wisconsin talk for someone with something sneaky up his sleeve; *hootenkacking,* an unusual Colorado word for talking somebody into something somebody doesn't want to do, including marriage, and *My sufficiency is fully serancified,* meaning someone's appetite is satisfied or he's had enough, which Cassidy heard from an eighty-year-old Norwegian man who couldn't tell him anything at all about where he got the mysterious word *serancified.* Another term investigators have had trouble with is *black ice.* A *DARE* field worker recorded this statement near Seattle: "We don't have much trouble with snow, but we do with black ice." Nobody has yet discovered what *black ice* means (it may be a river frozen over so that the water underneath appears black).

American dialects, specifically the New England accent, first came to the attention of British writers at about the time of the American Revolution (see Chapter 2). Most observers pointed out the relative freedom of American English from dialects, remarking that the differences in speech among Americans were far less than those found in Britain and other countries. This can be attributed to the mobility of Americans, who were constantly mingling with each other and homogenizing one another's speech, as well as to what one critic calls "the American instinct of conformity" and to the fact that English had been spoken in North America for at the most two centuries, as opposed to fifteen centuries in England. The Reverend John Witherspoon, the Scottish president of Princeton who coined the word *Americanism,* remarked in 1781 that the American common people, "being much more unsettled, and moving frequently from place to place . . . are not so liable to local peculiarities either in accent or phraseology." British traveler William Eddis had noted eleven years earlier that the language of Americans was "perfectly uniform and unadulterated; nor has it any provincial or national accent from its British or foreign parentage." Novelist James Fenimore Cooper, Yale president Timothy Dwight, and statesman John Pickering later agreed, as did the learned Reverend Jonathan Boucher, who in 1832 went so far as to say, "There is, properly speaking, no dialect in America" except "some scanty remains of the croaking, guttural idioms of the Dutch, still observable in New York; the Scotch-Irish . . . of some back settlers of the Middle States; and the whining, canting drawl brought by some republican, Oliverian and Puritan emigrants from the West of England, and still kept up by their unregenerated descendants of New England."

Wrote Isaac Candler, an English traveler, in *A Summary View of America* (1824): "The United States having been peopled from different parts of England and Ireland, the peculiarities of the various districts have in great measure ceased. As far as pronunciation is concerned, the mass of people speak better English than the mass of people in England. This I know will startle some, but its correctness will become manifest when I state that in no part, except in those occupied by the descendants of the Dutch and German settlers, is any unintelligible jargon in vogue. We hear nothing so bad in America as the Suffolk whine, the Yorkshire clipping, or the Newcastle guttural. We never hear the letter *H* aspirated improperly, nor omitted. . . . The common pronunciation approximates to that of the well-educated class of London and its vicinity."

Another explanation for the early comparative uniformity of American speech was suggested by a London editor in 1783: "[People] had assembled in America from various quarters [parts of Great Britain] and in consequences of their intercourse and intermarriages, soon dropped the peculiarities of their several provincial idioms, retaining only what was fundamental and common to them all; a process which the . . . universality of school-learning in North America must naturally have assisted."

But, subtle though they might be and slight compared to those of many other languages, there *were* regional dialects in America at the time these writers insisted there were none. The New England and Southern accents had already been acknowledged, and dialects in other regions were fast developing prior to 1800. As time passed and remote regions of the country were settled, differences became more pronounced. By 1860, Vermont linguist and pioneer conservationist George P. Marsh could report, "I think no Eastern man can hear a native of the Mississippi Valley use the *o* vocative, or observe the Southern pronunciation of *ejaculatory* or other emphatic phrases without perceiving a very marked though often indescribable difference between their and our utterance of the same things." Similarly, William Howard Russell of the London *Times,* reporting on a state dinner given by Abraham Lincoln a few weeks before start of the Civil War, observed: "There was a Babel of small talk around the table, in which I was surprised to find a diversity of accent almost as great as if a number of foreigners had been speaking English." There were several reasons for dialects developing at this time, principally that forms of transportation and communication were still crude and slow, making for less contact between people from diverse areas than when areas of settlement were closer together. Though most Americans could easily understand each other, regional language was more distinct during the first half of the nineteenth century than at any other time in our history. With improved forms of transportation and communication these differences began to iron out again toward the end of the century, until by 1919 George Philip Krapp, author of the influential *The English Language in America* (1925), could say that he had "little confidence in those confident experts, who think they can tell infallibly by the test of speech, a native of Hartford from a native of Providence, or a native of Philadelphia from a native of Atlanta, or even, if one insists on infallibility, a native of Chicago from a native of Boston." By 1929 the *Encyclopaedia Britannica* observed that "the differences in speech between Boston and San Francisco is less than what may be observed between two villages in Great Britain that are only a few miles apart."

Standardized British English is, of course, now understood practically everywhere in Great Britain, but American dialects, though they do exist and are by no means dying, still have far fewer differences between them. As Raven I. McDavid, Jr., put it: "To those familiar with the situation in European countries, such as France or Italy or even England, dialect differences in American English are relatively small." We have, H. L. Mencken said, "a general *Volkssprache* for the whole nation. . . . No other country can show such linguistic solidarity." Certainly we are closer knit linguistically than the thousands who speak Chukchi in northeastern Siberia; this language has what amounts to separate dialects for men and women—the letter *r,* for example, is pronounced *k* by men but *tsts* by women, so that the Chukchi for *walrus* is *kyrky* when men say the word and the radically different *tsytstsy* when women say it.

It wasn't until 1889, with the formation of the American Dialect Society, sixteen years after its British counterpart was established, that the study of American dialects began in earnest, its principal milestones being H. L. Mencken's *American Language* (1919), the quarterly *American Speech,* the Krapp study mentioned, the University of Chicago's *Historical Dictionary of American English,* Harold Wentworth's *American Dialect Dictionary* (1944), the various volumes of the still far from finished *Linguistic Atlas of the United States and Canada* initiated by Hans Kurath, and, one expects, the Cassidy dictionary of regionalisms soon to be published in its entirety. Remarkable scholarship has been done in the field, but critics maintain that too much of the work is based on folk speech found in rural areas, when more than three quarters of Americans live in cities and suburbs, though this situation is changing with studies like those of William Labov. The excessive focus on vocabulary has already been mentioned and too many of the scholarly works include unnecessary jargon.

An old Hindu proverb advises that dialects change every eighteen or twenty miles, and this may be true, but "scientific" estimates of the number of American dialects range anywhere from a basic three (New England, Southern, and the all-inclusive General American) to twenty-four and more. (Twenty-four varieties, in any event, have been recognized by the *Linguistic Atlas of the United States and Canada* and recorded on Linguaphone records under the direction of Columbia University experts.) I have at least touched upon sixty or so dialects and subdialects in these pages, but then, in liberally defining the term *dialect,* have included examples like Boontling (Chapter 9), which someone else might strictly call a "lingo," or an "American English jargon." Under a very loose, or precise, definition of "dialect," that old Hindu proverb is certainly more accurate than our modern dialectologists, for thousands of American cities and towns have their own unique words and ways of speech (see Chapter 10).

American dialects originated in several ways, but the traditional theory holds that they were born through the settlement of people speaking different dialects of British English, so that the British dialect spoken by the most immigrants to a region became the basis for the dialect of that region. An exception to this may be the General American dialect of the Midwest and Far West, which were settled by people from many other parts of the American colonies and territories speaking different regional dialects, as well as by many immigrants from foreign countries who spoke no English at all. Here pronunciation very likely followed the rule of schoolteachers in "sounding out" words by syllables. The current dialect that most of the TV networks use as a standard was probably born in the one-room schoolhouse.

General American technically includes at least six dialects: the New York City metropolitan area dialect (Chapter 3); the Middle Atlantic dialect; the North Central dialect; the Central Midland dialect (which is often divided into the Northern Midland and Southern Midland dialects); the Northwest dialect; and the Southwest dialect (the areas they cover can be seen on the map on page 17). General American thus extends from coast to coast, covering all areas that do not come under the New England or Southern dialects. While there are differences among the six dialects (and the subdialects and subsubdialects) General American encompasses, all have much in common, and because future exhaustive studies may show that they should indeed be treated as one dialect, the term *General American dialect* hasn't been completely abandoned yet, despite protests that it is a "prescientific concept." It seems very likely that if there weren't such a convenient term, one would have to be invented.

All of the dialects comprising General American are characterized by the retention of a strong *r* sound in all positions of words: that is, *car* is pronounced *caR*, and hard is *haRD*; this *r* is never rolled or trilled. Another General American characteristic is the use of the flat *a*, never shaded to *ah*, in such words as *class, brass, grass, dance, fast, ask, can't, path,* and *half.* This makes for the monotonous nasal quality many British critics complain of in American speech; whether or not it was brought over from England, as some writers suggest, seems incapable of proof, but one Cockney critic complained after seeing an American movie: "It ain't so much their bleedin' lingwidge; it's their blawsted neysel twang." (Interestingly, even Cockney rhyming slang has influenced American speech. The rhyming slang spread to America in the 1850s and one result was the word *alligator,* which rhymed with and meant "see you later." Rhyming slang never really caught on in

America and *alligator* in this sense didn't last long, but the full expression *See you later, alligator* remains with us.)

Compared with other American dialects, General American delivery is rather monotonous in the average speaker, the tendency to stress syllables not as prevalent as it is in other regions. There is also a tendency to pronounce certain vowels and diphthongs alike on the part of many if not all speakers; that is, they are pronounced as if only the first vowel existed, pairs often sounding identical, as in the case of *mourning—morning, horse—hoarse, for—four,* and *Mary—marry—merry.*

Speakers of General American commonly sound the unrounded *o* in such words as *not, pot, box, top, lot,* and *hot* almost as they would the broad *a (ah)* in *father.* There is generally less of a tendency to introduce a glide after vowels, as British English does in after the *o* in *note.* Most unstressed vowel sounds, no matter what the spelling of the word, are reduced to *UH, moment* thus becoming *mOHm-UHnt.*

General American speakers often drop the verb or auxiliary verb in such sentences as *Is this your mail?*, which becomes *This your mail?*, and adjectives are frequently preferred to adverbs, as in *He ran quick*—but these and most of their grammatical errors or preferences are common in all regions of the country. Speakers also favor certain words, such as *string bean* instead of *snap bean, earthworm* instead of *angleworm, skillet* instead of *frying pan,* and *creek* instead of *brook* or *branch,* but vocabulary varies among the dialects and subdialects of General American and these same terms are often preferred in other regions.

Though not standardized American English, General American is spoken by far more Americans than any other dialect. It is heard, in one slightly modified form or another, in such states and parts of states as Maine, New Hampshire, Rhode Island, Connecticut, New York (outside the metropolitan area), Vermont, Massachusetts, Ohio, Indiana, Illinois, Michigan, Wisconsin, Minnesota, Missouri, North Dakota, South Dakota, Nebraska, Kansas, Montana, Wyoming, Colorado, New Mexico, Texas, Idaho, Utah, Arizona, Washington, Oregon, Nevada, California, Alaska, and Hawaii. Many of the outstanding dialects and subdialects of these areas, such as the Texas or Western drawl and Brooklynese, will be treated in separate chapters, but General American will be constantly referred to and used for purposes of comparison throughout these pages as the dialect spoken by two thirds of all Americans over four fifths of the United States.

It should be stressed again, however, that General American is not a standard that should be aspired to; it is only mentioned so often here for purposes of comparison. The dialect here is considered neither the *acrolect* (from the Greek *acro,* topmost), the highest level of speech, nor the *basilect,* the lowest level. The truth is that everybody in the United States (and anywhere else) speaks a dialect, that there are no "illogical" or "unsystematic" dialects, that no dialect is a "corrupt" version of a standard language, and that while some dialects carry more prestige than others, one is as good as another, none is inherently inferior—each dialect has its place in the procession and our diversity is the main strength of our language. "A good standard," wrote Cornell professor C. K. Thomas fifty years ago, "is a national growth, not a manufactured article, and attempts to improve upon this standard (in dictionaries, academies or the like) are like attempts to graft wings on human shoulders; in other words, the voice of the people, in the last analysis, must decide and determine the voice of the people." The only thing even approximating a standard in America is the speech of the best or most educated speakers of a region. No one has ever found (or probably ever will find) the "perfect," "proper," or "natural" speech, not James I of Scotland, who by very questionable methodology determined that said language was Hebrew, nor Psammetichos of Egypt, who in the fifth century B.C. similarly declared that Phrygian was the primal tongue.

As the late Bergen Evans put it: "A language is as it is spoken, and by a happy dispensation most groups are inclined to regard their own twang or drawl or slur as divinely ordained and all deviations from it deserving of contempt and even death. Were not forty and two thousand Ephraimites slain at the passages of the Jordan because they mispronounced the first syllable of *Shibboleth?* Did not Jack Straw and his following, roaming London during the Peasants' Rebellion, kill any man who pronounced *bread and cheese* otherwise than they did? And did not Sicilians who revolted against the French in 1282 during the Sicilian Vespers kill all strangers who couldn't pronounce the word *cecceri,* chickpeas, the way they did? . . . In pronunciation usage is the last court of appeal. There is no 'correct' or 'perfect' pronunciation of any language."

Under the Influence:
English Words from Other Languages

This listing obviously offers only a sampling of the numerous foreign languages (and the many words from them) that have made contributions to the English language and influenced its structure and pronunciation, however subtly. A great number of these words are Americanisms and many more are given throughout the text. Some are corruptions of the original foreign language words, changed by mispronunciation and misspelling over the years.

ABORIGINAL AUSTRALIAN: boomerang, kangaroo, dingo, koala, wallaby, wombat, bellycan (water can)

AFRICAN LANGUAGES: *See* Chapter 6.

AFRIKAANS (THE TAAL): veldt, trek, commando, wildebeest, aardvark

AMERICAN INDIAN LANGUAGES: chocolate, tomato, potato, llama, puma, totem, powwow, papoose, squaw, caucus, Tammany, mugwump, Podunk, moccasin, sachem, potlatch, manitou, hogan, tepee, toboggan, wigwam, igloo, porgy, menhaden, quahog, catalpa, catawba, hickory, pecan, persimmon, tamarack, hominy, hooch, firewater, pokeweed, scupperwong, sequoia, squash, pone, bayou, pemmican, succotash, cayuse, wapiti, chipmunk, caribou, moose, muskrat, opossum, raccoon, skunk, terrapin, woodchuck

ARABIC: saffron, mattress, admiral, hazard, cotton, henna, camphor, alembic, alchemy, elixir, alkali, zenith, almanac, azimuth, cipher, gizmo, syrup, antimony, alcoran, mosque, sumac, bedouin, rebec, sash, algebra, monsoon, arsenal, assassin, jar, alcohol, apricot, giraffe, hashish, coffee, sirocco, fakir, emir, sherbet, alcove, sofa, harem, gazelle, minaret, zero, albatross, Allah, houri, magazine, genie, ghoul, candy, safari, tariff, coffee, café, and (possibly) so long (from *salaam*)

BASQUE: bizarre, jai alai, orignal (a mostly Canadian word for the American moose)

CELTIC: bin, crag, curse, dun, and (possibly) ass (perhaps a Celtic contraction of the Latin *asinus*); whiskey, clan, glen, heather, claymore, dirk, wraith, and plaid are Celtic, too, but are modern borrowings from Irish and from Scots Gaelic. Celtic words also survive in British place names, such as the Avon ("water") and Dover ("black"). Celtic includes Gaelic, Irish, Welsh, and Breton. (*See also* Gaelic.)

COPTIC: The Coptic language, now extinct, was superseded by Arabic, but it was the ancient Egyptian language most spoken in early Christian times. Two English words that come to us from Coptic: oasis and ebony.

DUTCH: Dutch and other Low German languages (Frisian, Flemish, and Plattdeutsch) have contributed a great many words to English. These include: date, dotard, bowsprit, golf, gin, uproar, wagon, liff, bounce, snatch, huckster, tackle (fishing), boy, booze, wainscot, hobble, splint, kit, mart, hop (plant), spool, rack, sled, excise, buoy, hoist, hose (stockings), bulwark, boor, loiter, snap, groove, luck, placard, brandy, stoker, smuggle, sloop, cruise, walrus, jib, yawl, knapsack, furlough, blunderbuss, sketch, stipple, decoy, slur, hanger, snort, snuff, hustle, snow, and mangle. Many Dutch words became part of American English. These include: bush, hook (of land), boss, patroon, Yankee, sawbuck, stoop (porch), hay, barrack, boodle, dingus, dope, dumb, logy, poppycock, Santa Claus, snoop, spook, skate, coleslaw, cruller, cookie, pit (of fruit), pot cheese, waffle, span (of horses), sleigh, caboose, scow, bedspan, bedspread, cuspidor, keelboat, landscape, and a good scout.

FINNISH: This remarkably constant language, which has changed little over the centuries and in which letters of the alphabet can be pronounced only one way, has only contributed a few words to English, the best known of these being the steam bath called a sauna.

FRENCH: French words came into English by the thousands after the Norman Conquest in 1066 and many had entered the language long before then. It would take a volume to list these basic contributions, but here is a brief sample of just those words that have come into American English: crappie (fish), gopher, pumpkin, cache, carry-all, pirogue, portage, voyageur, brioche, chowder, jambalaya, (pie) à la mode, praline, cent, dime, mill, bayou, butte, chute, crevasse, flume, levee, prairie, rapids, Apache (Indian) brave, Cajun, calumet, Canuck, lacrosse, lagniappe, parlay, picayune, rotisserie, sashay, bureau, depot, shanty.

GAELIC: Gaelic, still spoken by about 600,000 people in Ireland and Scotland, has contributed a number of words to English, including: bard, bog, glen, slogan, blarney, shillelagh, shamrock, colleen, brogue, galore (all Irish Gaelic); and clan, loch, and ptarmigan (Scots Gaelic).

GERMAN: English is of course structurally Germanic and is considered a Germanic language because of its Anglo-Saxon roots, but many words from Germanic languages have come into English at a later time in history, from the Middle Ages up until the present. A brief sample of these include: junker, lobby, carouse, plunder, saber, zinc, hamster, cobalt, shale, quartz, feldspar, gneiss, nickel, meerschaum, waltz, zig-zag, iceberg, poodle, spitz, dachshund, zither, leitmotiv, yodel, protein, paraffin, ohm, poltergeist, rucksack, semester, kindergarten, seminar, poker, and bum. Words in American English of German origin include the following: fresh (impudent), bub, hex, hausfrau, loafer, nix, ouch, phooey, wunderkind, spiel, Kris Kringle, Christmas tree, semester, seminar, noodle, sauerkraut, pretzel, lager beer, bock beer, frankfurter, hamburger, liverwurst, sauerbrauten, pumpernickel, schnitzel, delicatessen, snits, wienerwurst, zweiback, stollen, dunk, bake oven, and how!, cookbook, ecology, gabfest, check (restaurant tab), hold on, hoodlum, klutz, loafer, ouch, rifle, scram, slim chance, shyster, gesundheit, schnapps, standpoint, wisenheimer, wunderlust.

GREEK: Classical Greek and Latin borrowings possibly account for a majority of English words. Many Greek words have come into English, often through Latin and other languages. These include: anthology, barometer, Bible, catastrophe, cheer, cyclone, elastic, idiot, magic, tactics, tantalize, and hoi polloi.

HAWAIIAN: Hawaiian and South Sea Island languages like Tongan and Tahitian have contributed a number of words to English, including: tattoo, taboo, lei, atoll, muumuu, poi, ukelele, and sarong.

HEBREW: Among the many Hebrew words that came into English, sometimes through other languages, are: amen, hosanna, manna, rabbi, Sabbath, Satan, seraphim, cherubim, sapphire, babel, behemoth, leviathan, cabal, shibboleth, jubilee, kosher, shekel, Torah, kibbutz, and hallelujah. (*See also* Yiddish, Chapter 3.)

HUNGARIAN: Hungarian is not an Indo-European language like most European tongues, but it has contributed a few words to the English lexicon, including paprika, goulash, and coach.

INDIAN: It is estimated that nearly a thousand basic English words derive from words in Hindu, Sanskrit, and Romany, all Indian languages. Some of these are: panther, ginger, pepper, sandal, guru, pundit, nabob, punch (drink), chintz, mongoose, dungaree, cot, bungalow, juggernaut, tomtom, mugger, bandana, jute, sari, chit, myna, jingle, shampoo, puttee, cashmere, thug, pajamas, gazelle, dumdum, loot, dinghy, polo, chutney, zen (through Japan), loot.

INUIT There are only about eighty thousand speakers of Inuit, but even this little language has contributed words to the English lexicon: kayak, igloo, and makluk (a large bearded seal) are good examples.

ITALIAN: The contributions of Italian to English are vast, including three-quarters of our musical terms. Examples are: alarm, million, ducat, florin, brigand, bark (ship), tunny (fish), race, nuncio, artisan, doge, magnifico, mountebank, umbrella, gondola, carnival, mustachio, attack, cavalier, musket, squadron, battalion, citadel, bankrupt, contraband, carat, cornice, pedestal, piazza, stucco, portico, grotto, balcony, corridor, sentinel, catacomb, dado, concert, madrigal, viol da gamba, fugue, pastel, fresco, volcano, sonnet, stanza, canto, caprice, regatta, lagoon, balloon, muslin, mercantile, risk, opera, serenade, sonata, spinet, largo, piano, intaglio, profile, vista, miniature, cartoon, chiaroscuro, burlesque, ghetto, incognito, broccoli, sketch, casino, mafia, vendetta, malaria, influenza, bronze, area, lava, braccia, travertine, mezzanine, figurine, soprano, trombone, viola, cantata, trio, concerto, aria, violin, quartet, finale, andante, adagio, crescendo, tempo, bravo, piccolo, prima donna, sextet, scherzo, contrapuntal, fiasco, imbroglio, tirade. Italian words that have entered American English include: spaghetti, pasta, lasagne, tortoni, spumoni, tutti-frutti, antipasto, minestrone, Chianti, provolone, and many other food and drink terms. America itself, named after Amerigo Vespucci, could also be said to be an Italian word, as could Washington, D.C., the District of Columbia (from Columbus's name). Even the derogatory word *wop* is of Italian origin.

JAPANESE: Among Japanese words that have enriched English over the centuries are: kimono, karate, judo, tycoon, kamikaze, sukiyaki, samurai, hara-kiri, haiku, kabuki, geisha, sake, and Nisei.

LAPP: Even a little-known language like the Lappish spoken by Laplanders has contributed a few words to our English vocabulary, these including lemming and tundra.

LATIN: Though many Latin words and phrases are the basis for words in the English lexicon, very few can be traced directly back to the Roman occupation of Britain, which lasted almost four hundred years, A.D. 43–410. Strangely enough, there are more ruins than there are words attesting to the Roman stay, the latter including port, portal, mountain, and the *cester* (from the Latin *castra*, camp) that forms part of place names such as Winchester and Manchester. Latin words form about half of the English vocabulary, but the great majority entered the language during and after the Renaissance.

MALAGASY: Malagasy, the Malayo-Polynesian language of Madagascar, has contributed several words to English, including bantam and kapok.

MALAY, TAMIL, AND TELEGUE: These Dravidian languages give us a number of English words, including: calico, mango, copra, curry, coolie, pariah, junk, atoll, teak, ketchup, bamboo, gong, orangutang, fetish, caste, anaconda, catamaran, and mulligatawny.

MAORI: kiwi, mako

PERSIAN: Persian words that became English words, usually through other languages, are: tiger, paradise, pard, scarlet, chess, checkmate, checkers, azure, salamander, taffeta, arsenic, roc, mummy, spinach, jasmine, lilac, seersucker, khaki, scimitar, bazaar, shawl, lemon, divan, and van (from caravan).

PORTUGUESE: Portuguese words that came into English, often through Spanish, include: apricot, molasses, marmalade, verandah, junk (via Javanese), and cuspidor (possibly through Dutch).

RUSSIAN, POLISH, AND SLAVIC: Russian and Slavic words are the basis for a number of English ones, including: ruble, czar, kvass, sable, mammoth, knout, cravat, ukase, vodka, droshky, astrakhan, samovar, mazurka, polka, troika, steppe, pogram, bolshevik, commissar, soviet, intelligentsia, kulak, robot, sputnik, babushka.

SCANDINAVIAN: The Vikings, who conquered nearly half of England, the Danelagh, and were later absorbed into the population, contributed thousands of words to the English language—at least 1,500 places in England have Scandinavian names. Words that we owe to their northern Germanic language include: steak, knife, law, gain, birth, dirt, fellow, guess, leg, loan, seat, sister, slaughter, thrift, trust, want, window, flat, ill, loose, low, odd, tight, weak, call, die, egg, get, lift, rid, same, scare, though, till, both, husband, skin, hit, happy, rotten, ugly, wrong, and fell.

SINHALESE: Sinhalese, spoken in Sri Lanka, has contributed several words to English, including beriberi and tourmaline.

SPANISH: There are probably five hundred words in American English alone that are borrowed from Spanish. Some of the more common ones include: cork, cask, anchovy, sherry, spade (cards), galleon, grenade, armada, comrade, sombrero, cannibal, Negro, iguana, alligator, armadillo, sassafras, sarsaparilla, mosquito, banana, cargo, desperado, matador, lime, embargo, parade, guitar, siesta, peon, chinchilla, cockroach, vanilla, barracuda, avocado, barbecue, tortilla, plaza, ten-gallon hat, chaps, serape, poncho, adobe, cafeteria, patio, plaza, pueblo, breeze, buckaroo, chaparral, cinch, corral, hacienda, lariat, lasso, machete, ranch, reata, rodeo, stampede, wrangler, alfalfa, marijuana, mesquite, yucca, bronco, buffalo, burro, barracuda, bonito, pompano, coyote, mustang,

palomino, pinto, chile con carne, en-
chilada, frijole, jerky, mescal, piñon
nuts, taco, tamale, tequila, calaboose,
hoosegow, vigilante, incommunicado,
arroyo, canyon, mesa, sierra, couch,
coon, creole, junta, mulatto, fiesta, filibuster, hombre, loco, marina, mosey,
pronto, rumba, samba, savvy, steve-
dore, tornado, vamoose. Some of these
are covered fully in this book.

SUMERIAN (The world's oldest known language,
dating back to the late fourth millen-
nium B.C.): abyss, acre, Eden.

TURKISH: Turkish words that have enriched the
English language include the ancestors
of: turban, tulip, yogurt, caviar, horde,
fez, and vampire.

2 The Boston, or Haavaad, or New England Yankee Accent

★

The King's English, or "standard" English, is spoken only in Boston, Richmond, Virginia, and Edinburgh, or so an Oxford professor of English, George Gordon, pronounced back in the 1920s. In a study three decades later, the American Linguistic Institute polled "experts" to discover just where they thought the best English was spoken in the United States, the three winners being Boston, Nashville, and Washington, D.C. (with New York City coming in last!). At about the same time, on March 10, 1948, the "Director of Speech Improvement" for the Boston public school system intoned that "Bostonians certainly speak the purest cultural English of any section of the country," a blessing she attributed to Boston's geographic location near the ocean, because "the salt in the air makes our Boston speech more forceful, gives it more strength."

It is probably safe to bet that the majority of Americans agree with the Director of Speech Improvement & Co. and still regard the Boston or New England accent as the "purest" English in the country—possibly because Harvard College has long been located there (the accent is, in fact, often called the Haavaad accent by admirers), or perhaps because so many of our earliest literary lights and statesmen were New Englanders, or maybe just because the Cabots, who spoke only to God, would be expected to do so in high style (though that would surely be a sin of pride). Then there is the "dominant WASPs" theory, explained by Bergen Evans: "It is more likely that God is conceived of as belonging to the dominant group. If He no longer speaks in Hebrew or Latin, He at least has a Boston accent."

All stuff and nonsense, certainly. What impresses most people about the Boston accent, for example, is its elegant or affected (depending on one's ear or psychology) pronunciations of words like *ask, brass, class, grass, half, fast, dance, bath,* or *can't* with the broad *ah* sound (*bah-th, cah-nt, dahnce,* etc.). Granted, this is King's English, too, but most people fail to realize that the broad *ah* sound in such words, the so-called Boston Brahmin *a,* is quite possibly an affectation introduced on the stage by the famed English actor David Garrick in the eighteenth century. Others say that the broad *a,* which a 1790 British pronouncing dictionary called "a characteristic of the elegant and learned world," is ironically of "vulgar" Cockney origin! In any case, it was unknown in polite circles during the Elizabethan era (when *a cahff came down the pahth to take a bahth* was simply pronounced *a calf came down the path to take a bath*), and is relatively a pompous upstart, the "flat" sound of *a* in words like *dance* and *bath,* which is common to General American speech, preceding it by many, many years. It is interesting to note that the broad *a* is far from universal in England today. John Braine's lower-class heel of a hero in *Room at the Top* (1965), who is clawing his way up the social ladder, says before he gets to the top rung: "I was going to pronounce *Aunt* with a broad *a,* but decided not to attempt it yet."

Besides sometimes pronouncing *a*'s broad enough to launch a missile from, New Englanders lengthen the *a* sound in such words as *far, park, dark,* and *heart,* producing a sound somewhere between the one most Americans make in pronouncing *hat* and *father.* This characteristic is also found in the Southern Tidewater region, especially in eastern Virginia. A minority of dialectologists call it the Boston *a* and believe that it may have come over with the Irish in the 1830s—those same Irish that Boston Mayor Theodore Lyman believed with Yankee Certitude were "a race that will never be infused into our own, but on the contrary will always remain distinct and hostile"!

The lack of consonantal strength of the *r* in the New England accent is also a development that most likely began in southern England, proceeding until the end of the eighteenth century, when the *r* was finally heard no more in a Londoner's pronunciation of words like *car*. In 1791 *Walker's Critical Pronouncing Dictionary* observed that "in England, and particularly in London, the *r* in *bar, bard, card, regard,* etc. is pronounced so much in the throat as to be little more than the middle or Italian *a,* lengthened into *baa, baad, caad, regaad.*" New England settlers brought this mannerism with them, and their slighted *r,* along with the broad *a* sound previously mentioned, eventually provided the color of the so-called Haavaad accent, which yields uranium like *Pahk the cah in Hahvahd yahd* (Park the car in Harvard yard). It should be noted, however, that the *r* is *not* dropped before vowels, as in *carry,* or *Tory,* which are pronounced *carry* and *Tory.* Anyway, New Englanders were consistently dropping their *r*'s midway through the eighteenth century, the reason *liberty* is so often misspelled *libety* in early documents. The surest proof that *r* was not formerly sounded as *ah,* as it is in eastern New England and in parts of the South today, is the fact that it was once called "the dog letter." Since Roman times *r* had been thought of as the "dog's letter," or "the snarling letter," because its sound resembles the snarling of a dog—*r-r-r-r-r.* Said Ben Jonson, in his *English Grammar Made for the Benefit of all Strangers* (1636): "R is the dog's letter, and hurreth in the sound; the tongue striking the inner palate, with a trembling about the teeth." Shakespeare has Juliet's nurse in *Romeo and Juliet* call *r* the "dog name" when she tells Romeo that his name and rosemary, an herb associated with weddings, both begin with *r.* Today, however, *r* is pronounced as the dog letter only in parts of Scotland. In Anglophone North America *r* has become "a vocalic glide or a retroflexed central vowel" (that is, sounded with the tip of the tongue curled back)—except, of course, in the coastal Southern states, New York City, and eastern New England, where the *ah* sound holds forth.

"R-dropping" America has inspired a humorous theorem called the Law of Conservation of R's (formulated by Edward Scher in 1985), which holds that an *r* missing from one word will turn up in excess in another: *fawth* (fourth), for example, is balanced by *idears* or the common second *r* in *sherbert!* "R-dropping" reached its zenith of popularity in the early 1960s, when John F. Kennedy was President. "Politicians all over the country began affecting his nasal *r*-dropping style of speech," columnist

Mike Royko wrote in a recent nostalgic piece. "I can remember a member of the Cook County [Chicago] Board, who had been born and reared on the West Side, standing up at a political gathering, tucking his hand into his coat pocket, hunching his shoulders, and trying to talk like Kennedy. The effect on the audience was electrifying. Between his native West Side accent and his attempt to sound Boston Irish, nobody in the hall understood a word he said and thought he was drunk. The mayor was so alarmed at this kind of behavior that he ran the man for judge."

The vagrant *r* is lucky when its fate is compared to that of *t* and *d* in regional speech, according to one New Englander. "Harsher is the fate of *t* and its soft sister, *d,* which often vanishes outright, albeit to a saving of time," William Howells of Kittery Point, Maine, observed in a letter to *The New York Times.* "In long words, it is usually every other *t* that goes, so I call the syndrome the all-knit *t*. Thus, in the television weather report: *Sal light pictures show inner mitten showers.* My favorite evening television newscaster manages to say nightly news with no *t* at all (he uses what cognoscenti call a glottal stop). By dispensing with many *t*'s and *d*'s he can save a *hun ridden twenny* seconds in half an hour, which translates into a lot of money."

While there is no such thing as the "correct" pronunciation of American, there is little doubt that New England, along with Virginia, still echoes accents of the *earliest* English immigrants to America, who came mainly from the eastern and southern counties near London, or that speech in the area is closest to "English English," the standard English spoken in England, than any other American dialect. It is the one region in the United States where the dialect clearly owes most to the migration of people from England, specifically Puritans from East Anglia, who constituted two thirds of the 15,000 colonists who sailed to New England from 1620–40. Even the nasalization or "nasal twang" that the British twitted New Englanders (and Virginians) about had its origins in England, specifically in places where the Puritans held sway. English writers for many years associated this nasal twang (also called a *whine* and said to be affected to show piety) with the Puritans of East Anglia, Shelley describing a rather nasty pious Puritan in this way:

His eyes turned up, his mouth turned down;
His accent caught a nasal twang.

Some New Englanders, their tongues arched up in the mouth, the pitch of their dialect somewhat higher than General American, still nasalize *cow* as *keow,* a pronunciation old Ben Franklin kidded them about and a habit that also results in the pronunciation of *k* and *g* as *ky* (*kyat,* cat) by many speakers. The *y* glide of the *u* sound after *d, n,* and *t,* resulting in pronunciations like *nyu* (now), *dyu* (due), and *tyune* (tune), is responsible for the "Yankee drawl" that Noah Webster tried to explain in terms of Yankee inferiority. Webster noted in his *Dissertations on the English Language* (1789) that Yankees were not used to commanding slaves and servants and didn't possess "that pride and consciousness of superiority which attend birth and fortune," all of which made them "give their opinions in an indecisive tone" and drag out their words uncertainly.

But there is generally a sharp, clipped quality to New England speech—"a dryness that almost crackles," as one writer put it. A common characteristic is the glottal stop in the place of a final *t* or *nt,* so that *twant* (it was not) often becomes *twan.* New Englanders also commonly pronounce the *o* in words like *not, box, pot,* and *hot* as an open *o* sound, with the lips rounded, while the rest of America generally voices the *o* more like the broad *a* in *father.*

Another characteristic New England dialect feature is the vowel shift of *au* to *ah, Boston* thus becoming *Bahston* and *caught* transformed into something like *caht.* However, while this is common in the Boston area, the reverse is true in some New England areas, especially in Cape Cod, where *Cape Caud* is surrounded by *wotta.* Cape Codders, whose speech is less nasal than that of most New Englanders, also differ from Bostonians in not only dropping their *r*'s but in adding another syllable as well; a Cape Codder's *there* thus becomes *they-uh* (instead of the Bostonian's *theah*) and *air* becomes *ey-uh.*

Obviously, then, the Boston or New England accent is not the same in all parts of New England. Perhaps the designation *Boston accent* has stuck because the accent is so strong in the city, specimens like the following commonly heard on streets around the Common:

a gull—a girl	such—search
shop—sharp	dock—dark
gahd—guard	bee-ad—bad
cod—card	hot—heart
owah—hour	otter—order
noo-klee-eh—nuclear	bey-eh—bear
moa—more	bee-eh—beer
back—bark	cotton—carton
potty—party	sutton—certain
shut—shirt	waw—war

More likely the term *Boston accent* is so often heard because Boston is the eastern New England dialect's "focal area"—that is, an area that strongly influences the speech of surrounding areas because of cultural, commercial, political, and other factors. But the differences remain within the region. Another is the pronunciation of *home* and *stone* as *hum* and *stun,* once common in many New England areas but now largely confined to Maine, which has in many respects a dialect unto itself. While the *u* in words like *up* is generally pronounced *aw* in New England, it is pronounced as a deep-back-of-the-throat *ah* in Maine: *AHp.* Mainers also pronounce the "pure" New England *ay* sound of *maybe* as *eh,* saying *mehbe.*

To give still another example of differences within the region, rural New Englanders often pronounce *far* not with the typical New England broad *a,* but as *fu-uh.* Rhode Islanders speak differently from Bostonians and New Havenites speak differently from both of them. There are, in short, many subtle pronunciation variations throughout the speech region, even among the "focal area" residents of Boston.

Vocabulary also varies throughout New England. Nantucket, for instance, has the local expression *greasy luck* (good luck), a carryover from whaling days, when well-wishers hoped that a whaleman would fill his ship with oil on a voyage. The national expression *I wouldn't know him from Adam's off ox* (the ox in the yoke farthest away from the driver) also began life as a Nantucketism, originally having been *I wouldn't know him from God's off ox,* the *Adam* substituted as a euphemism. *Coof,* Nantucket talk for a summer

visitor and "off-islander," may derive from a Scottish word meaning "a dull, spiritless person."

The expression *swatson* (to chat or chew the fat—probably from
the German *schwatzen*) possibly originated in the Connecticut
area, while *guzzle*, for a small channel between two sandbars of a
stream through a marsh, comes from Cape Cod. *Schooner* sup-
posedly came to life in Gloucester, where an onlooker is said to
have exclaimed, "Oh, how she scoons!" when Captain Andrew
Robinson launched the first vessel of this kind back in 1713 and
she glided gracefully over the water. Captain Robinson, overhear-
ing the remark, dubbed his ship a *scooner*, which came to be misspelled *schooner* over the years (*scoon* itself probably derives from
the Scottish *scon*, to skip a flat stone over the water).

One of the earliest New Englandisms was the amusing Vermont
term *guyascutus* for a cow with shorter legs on one side so that it
could better walk around the steep Vermont hills! The rutted
roads winding over New England's hills in early times gave us the
expression *kiss-me-quick*, for a ridge or depression in a roadway, one
that caused a carriage to jolt and possibly throw a girl into her
young man's arms. Similarly, *thank-ye-ma'am* is an American courtship term that dates back to nineteenth-century New England.
Roads at the time had diagonal earthen ridges running across them
that channeled off rainwater from the high to the low side and
prevented washouts. Rural Casanovas driving their carriages along
these rude roads made sure that they hit these ridges hard so that
their female companions would bounce up in the air and bump into
them. With the head of his sweetheart so close, the gentleman
could steal a kiss, and usually expressed his gratitude with a *Thank-
ye-ma'am*, that expression becoming synonymous for a quick kiss or
for any hole in the road that caused riders to bump up and down. It
wasn't long before some salacious wit took this innocent phrase
between the sheets, or to the side of the road somewhere, and
elaborated on it, for in 1895 we find recorded the related expression *wham bam (thank-ye-ma'am)* for quick coitus. As a matter of fact,
the first recorded use of both expressions occurs in that year.

Two seldom (if ever) recorded New England expressions that
are very typical of the area are *mighty small potatoes and few in a hill*
(something or somebody of little consequence) and *he has too many
shingles to the weather* (he's trying to do too many things at one

time). As would be expected, New England nautical life is responsible for many national and local expressions. *Switchel,* for example, is old Yankee sailor slang, origin unknown, for a very thirst-quenching drink of molasses and water seasoned with vinegar and ginger; and *quoddy boats,* the double-ended keelboats used in lobstering, take their name from the Passamaquoddy Bay between New Brunswick, Canada, and Maine, where they were first used. *Blue lights,* an early American term for traitors, originated during the War of 1812 when pro-British Americans flashed blue lights to British ships off the coast as a signal that Commodore Stephen Decatur's two frigates would soon be sailing from their New London, Connecticut, harbor. The British acted on this information and blockaded the port.

Son of a sea cook, which can mean either a "good guy" or a "mean SOB," depending on the context, really has little to do with the sea, but it does concern New England. It seems that the earliest American settlers appropriated the word *s'quenk,* for "skunk," from the Indians around the Massachusetts Bay Colony, pronouncing it *sea-konk.* Thus, a *son of a sea-konk* was first a stinking son of a skunk. But *sea-konk* sounded something like *sea-cook* and came to be pronounced that way long after the Indian word was forgotten. The fact that sea cooks were often cantankerous old men (but did dispense the food) probably reinforced the term's present ambiguous meaning.

The term *codfish aristocracy,* for any pretentious newly rich person, apparently comes from the Boston area. It's hard to think of any group haughtier than the Lowells and Cabots (who spoke only to God in the land of the bean and the cod), but the Boston nouveau riche who made their money from the codfishing industry in the late eighteenth century apparently gave a grandiose imitation of those haughty Yankees in Back Bay Boston. As Wallace Irwin's old poem goes:

> *Of all the fish that swim or swish*
> *In ocean's deep autocracy,*
> *There's none possess such haughtiness*
> *As the codfish aristocracy.*

The word *Yankee* itself was first applied, in America, to Yankee sailors. The most popular of dozens of theories holds that *Yankee* comes from *Jan Kee* (little John), a Dutch expression the English used to signify "John Cheese" and contemptuously applied to New England seamen. From a pejorative nickname for New England sailors, the term *Jan Kee,* corrupted to *Yankee,* was applied to all New Englanders and then to all Americans during the Revolution, the most notable example of this being found in the derisive song "Yankee Doodle." Nowadays, the British and others use *Yankee* for an American; Southerners here use it for Northerners; and Northerners use it for New Englanders, who are so proud of the designation that they gladly call themselves Yankees.

As for *New England* itself, Captain John Smith thought that the area called New England in North America greatly resembled England. He was the first to record the name on a map he made in 1616: "That part we call New England . . . betwixt the degree 41. and 45."

There are, of course, thousands more words and pronunciations characteristic of New England Yankee speech than those already mentioned. Among vowel changes, for example, the following stand out prominently:

★ The General American *aw* of *all* and similar words usually becomes *ah,* except when preceded by *w* or followed by *r,* when it becomes an *o* sound (wash = *wosh*).

★ The *aw* of *cough* is often pronounced *o (kof)* by New Englanders.

★ The *aw* of *more* becomes *oh (mohuh).*

★ The long *ee* of *he* changes to *i (hi).*

★ The *eh* of *there* becomes *aa (thaauh).*

★ The *er* of *curb* changes to *u (kub),* especially in rural areas.

★ In many but not all words, the long *oh* of *home* often resembles *uuh,* pronounced with a faint glide *(huuhm).*

Among changes in New England consonant pronunciation from General American:

★ *D* at the end of a word is dropped after an *n (sand* becomes *san).*

★ *H* is frequently added to *ain't,* yielding *hayn't.*

★ In *ing* endings the nasalized *ng* is usually dropped (especially

north of Boston and on the East Coast) and replaced by a clear *n*, *pudding* thus becoming *pudin*.
★ Outside of Boston the initial *wh* sound is generally pronounced *w*—*where*, for example, becoming *waa*.

In an old joke a New Englander just back from Europe and hungry for a fish dinner directs the airport cabbie to "Take me where I can get scrod." "O.K.," the cabbie says, heading toward a brothel, "but I must say that's the first time I ever got the request in the past pluperfect tense." I don't know that many or any New Englanders change *screw* to *scrod* in the "past pluperfect tense," but the dialect does have its share of typical grammatical "errors" or differences, mainly used by rural or uneducated people and all becoming less common in recent times. Among those historical examples not already noted, the following stand out conspicuously:

★ *Be* used in place of *are* (How *be* you today?).
★ *Like* substituted for *almost* (He *like* to drowned).
★ *Knowed* used for *knew* (I *knowed* he was coming).
★ Verb and subject often don't agree, as in *Where's them boats?*
★ The singular is used instead of the plural for quantitative words, as in *It's been eighty year now.*
★ *Are* is omitted after *where* (*Where you going?*).
★ *Shouldn't wonder* takes the place of *think* (*I shouldn't wonder but what it's true*).
★ *Should* is used in place of *to* after the word *want* (*He wants you should stop it*).

Most of western New England speaks what is often called Inland Northern, a branch of the General American dialect (see Chapter 1). What is properly the New England dialect, with numerous variations, is spoken from the Connecticut River north- and eastward through the eastern strip of Connecticut and Rhode Island, the eastern half of Massachusetts, and Vermont, all of New Hampshire except in the mountains, and all of Maine. The dialect was the first to be recognized by visitors to the colonies and is probably the earliest in the United States to be honored (or derided) with a name, *New England dialect*, first recorded in 1788, when the phrase was noted in the diary of a visitor to the region. A year before that the "Yankee type" made his debut on the stage in the first comedy written by an American, Royall Tyler's *The Contrast*. Jonathan, the trusty Yankee retainer of the serious-minded American Revolutionary War officer Colonel Manley, is a servant full of homespun shrewdness, regional sayings, and downeast dialect. Tyler's play also marks the first recorded use of the popular American expression *to be left holding the bag* (to be made a scapegoat); after referring to Shay's Rebellion, a 1786 revolt of Massachusetts farmers against high land taxes, Jonathan says: "General Shays has sneaked off and given us the bag to hold."

The Yankee type was elaborated upon by many humor writers, including Seba Smith, who invented the Yankee peddler Major Jack Downing, whose shrewd commentaries on politics, under the guise of simplicity, made him the first in a long line of American political and social humorists, including James Russell Lowell and his Hosea Biglow, Finley Peter Dunne and his Mr. Dooley, Mark Twain, Will Rogers, and, in our day, Art Buchwald and Russell Baker, among others. Numerous cartoons of Major Downing appeared in the newspapers of the time and the popular Yankee was widely considered a uniquely American character, his likeness becoming the prototype for Uncle Sam.

Another Yankee fictional character who greatly influenced American humor was the itinerant clockmaker Sam Slick, created by Canadian humorist Thomas C. Haliburton, who combined shrewd New England talk with the boastful tall talk of the frontier. Sam Slick consistently said "Yankee" things like: "Now, Marm Pugwash is like the minister's apples, very temptin' to look at but desperate sour." Haliburton coined, or first recorded, a great many popular American words and expressions in the various adventures of Sam Slick. He apparently invented the common Americanism *as poor as Job's turkey* in one of his tales, explaining that the turkey was even poorer than the Biblical Job, who had been stripped of all his worldly goods by Satan, Job's turkey so poor that it had but one feather to its tail, and so poorly fed that it had to lean up against the fence when it gobbled, lest the exertion make it fall down. In *The Attaché, or Sam Slick in England* (1844), Haliburton may have coined the still-popular expression *to fly off the handle* (to lose one's self-control or head, as an ax sometimes loses its head when wildly wielded). He was among the first to record *to get one's dander up* (to become angry) and *to cut a wide swath* (to swagger), his stories popularizing these and many other expressions. Our "Mark Twain of the early nineteenth century" may also have invented the Americanism *to cry over spilt milk* in *The Clockmaker* (1863), and the just as popular *lock, stock and barrel* (everything), which refers to the three main components of a rifle: the barrel, stock, and lock, or firing mechanism. This only reflects expressions I have chanced upon in my reading; a thorough study might well reveal a host of genuine New England Americanisms that this premier humorist introduced—more, perhaps, than any other early writer.

The Yankee humorist tradition came to its apotheosis in James Russell Lowell's *The Biglow Papers* (1848 and 1867), two series of satirical verses written in Yankee dialect. New England farmer Hosea Biglow is the purported author of most of the "letters" in the work, and while Lowell's Yankee dialect has been criticized roundly on technical grounds, it is accepted by many scholars as "an effective literary presentation of rural New England speech of the early nineteenth century." There is no doubt that American humor had never before been put to more serious purposes, the first series of verses written in opposition to the Mexican War, which Lowell saw as an immoral one, and the second series supporting the North in the Civil War. In one stanza of the earlier series he writes:

> *Ez for war, I call it murder,—*
> *There you hev it plain an' flat,*
> *I don't want to go no furder*
> *Than my Testymunt fer that!*
> *God hez sed so plump an' fairly,*
> *It's ez long ez it is broad,*
> *An' you've gut to get up airly*
> *Ef you want to take in God . . .*
> *Wut's the use o' meetin'-goin'*
> *Every Sabbath, wet or dry,*
> *Ef it's right to go amowin'*
> *Feller-men like oats an' rye? . . .*

In a verse letter from Birdofredum Sawin to Hosea, Lowell has Birdofredum add:

> *Thet our nation's bigger'n theirn an so its rights*
> *air bigger,*
> *And thet it's all to make em free thet we air pullin'*
> *trigger,*
> *Thet Anglo Saxondom's idee's abreakin' 'em to pieces,*
> *An thet idee's thet every man doos jest wut he damn*
> *pleases . . .*

Certainly no Hosea Biglow or Birdofredum today, the "typical" New Englander would be impossible to define, given the great variety of people in the region. But traditionally the native son or daughter has been depicted as a dry, conservative, unemotional, cautious, prudent person not much given to change or "newfangled" ideas or the latest fashions, a type that doubtless exists in great numbers everywhere. Albert Bigelow Paine (the title of one of whose plays gave the familiar nickname *The Great White Way* to New York's theatrical district) described a typical New Englander like this in his turn-of-the-century dialect poem "Mrs. Smith":

> *All day she hurried to get through,*
> *The same as lots of wimmen do;*
> *Sometimes at night her husben' said,*
> *"Ma, ain't you goin' to come to bed?"*
> *And then she'd kinder give a hitch,*
> *And pause half way between a stitch,*
> *And sorter sigh, and say that she*
>   *Was ready as she'd ever be,*
>   *She reckoned.*
>
> *And so the years went one by one,*
> *An' somehow she was never done;*
> *An' when the angel said as how*
> *"Mis' Smith, it's time you rested now,"*
> *She sorter raised her eyes to look*
> *A second, as a stitch she took;*
> *"All right, I'm comin' now," says she,*
>   *"I'm ready as I'll ever be,*
>   *I reckon."*

The word choice of New Englanders does seem to lean toward the dry, lean, and laconic, the reserved and prudent; *I calculate* is often used, for example, in place of *I know* (*I calculate he's coming*). Typical New England words and phrases would fill a good-sized book, but an attempt at a sampler of sorts follows. Some of these characteristic expressions are heard only in certain areas of New England and others are used mainly by older people, a number of the terms well along on the road to obsolescence, just as *to home* (for *at home*), *trading* (for *shopping*), and *clothes press* (for *closet*) are already obsolete in New England. As a further qualification it should be added that many of these expressions, such as *conniption fit, scrimp, pesky,* and *snicker* (four New England terms that come directly from England's Essex dialect), have national currency today, though they did originate in the region:

* The New England word for pail is *bucket*.
* An earthworm is an *angleworm*.
* To swim is *to bathe*.
* A hero sandwich is a *grinder* (because you need a good set of grinders, or teeth, to chew one).
* *Cape Cod turkey* means baked cod.
* *'Lowed* or *allowed* is used for *thought* (*She 'lowed it was true*).
* *Ary* is used for *either* (*Ary one or the other*).
* *Master* is a synonym for *excellent* (*He did a master job*).
* *Aim* often takes the place of *intend* (*I aim to go*).
* *Look here* becomes *look-a-here*, especially in rural areas.
* *Flummydiddle* is *nonsense*.
* A *body* frequently means a *person* (*What's a body got to do to get something to eat around here?*).
* *Up and died* is used instead of *died*. This is preserved in doggerel about *Anadama bread*, a Yankee cornmeal recipe. One tale claims there was a Yankee sea captain who endearingly referred to his wife as "Anna, damn'er." Anna's cornmeal bread was much loved by his crew because it was both delicious and wouldn't spoil on long sea voyages. The captain is said to have written the following epitaph for his wife:

> *Anna was a lovely bride*
> *But Anna, damn 'er, up and died.*

The bread was thereupon named *Anadama bread* in her honor.

★ *Spell* often replaces *while (Let's set for a spell)*.

★ *Fetched* is used instead of *gave (He fetched the dog a kick)*.

★ A cleaning woman or girl is more politely called a *cleaning lady*.

★ *Nearly often* becomes *nigh (It's nigh on five miles down the road)*.

★ A cemetery is a *graveyard*.

★ *The other* often becomes *t'other (Give me t'other one)*.

★ The verb *address* becomes *back (Please back this letter for me)*.

★ The movies is the *show*.

★ *Tolerable* is used for *rather* and also for *pretty well* or *fair to middlin' (He was a tolerable big man; I'm feelin' tolerable)*.

★ Plain, thick unsalted crackers used with chowder are called *common crackers*.

★ A basement is a *cellar*.

★ *Nary* is used for *none (I ain't got nary one)*.

★ A sycamore tree is a *buttonwood*.

★ Sneakers can be *tennis (Put on your tennis)*.

★ *That wasn't* sometimes becomes *twant (Twant no way to do it)*.

★ One doesn't mow a lawn, but *cuts* it.

★ *Dast* is sometimes used for *dare* and *dassn't* for *didn't dare (He don't dast go; he dassn't come)*.

★ A water cooler is a *bubbler*.

★ "Regular" coffee, which is generally coffee with cream and sugar on the side, is in Boston and other New England areas coffee with cream added and sugar on the side.

★ The zeroes in dates are sometimes pronounced *ought* (19 ought 3 = 1903), especially by old-time Mainers.

★ *Please* is sometimes replaced by *thank you kindly (I'll thank you kindly to leave)*.

★ A milkshake is a *cabinet*.

★ A refrigerator is often an *icebox*.

★ A gardener is a *yardman*.

★ To *play hooky* is sometimes to *slunk school*.

★ *I can't be sure* is often *I can't rightly know for sure*.

★ *Sitting* is often *setting*.

★ E. B. White's beloved *Moxie* is a tart New England brand of soft drink that gives us the word *moxie* for courage. (See page 56.)

★ *Let on* often takes the place of *pretended* (*He let on he was ailing*).
★ *Being as* sometimes replaces *now that* (*Being as I'm here, let's start*).
★ Soured milk is *barney clapper*.

There are many many others, including a *hummer* for any bad guy with some saving grace, such as a sense of humor, and the *banking* or *tree belt* for the stretch of grass between the curb and the sidewalk (New York City has no name for this, while it is a *tree lawn* in Cleveland, a *boulevard* in Minneapolis, and the *devil's strip* in Akron). Common regional similes, at least ones I (not a native New Englander) have heard, include: *bright as a button; as blue as calm water; cool as a cucumber; leak like a sieve* (or *riddle*); *sharp as a meat ax; big as all outdoors; acts like folks; cross as Sam Patch; mad as a hopper; crazy as a loon; homely as a stone fence; like all get out; sleek as a whistle; tall as a beanpole; fast as a cat in a gale; slick as a whistle;* and *soft as mush.*

Tangy similes I haven't heard, and which probably aren't used much except by older people, include: *more airs than a country stud horse; puffing like a grampus* (whale); *easygoing as old Tilly; as mean as turkey bitters; deafer n' a coot; as true as preaching; as bad as all possessed; sour as swill; tough as a boiled eel; right as bean water;* and *meaner than goose grease.*

New England cooking terms are among the most distinctive in the country. *Johnnycakes,* (see "More Yankee Words and Phrases," following) *journey cakes* (they were used as food on long journeys), were invented in New England. The area is also historically noted for *bean porridge,* pronounced to rhyme with *Norwich,* as in *There was a young man from Noritch / Who burnt his mouth on bean porritch.* New England's butternuts are called *oil nuts.* In Maine, *huff-puffs* are small balls of raised bread dough fried in deep fat; they are called *holy pokes* in Connecticut and *Baptist bread* elsewhere. *Sap coffee* is a New England coffee in which maple sap has been substituted for the water. *Bean swagger* is stewed dried beans cooked with salt pork pieces, and *bloaters* are large cured herring. *Beanhole beans* are beans cooked for twenty-four hours in a hole lined with coals and covered with soil; a *dido* is the slash made in a pie crust to let out steam; *garden sass* is rhubarb; and *slip gut* is an old-fashioned pudding. *Hasty pudding,* which of course has odes written to it, is a New England invention that has the honor of being the only food besides macaroni mentioned in "Yankee Doodle":

> *But father and I went down to camp,*
> *Along with Captain Goodwin,*
> *And there we saw the men and boys,*
> *As thick as Hasty Pudding.*

Our word *squash* comes from the vegetable's Narragansett Indian name, *asquatasquash* (eaten raw), which came to be pronounced *squash* by New Englanders, while the noted Hubbard squash takes its name from Mrs. Elizabeth Hubbard, the Massachusetts lady who first cultivated it. Similarly, the corn-and-bean mixture called *succotash* was early taken by New Englanders from the Algonquian *misickquatash* (kernel of corn), and the name of the fish called the *menhaden* was adapted from the Algonquian *munnoquohatean* (that which enriches the soil).

In New England place names reside many stories. To take just the Boston area, Milk Street is so named because country slickers used to water their milk at a stream there before selling it to city bumpkins; Beacon Hill recalls a beacon on a high pole there that guided ships into Boston Harbor; the Common was once used "in common" by all the people for grazing their cattle; and Damnation Alley was wide enough for only one oxcart, so that whenever two teamsters met going in opposite directions the air was blue with *damns* and much stronger curses. Pronunciation of New England place names is no easy matter, and there are no easy rules to follow. Groton, for example, is pronounced *Graw-ton;* Quincy is *Kwin-zi;* and Billerica is *Bill-rikker.*

New England exclamations aren't often euphemisms anymore and aren't heard as much today as in earlier times, even as recently as 1933, when Hans Kurath listed no fewer than forty-two New England euphemisms for the virile *bull,* the most widely used of these being, in order of popularity: *gentleman cow; male; toro; sire; animal; gentleman ox; critter; creature; gentleman; beast; male animal; male cow; he-cow; male ox; he-creature; old man; top steer; gentleman heifer; male critter; man-cow; cow-man; bullock; cow topper; doctor; bullit; paddy;* and *bungy.* The euphemistic exclamations most commonly associated with New England, at least in historical or literary use, would include the following, in no particular order:

Pshaw!; land sakes alive!; lands sakes!; sakes alive!; gee whittakers!; godfrey!; dad blame it!; my gracious!; what in tarnation!; what in tunket!; don't that beat all get out!; chowder!; Jerusalem crickets!; ginger!; blow my shirt!; jumpin' gehosephatt!; I swear!; I'll be blowed!; I'll be jiggered!; I'll be dinged!; I'll be danged!; not by a jugful!; and *gracious me!*

To which I finally should add the rather archaic but rather nice exclamation my dear old grandmother (a New Englander) used to exclaim:

My stars and body!

More Yankee Words and Phrases
(Expressions that originated in New England)

★

WOULDN'T TOUCH IT WITH A TEN-FOOT POLE

This expression may have been suggested by the ten-foot poles that New England boatmen used to pole their boats along in shallow waters. Possibly the words were first something like *I wouldn't touch that with the ten-foot pole of a riverman,* this shortened to the present phrase with the passing of pole boats from the American scene. The image first appears in the Nantucketism *can't touch him with a ten-foot,* meaning "he is distant, proud, reserved." In the sense of not wanting to get involved in a project or having a strong distaste for something, the words aren't recorded until the late nineteenth century.

★

TARRED AND FEATHERED

At Salem, Massachusetts, on September 7, 1768, an informer named Robert Wood "was stripped, tarred and feathered and placed on a hogshead under the Tree of Liberty on the Common." This is the first record of the term *tarred and feathered* in America. Tarring and feathering was a cruel punishment in which hot pine tar was applied from head to toe on a person and goose feathers were stuck in the tar. The offender was then ignited and ridden out of town on a rail (tied to a splintery rail), beaten with sticks and stoned all the while. A man's skin often came off when he removed the tar. It was a common practice to tar and feather Tories who refused to join the Revolutionary cause, a practice much associated with the Liberty Boys, but known long before the Revolution, dating back at least to the days of Richard the Lion-Hearted. Though no one has been tarred and feathered or ridden out of town on a rail in recent years, the expression remains to describe anyone subjected to indignity and infamy.

★

LET'S TALK TURKEY

According to an old story, back in colonial days a white New England hunter unevenly divided the spoils of a day's hunt with his Indian companion. Of the four crows and four wild turkeys they had bagged, the hunter handed a crow to the Indian and took a turkey for himself, then handed a second crow to the Indian and put still another turkey in his own bag. All the while he kept saying, "You may take this crow and I will take this turkey," or something similar, but the Indian wasn't as gullible as the hunter thought. When he had finished dividing the kill, the "ignorant savage" protested: "You talk all turkey for you. You never once talk turkey for me! Now I talk turkey to you." He then proceeded to take his fair share. Most scholars agree that from this probably apocryphal tale, first printed in 1830, comes the expression *let's talk turkey* (let's get down to real business).

★

GERRYMANDER

Above editor Benjamin Russell's desk in the offices of the *Centinel,* a Massachusetts Federalist newspaper, hung the serpentine-shaped map of a new Essex County senatorial district that began at Salisbury and included Amesbury, Haverhill, Methuen, Andover, Middleton, Danvers, Lynnfield, Salem,

Marblehead, Lynn, and Chelsea. This political monster was part of a general reshaping of voting districts that the Democratic-Republican–controlled state legislature had enacted with the approval of incumbent Governor Elbridge Gerry. The arbitrary redistricting would have enabled the Jeffersonians to concentrate Federalist power in a few districts and remain in the majority after the (then-yearly) gubernatorial election of 1812, and was of course opposed by all Federalists, though a fairly common practice of the times. So when the celebrated painter Gilbert Stuart visited the *Centinel* offices one day before the elections, editor Russell indignantly pointed to the monstrous map on the wall, inspiring Stuart to take a crayon and add head, wings, and claws to the already lizardlike district. "That will do for a salamander," the artist said when he finished. "A *Gerry*-mander, you mean," Mr. Russell replied, and a name for the political creature was born, *gerrymander* coming into use as a verb within a year.

★

SCROD

Deriving from the Middle Dutch *schrode*, *scrod* means a strip or shred. New England scrod may be immature cod or haddock weighing one and a half to two and a half pounds. Sometimes the term is applied to cusk of about the same weight, or to pollack weighing one and a half to four pounds. When New England fishermen use the word, they are usually referring to gutted small haddock.

★

TO MAKE THINGS HUM

Since at least the early eighteenth century, *humming,* suggesting the blending of many human voices or the activity of busy bees and other insects, has been used to express a condition of busy activity. Two hundred years later, the expression *to make things hum* was invented in New England. Possibly the hum of machines in New England textile factories was the source for the phrase, in reference to the fabled Yankee mechanics who made things hum again when the machines broke down.

★

NOT TO KNOW BEANS

Not to know beans was initially a Boston expression, referring to the fact that anyone who didn't know how to make beans in Boston, "the home of the bean and the cod," would have to be incredibly ignorant.

★

DRY-GOODS STORE

Dry-goods stores possibly take their name from stores run by New England shipowners, many of whom were merchants in colonial times. Their two chief imports were rum and calico, which were usually displayed on opposite sides of the store —a wet-goods side containing the rum, and a dry-goods side containing the calico. Though *wet goods* are still called dry-goods stores.

★

ON YOUR OWN HOOK

This expression comes to us from New England fishermen working the Grand Banks on big boats in the nineteenth century. They were paid according to what they caught individually on their own hooks and lines, to which practice we owe the expression *to be on your own hook*, to be on your own.

★

BRISTOL

This Connecticut city takes its name from its sister city in England. Bristol, England, in turn got its name from the habit its residents had of tacking an *l* onto words ending in a vowel. This local dialectical eccentricity, which persists there today, changed the seaport's name from Bristowe to Bristol.

★

MOXIE

Wrote the late E. B. White of this soft drink: "I can still buy Moxie in a tiny supermarket six miles away. Moxie contains gentian root, which is the path to the good life. This was known in the second century before Christ and is a boon to me today." The rather tart flavor of Moxie, a popular New England tonic (as soda pop is often called in the area), may be the reason it yielded the slang word *moxie* for courage, nerve, or guts. Or maybe Moxie braced up a lot of people, giving them courage. These are only guesses, but the tonic, a favorite since at least 1927, is definitely responsible for *a lot of moxie* and other phrases, which, however, aren't recorded until about 1939. I've read that Moxie was originally a nerve tonic, dating back to the 1880s. This would go far in explaining *moxie* (nerve or courage), if earlier uses for the term could be found.

★

LOLLYGAG

One source says "Lolly-gaggin' was Grandmother's word for lovemaking." Maybe so, but I never knew Grandmother meant that by it. She always used the word *lollygag* to mean fooling around, wasting time, talking idly. The word was first recorded in 1868, but its origin is unknown, though it may have something to do with the British dialect *lolly* (tongue).

★

ONE PERRY AND ONE PORTER
WERE TOO MUCH FOR JOHN BULL TO
SWALLOW!

A popular Yankee slogan after the War of 1812, this punning expression refers to American naval heroes Oliver Perry, whose last name means a hard cider made of pears, and David Porter, whose last name means a strong, dark beer. John Bull, of course, is the national nickname for England.

★

O-GRAB-ME

The Embargo Act of 1807, and acts of following years, restricted American ship departures to prevent hostilities on the seas. But since it hurt our British and French enemies less than it hurt Americans, New England shipowners began spelling *embargo* backward and called the acts the *o-grab-me acts.*

★

THE SCOOTS; SCOOTBERRY

The *scoots* was nineteenth-century New England slang for diarrhea (which sent one scooting to the outhouse), and because the sweetish red berries on the shrub *Striptopus roseus* almost always acted as a physic on youngsters who eagerly ate them, the plant was named the *scootberry.*

★

JOHNNYCAKE

"New England corn pone," someone has dubbed this flat corn bread once cooked on a board over an open fire. Most scholars agree that no cook named Johnny had a hand in inventing the bread. *Johnnycake* is usually traced to *Shawnee cakes,* made by the Shawnee Indians, who even in colonial times were long familiar with corn and its many uses in cooking. Not everyone agrees, though, one popular theory holding that *johnnycake* is a corruption of *journeycake,* which is what early travelers called the long-lasting corn breads that they carried in their saddlebags. However, *johnnycake* is recorded before *journeycake* in the form of *joninkin,* "thin, waferlike sheets, toasted on a board . . . eaten at breakfast with butter," a word still used for the griddle cakes on the eastern shore of Maryland. The word apparently progressed from *Shawnee cake* to *jonnikin* and *johnnycake,* and then to *journeycake.* When people no longer needed to carry the cakes on journeys, *johnnycake* probably became popular again.

★

KILROY WAS HERE

No catchphrase has ever rivaled *Kilroy was here* since it appeared on walls and every other surface capable of absorbing it during World War II. It was first presumed that *Kilroy* was fictional; one graffiti expert even insisted that *Kilroy* represented an Oedipal fantasy, combining *kill* with *roi* (the French word for "king"). But word sleuths found that James J. Kilroy, a politician and an inspector in a Quincy, Massachusetts, shipyard, coined the slogan. Kilroy chalked the words on ships and crates of equipment to indicate that he had inspected them. From Quincy the phrase traveled on ships and crates all over the world, copied by GIs wherever it went, and Kilroy, who died in Boston in 1962, at the age of sixty, became the most widely published man since Shakespeare.

★

3 The Kings (County) English, or How Youse Too Can Tawk Noo Yawk

✦

No dialect these days winds more gently through my ears than Brooklynese (interchangeably called "Noo Yawkese" here), the clipped 78-rpm patois to which I was to the manner born in Kings County (Brooklyn) and to which (the first few times I hoid my verse played back on a tape recorder) I invariably reacted by cringing slightly, if not by shuddering and clapping my hands over my ears.

Far sweeter sounds have I heard, but I've become comfortable *(cumtabull)* with my cacophonous birthright, so often slurred as "Slurvian" and much worse, perhaps so long as I can delude myself into thinking I am not really speaking it, except when or because I wanna. Why, da goils love it—look at da verse of da Fonz!—and I have hoid the most gifted, the most brilliant, the most beautiful of people speak in Brooklynese—and dere is poetry in da dialect, which Orter Anonamous certainly proved more than half a century ago, when he wrote what has been called "Da Brooklyn National Antem":

> Da Spring is sprung
> Da grass is riz
> I wunneh weah da boidies is?
> Da boid is on da wing?—dat's absoid!
> From what I hoid da wing is on da boid.

To be a bit more serious, Brooklynese, or Noo Yawkese, has been defined as what you have a bad case of if you recite the sentence: *There were thirty purple birds sitting on a curb, burping and chirping and eating dirty worms, brother,* and it comes out: *Dere were toity poiple boids sittin onna coib, boipin and choipin an eatin doity woims, brudda.*

"Whadsa madda wid dat?" Well, maybe nuttin', brudda, and a better explanation of Brooklynese is surely called for. The dialect's most noticeable "peculiarity," as Mencken kindly put it (as kindly as the old aristocrat put anything), is the reversal of the *er* and *oi* diphthong sounds. Thus the *er* sound (which can also be spelled *ear, ir,* or *ur*) changes in words like *nerve, pearl, girl,* and *murder*—these good words becoming *noive, poil, goil,* and *moider.* Conversely, the *oi* sound (which can be spelled *oy* as well) changes in words like *boil* and *oyster,* so that we are left with *berl* and *erster.* There are many more examples, including *coil* (curl), *foist* (first), *adjern* (adjoin), *thoid* (third), *loin* (learn), *toin* (turn), *terlet* (toilet), *nerz* (noise), *hersted* (hoisted), and *Greenpernt* (Greenpoint). However, when the *er* sound is last in a word, but isn't a suffix, it should be pronounced *uh* in Brooklynese: as in *were,* which is pronounced *wuh;* or as in *her,* which becomes a grunted *huh.*

The pronunciation of the voiced and unvoiced forms of *th* as *t* and *d* (try *wit* and *dat* for *with* and *that*) isn't as common in Brooklynese as it used to be, thanks to several generations of dedicated schoolmarms stressing fundamentals on fundaments, or banging their rulers on desks and blackboards. The first writer to comment on the pronunciation, back in 1896, noted that it "does not take place in all words, nor in the speech of all persons, even of the lower classes; but the tendency exists beyond all doubt." This could still be said. And so we have *muddas, faddas, bruddas,* and *uddas* as well as the *dems, deses,* and *doses* that experts trace to the Dutch settlers of New Amsterdam or to later immigrants. But there are subtle differences in the use of all these forms, depending on both the speaker's audience and what he is talking about. In the case of *dis* and *dese,* for example, Professor William Labov listened intently and found that some New Yorkers say *dis* for *this* and *dese* for *these* when talking about an emotion-charged event, such as a bad accident or a close call. When talking to teachers or reading aloud—that is, when watching themselves —New Yorkers tend to say *dis* and *dese* much less frequently.

Other important parts of the Brooklyn or New York dialect (Brooklynese may strictly be a subdialect of New Yorkese, but it's hard to see why it shouldn't be termed just an exaggeration of it) are the *aw* sound in words like *tawk* (talk), *fawk* (fork), *wawk* (walk), and *Noo Yawk;* the dropped *r*'s that transform *paper* into *papah, bar* into *bah, beer* into *beeah,* and *super* into *soupa;* the omission of the letter *d* within contractions, making *didn't* into *dint;* and the *k* and *g* clicking sounds that can best be explained by the example of *Lunk Guylin* (Long Island), home now to possibly half of old Brooklyn.

By no means is that all of it. *Oncet* and *twicet (once* and *twice)* are bona fide Brooklynese, even though they were first recorded in Philadelphia and Baltimore by Noah Webster and are also heard in the Ozarks. And New Yorkers, like others, frequently add an *r* in words such as *idea (idear)* and *sofa (sofer).* Middle-class New Yorkers pronounce all their *r*'s more than the poor or the rich do, however, out of concern for speaking "properly," being grammatically "correct." Contractions, too, are plentiful in Brooklynese, telescoped words and phrases unconsciously tailored to meet the needs of the hurried, harried city dweller. *Finstins,* just a few samples that come to mind are *shudda* (should have), *dijuh* (did you), *ongana* (I'm going to), *alluh* (all the), *smatter* (what's the matter), *wuntcha* (wouldn't you), *juhhimee* (do you hear me), and of course the word *for* almost always blended into the following word, as in *finstins* (for instance). Then there are the many verbal shortcuts such as *Lex* for *Lexington Avenue,* the *Met* for the *Metropolitan Opera House,* and the *Garden* for *Madison Square Garden.*

Typical Brooklynese grammatical "errors" or differences include the use of *should* for the infinitive *to (I want you should see it* instead of *I want you to see it);* using *leave* instead of *let (Leave me alone);* overuse of *like (Like, I like her);* using *on account* instead of *because (I did it on account of her);* and the use of *being* for *because (Being that I'm sick, I can't leave,* instead of *I can't leave because I'm sick).* Among a host of similar expressions, *that* is often substituted for *who (She's the one that went* instead of *She's the one who went),* and *if* is omitted in dependent clauses *(She asked him would he go* instead of *She asked him if he would go).*

Speakers of Brooklynese are not nearly so rude as they are portrayed. Instead of a simple *thank you,* New Yorkers will often say *I really appreciate it.* One of the most common terms heard in

New York (City) is the apologetic *personally,* as in *Personally, I don't believe it,* instead of the franker *I don't believe it.* While this addition serves to show a certain humility, or worldliness—really one and the same thing—other typical interjections are completely superfluous, such as the *already* in *Let's go, already; here* in *This here book is mine;* and *there* in *That there coat is hers.*

A feature of New York speech that seems to be fading led to the popular designation *a Joe Echoes* a hundred years ago. People known as *Joe Echoes* (or *Johnny Echoes, Eddie Echoes,* etc.) in late-nineteenth- and early-twentieth-century New York weren't so called because they echoed *other* people's words. Those bearing this common nickname, usually the offspring of poor, recent immigrants, often echoed *themselves* in sentences such as *I betcha ya can't do it, I betcha,* or *I tell ya it's mine, I tell ya!*

Youse—the so-called generous plural—is a class by itself as a New Yorkism, though the expression is definitely heard in several parts of the country, including other Eastern cities and the Midwest. New York editor and author Barbara Burn, a New England transplant with a fine ear for regional speech, theorizes that *youse* is usually employed when a speaker is referring to the second person plural, helping the speaker differentiate between one person in the group he is speaking to and the group as a whole. It is the New York counterpart of the Southern *you-all* (a Biblical precedent for which can be found in Job 17:10), the "mountain tawk" *you-uns,* and the localized *mongst-ye* heard in Norfolk and on Albemarle Sound.

New Yorkers would not qualify as gentlemen under Palm Beach sportsman Charles Munn's definition of the species: "someone whose family has pronounced tomato *toe-mah-toe* for three generations." New York families have been pronouncing it *tamater,* and calling pretty girls the same, for that long and longer. I have known only one native middle-class or poor New Yorker who pronounced the word *toe-mah-toe* and she, dear lady, suffered from delusions of grandeur worse than most of us do.

New Yorkers, too, have their special names for things. That long sandwich crammed with edibles on Italian or French bread and called a *poor boy* in the South and a *grinder* in New England is a *hero* in most of the metropolitan New York speech area. A *stoop* (from the Dutch for *step*) is the front porch and steps of a New York house, while a sliding *pond* (possibly from the Dutch *baan,* track) is a metal slide in a New York playground but nowhere else (see Chapter 1). A *patsy* (one who is readily deceived or victimized) is another term that originated in New York. The word comes from the Italian *pazzo* (a crazy person or fool) and is first recorded in 1909. *Pazzo* may also be responsible for *potsy* (a New York City name for hopscotch), which may take its name from the *potsy* (object thrown into the hopscotch boxes)—like a victimized *patsy,* the *potsy,* too, is kicked around.

"I shuddah stood (stayed) in bed widda doctor!" is early Brooklynese rarely heard anymore in this life. But native New York kids still *have a catch* (whereas other American youngsters *play catch*), their parents often omit the preposition *to* and *go over Harry's house* or *go down the store,* where (as they did in the schoolyard when the teacher kept them "in line," or orderly "on line") they stand *on line,* not *in line* as other Americans do, to pay for their groceries (though once they are *on line* they ideally *stay in line*). The New Yorker will usually ask for change *for* a dollar, not *of* a dollar, and he will *get a haircut* or, less frequently, *take a haircut,* never *have a haircut.* He will rarely today use *on* for *with,* as in *Do you want zucchini or salad on your spaghetti?* (at least I don't hear the usage much anymore). While New Yorkers do say they *go to work,* they sometimes go to *business,* too, and they often *play piano* (without the *the*) as well as *play the piano.* They always *go to the beach,* never *go to the shore,* as neighboring Jerseyans put it. They don't go to the supermarket but to Waldbaum's, Gristede's, etc. Their frequent synonym for *You're welcome* is a modest *No problem.*

Stuart Berg Flexner tells us in *Listening to America* that the immortal intonation "The *li-on* is busy" is said "to have first been used at the Metropolitan Telephone and Telegraph Co.'s old Nassau exchange in New York City, by a Brooklyn-born operator around 1882." "Number Please?" spoken with rising inflection, is, however, a Chicago invention.

New Yorkers call New York City *the City* or *New York,* never New York City. If they come from any of the other four boroughs and are going into Manhattan, they say, *I'm going to the City.* But when asked where they hail from, the answer is always *I come from the City,* or *I come from New York,* and this includes anyone who hails from any of the five boroughs, not just Manhattan. Practically no one says *I'm going to Manhattan,* either, and *au courant* expressions like the *Butcher Shop* are used jokingly or sparingly, if at all. As for the borough of the Bronx (Fred Allen used to call it South Yonkers), it is always called just that—*the Bronx*—not *Bronx*. *Let's go to Queens (or Brooklyn, or Staten Island, or the City)* is fine, but never *Let's go to Bronx*. Staten Island, incidentally, is never called Richmond County or Richmond. And when people in the Bronx go *downtown* they're going to Manhattan; Queens and Brooklyn commuters go *uptown* to Manhattan.

Outlanders often call New York *the Big Apple,* but this foreign term is rarely used seriously by New Yorkers. A nickname for New York City since the 1960s, *the Big Apple* was first used in New Orleans. In about 1910, jazz musicians there used it as a loose translation of the Spanish *manzana principal* (the "main apple orchard"), the main city block downtown, the place where all the action is, bro.

It isn't generally known that New York is ultimately named for a Duke of New York who ruled over York in England. It gets complicated. The name *York* itself comes from the Celtic *Eburācon* (the place of the yew trees). This became the Latin *Eburacus,* but to the Anglo-Saxons who ruled England after the Romans, *Eburacus* sounded like *Eoforwic* (their "boar town"), and to the Vikings, who invaded after the Romans left, *Eoforwic* sounded like *Iorvik.* Over the years *Iorvik* was shortened to *Iork,* which was finally transliterated into *York.* Then in 1664 James, Duke of York and Albany, was granted the patent to all lands in America between the Delaware River and Connecticut by his older brother, King Charles II. The Duke gave away the Jersey portion, but held on to what was then the Dutch colony of New Netherlands. York became the patron of Colonel Richard Nicholls, who that same year set sail for the New World, captured New Amsterdam from the Dutch, and named both the city of New Amsterdam (New York City) and the colony of New Netherland (New York State) after the Duke. New York State's capital, Albany, is also named for the same Duke of York and Albany.

According to one astute statistician, the Algonquin Manhattan Indians who sold *Manhattan* Island to the Dutch for $24 in trinkets probably got the best of the deal. He figures that if the Indians had invested their $24 at the prevailing interest rates, they would now have some $13 billion—$4 billion more than all the real estate in Manhattan is worth. Since 1898 Manhattan has been the name of New York's central borough and has always been a synonym elsewhere for New York City itself. From the same Manhattan Indians, indirectly, the world also has the *Manhattan* cocktail, made with whiskey, sweet vermouth, and bitters, first mixed about 1890; *Manhattan clam chowder,* made with *tamaters,* unlike the traditional New England (milk) clam chowder; and *Manhattan Project,* the code name for the secret scientific group that developed the first atomic bomb. *Manhattanization* is a word that seems to have originated only recently. In the 1971 fall elections, San Francisco residents were urged to vote for an amendment halting the construction of tall buildings, to avoid "the *Manhattanization* of San Francisco."

Wall Street, which is both a street and a term symbolizing varying views of American capitalism in general, is of course located in downtown Manhattan, at the southern end of the island, and takes its name from the wall that extended along the street in Dutch times (a wall parts of which the Indians it was erected against used for firewood). The principal financial institutions of the city have been located there since the early nineteenth century. *Wall Streeter, Wall Street broker, Wall Street plunger,* and *Wall Street shark* are among American terms to which the street gave birth, *Wall Street broker* used as early as 1836, and Wall Street being called *The Street* by 1863. The *New York Stock Exchange (NYSE)* was first named the *New York Stock and Exchange Board* (1817), taking its present name in 1863. The *American Stock Exchange (AMEX),* which took its present name in 1953, was formed as the *New York Curb Exchange* in 1842 (because it was composed of *curbstone* brokers who were not members of the New York Stock and Exchange Board).

Flea markets across the country also owe their name to New York, as does every tough district called a *tenderloin. Flea market* as an American expression goes as far back as Dutch colonial days, when there was a very real Vallie (Valley) Market at the valley or foot of Maiden Lane in downtown Manhattan. The Vallie Market came to be abbreviated to *Vlie Market* and this was soon being pronounced *Flea Market.* The original *tenderloin* was the area from Twenty-third to Forty-second Street west of Broadway in Manhattan. Gambling and prostitution flourished in this district, giving police officers "delicious opportunities" for graft. In fact, one cop, named Williams, was so happy to be assigned to the old Twenty-ninth Precinct covering the area in about 1890 that he said he had "always eaten chuck steak" but from now on he'd "be eating tenderloin." His remark led to the area's being dubbed *the tenderloin,* and that name was eventually transferred to similar places throughout the country. Many residents of New York's *tenderloin* were sent *up the river;* the river referred to is the Hudson in New York City, and *up it,* at Ossining, is *Sing Sing Penitentiary,* which was founded in 1830.

The *Bronx,* one of New York City's five boroughs, takes its name from Jonas Bronck, a Dane who first settled the area for the Dutch West India Company in 1641. The *Bronx* cocktail was named in honor of the borough, or invented there, in about 1919. Long associated with baseball, the razz or raspberry called the *Bronx cheer* wasn't born at the borough's Yankee Stadium, home of baseball's New York Yankees, as is generally believed. It may derive from the Spanish word *branca* (rude shout) or have originated at the National Theatre in the same borough of the Bronx, however; we only know certainly that the term is first recorded in 1929.

Since we've dwelt nostalgically upon New York and the Bronx, it's only fair that the origins of New York City's remaining three counties or boroughs be mentioned. *Kings County,* better known as Brooklyn, is named for England's King Charles II; *Queens County* honors Catherine of Braganza, Charles's Queen; and *Richmond,* better known as Staten Island, is named for King Charles's son the Duke of Richmond. Since New York County, or Manhattan, was named for King Charles's brother James, Duke of York, that leaves only the Bronx of New York City's five boroughs that isn't named for Charles II's royal family.

The *Coney* in Brooklyn's illustrious (and soon to be renovated) *Coney Island* should really be pronounced (but never is) to rhyme with *honey* or *money.* The word derives from *cony* (or *coney* or *cuny*), meaning the adult long-eared rabbit *(Lepus cunicula)* after which the place was named. However, *cony* (pronounced *cunny*) came to mean *cunt* in English slang. Proper Victorians stopped using the word, substituting rabbit, which previously meant just the young of the cony species. The only trouble remaining was that *cony* (pronounced *cunny*) appeared throughout the King James Bible, which had to be read aloud during church services. Proper Victorians solved this problem by changing the pronunciation of *cony* *(cunny)* to *coney* (rhymes with *Tony*), which it remains to this day in *Coney Island* as well as in pulpit readings from the Bible.

The fabled American *hot dog* also has a Coney Island connection. According to concessionaire Harry Stevens, who first served grilled franks on a split roll in about 1900, the franks were dubbed *hot dogs* by that prolific word inventor and sports cartoonist T. A. Dorgan after he sampled them at a ballgame. "Tad" possibly had in mind the fact that many people believed frankfurters were made from dog meat at the time, and no doubt heard Stevens's vendors crying out, "Get your red hots!" on cold days. Dorgan even drew the *hot dog* as a dachshund on a roll, leading the indignant Coney Island Chamber of Commerce to ban the use of the term *hot dog* by concessionaires there (they could only be called *Coney Islands, red hots,* and *frankfurters*).

Coney Islands and *Coney Island bloodhounds* are rarely used to mean a hot dog anymore. Similarly, no dictionary of slang records the Americanism *Coney Island whitefish* for a disposed condom floating in the water, though I've heard it twice that I can remember and guess that it dates back to about the 1930s. In typical New York humor it says much about the often dirty waters off the famous resort.

Even more famous worldwide than Brooklyn's Coney Island are Brooklyn's incomparable Brooklyn Dodgers, who became comparable after their move to Los Angeles in 1958. The team was dubbed *the Dodgers* because Manhattanites contemptuously referred to all Brooklynites as "trolley dodgers" at the turn of the century, the bustling borough being famed for its numerous trolleys, especially in the central Borough Hall area. Attempts were made to change the name to the Superbas, the Kings, and the Robins, all to no avail.

The legendary nickname for the Brooklyn Dodgers beloved of memory was given to them by an irate fan seated behind home plate at a home game in Ebbets Field during the Great Depression. Particularly incensed by one error he shouted, "Ya bum, ya, yez bums, yez!" and his words, reported by a baseball writer, stuck as an endearing nickname for the team. *Dem bums* are responsible for the national expression *Nice guys finish last.* The cynical proverb has been attributed by *Bartlett's* to former Brooklyn Dodger manager Leo Durocher, who has written a book using it as the title. Back in the 1940s Leo was sitting on the bench before a game with the New York Giants and saw opposing manager Mel Ott across the field. "Look at Ott," he said to a group of sportswriters. "He's such a damn nice guy and they'll finish last for him." One of the writers probably coined the phrase *Nice guys finish last* from this remark, but the credit still goes to the Lip. This is one of the few baseball expressions that have become proverbial outside the sport.

No one has been able to prove beyond a doubt the origin of Brooklynese. The dialect is native to the Bronx, Manhattan, Queens, Staten Island, and Nassau and Westchester counties, as well as to the borough of Brooklyn. A misnomer, indeed, Brooklynese even extends across the river into Joisey's Hudson, Bergen, and Essex counties, among others, finding some of its most accomplished practitioners in Hoboken. It is the language of tens of millions, and you will in fact come upon it anywhere within a 100-mile circle, using Manhattan as a fulcrum, which would include southeastern Connecticut, Rockland County (to the north of Westchester), and northeastern New Jersey—though not always in its purest form. Echoes of Brooklynese can be heard in Chicago, Miami, the Gulf Coast area (where politicians commonly refer to "mah woythy opponent"), San Francisco, which New Yorkers were prominent in settling, and the Jewish district of west Los Angeles, which for half a century has been well known for its perpetuation of New York City dialect and idiom. Recognized immediately all over the world, echoes of it are heard in parts of Britain and Australia.

Stretching the point a bit, one could say that Brooklynese is also spoken (without any derogatory associations, by the way) in South Carolina, New Orleans, and other Southern areas where the peculiar *uh-ee* diphthong in words like *thirty (toidy)* is heard almost as commonly as in New York—though most scholars would say the opposite: that *toidy boids,* etc., flew north from Dixie. People have persisted in calling the accent Brooklynese (often to the dismay of speech experts) because the borough has always been the butt of jokes and because the accent was once at its exaggerated best in northern Brooklyn, especially Williamsboig and Greenpernt.

Denounced as "vulgar" by H. L. Mencken in his seminal *The American Language,* Brooklynese may have its roots in German or Yiddish. Certainly the characteristic melodic rhythm of the dialect, which rises and falls in the midst of a sentence and is so sung by most all of us speakers (whether we know Yiddish or not), seems to be Yiddish-influenced. Yiddish has contributed hundreds of expressions to those who *schmooz* (stand around and gab)

New Yawkese, but research doesn't bear out the theory that Brooklynese is simply an offshoot of Yiddish, as many people believe. Though Yiddish strongly influenced the dialect, Noo Yawk tawk has had influences too numerous to mention since the Dutch and Indians gave it words and ways of speaking, especially regarding vocabulary. Nevertheless, Yiddish terms do abound in Brooklynese. New Yorkers use such originally Yiddish words as *bagel, bialy, blintz, borsht, bubie* (a term of endearment, from *bubeleh*), *chutzpa* (gall, brass: "a man who kills his mother and father and throws himself on the mercy of the court as an orphan" has it in spades), *cockamamy* (ridiculous, muddled, not credible), *dreck* (shit), *fin* (five dollars), *gefilte fish, gelt, gesundheit, oy gevalt!, glitch, kibitzer, klutz, knish, k'nocker* (a boastful big shot), *kosher, kvetch* (complain, among other meanings), *lox* (this fabled fish food invented in New York City), *matzoh, maven* (expert), *mazel tov, mazuma, megillah, mensh* (a decent human being), *meshugge* (crazy), *mish mosh, nebbish, nosh, nudnik* (one whose purpose in life is to bore everyone else), *Phudnik* (a *nudnik* with a Ph.D), *putz* (fool), *schlemiehl, schlep, shekel, shlock, shmaltz, shmeer* (to spread), *shmegegge, shmo, shmuck, shnook, shnorrer* (beggar, cheapskate, bargain hunter), *shnoz, shtik* (a piece of clowning, a prank), *tsimmes* (troubles), *tsouris* (troubles), *tummler* (a clown, prankster), *yenta*, and *zaftig*. These fifty or so are only a small fraction of the yeasty guttural Yiddish words and phrases that have enriched the dialect. Leo Rosten's *The Joys of Yiddish* (1968) alone collects over a thousand more. This does not include expressions such as *Who needs it?* and *Get lost!*, which owe their presence in New York talk to Yiddish or Jewish influence. Other such phrases and inflections include:

> I should have such luck.
> Wear it in good health.
> It shouldn't happen to a dog.
> This I need yet?
> I need it like a hole in the head.
> He's a real nothing.
> It's O.K. by me.
> All right already.
> He's a regular genius.
> My son, the doctor.
> Excuse the expression.

And many, many, many more. *Webster's Unabridged* contains some five hundred Yiddish words common in American English, especially in the New York area. Almost any expression can take on Yiddish or Jewish coloring by what Rosten calls "unusual word order" *(Smart, he's not)*, "blithe dismissal via repetition" *(Fatshmat, so long as she's happy)*, "contempt via affirmation" *(My son-in-law he wants to be)*, and other linguistic devices that convey "exquisite shadings of meaning" and have been adopted, often subconsciously, by almost all New Yorkers.

One of the better-known Yiddish–Noo Yawkese expressions, *mazel tov,* is often believed to mean "good luck." However, Rosten says it has come to mean " 'Congratulations" or 'Thank God!' rather than its literal meaning of 'Good luck.' " Advising us that this "distinction is as important as it is subtle," he offers an example: "Say *mazel tov!* to an Israeli ship captain when he first takes command: this congratulates him on his promotion; don't say mazel tov! when the ship reaches port; this suggests you're surprised he got you there." Though Rosten and most others say *mazel tov* literally means "good luck" (from *mazel,* luck, *tov,* good), *mazel* is actually the Hebrew for "star," so the expression literally means: "May a good star shine upon your days."

The common greeting *What's new?* has been traced back to 1880s New York and is thought to be a translation of the *Was ist los?* of German-Jewish immigrants, as is the similar expression *What's with you?* Interestingly, one respected authority offers the surprising theory that *kike,* a vulgar, highly offensive term of hostility and contempt, often used by anti-Semites, offends not only persons of Jewish descent and religion but the Italians and Irish as well. The *Random House Dictionary of the English Language* suggests that it is "appar modeled on *hike.* Italian, itself modeled on *mike* Irishman, short for Michael." In other words, the deliberately disparaging term painfully illustrates the transfer of prejudice from one newly arrived immigrant group to the next. This view runs counter to the prevailing theory, however. Mencken and others, including *Webster's,* believe that the word "derived from the *ki* or *ky* endings of the surnames of many Slavic Jews." Neither theory seems susceptible of absolute proof.

The New Yorker's habit of "talking with his hands," a kind of frenetic ballet accompaniment to the music of his voice, is often associated with Yiddish, but it is a habit common to many language groups in the city, especially to Italian speakers. One wonders if American Indians could have communicated with New Yorkers unknown to them through ideographic signs, as late-nineteenth-century experiments showed they were able of doing with deaf-mutes! In any case, New Yorkers use a good number of the "700,000 distinctive movements of the hands, fingers, arms and face by which information can be transferred without speech" —perhaps more of them than any other Americans. Watch a New Yorker talking in a silent film and you might think he is speaking some form of Ameslan (*American Sign Language*).

H. L. Mencken considered Brooklynese a class dialect rather than a regional or geographical one. Originally it was "Bourgese," the Sage of Baltimore noted, a New York City speech pattern associated with "lower-class" colloquial speech. The word *Brooklynese* itself doesn't seem to have been coined until the late 1920s, though the dialect that grew in Brooklyn was observed and joked about fifty years earlier.

Called "The English of the Lower Classes" by E. H. Babbitt, the Columbia professor who first gave it scholarly attention in 1896, Brooklynese may well be rooted in Gaelic. The theory here is that the dialect first appeared after a late-nineteenth-century tsunami of immigration from Ireland flooded New York with future cops, firemen, cabbies, longshoremen, socialities, politicians, poets, and baseball fans. Francis Griffith, a retired Hofstra University professor who has studied the Brooklyn dialect nearly half a century, argues that the trademark Brooklyn diphthong *oi* (as in *moider*), which exists in no British dialect, is found in many Gaelic words, such as *barbaroi* (barbarian) and *taoiseach* (leader). Griffith, who used to have a sign over his blackboard admonishing "There's no joy in Jersey" when he taught public school in Brooklyn, doesn't accept the traditional Dutch derivation for *dese* and *dem,* pointing out that neither Gaelic nor Brooklynese has a *th* sound. *Th* becomes a hard *t* or *d* in both languages, giving us rough Brooklynese diamonds like *da dame wid tin legs.* It should be noted, however, that in addition to the Irish, none of New York's polyglot immigrants (into the 1930s New York City subways had No Smoking signs printed in English, German, Italian, Yiddish, Chinese, and Russian) pronounced *th* or *dh* sounds in their native languages and also substituted the nearest equivalents, *t* and *d,* for them.

A number of classic Brooklynese expressions do come directly from Gaelic. A *card* (as in *Wudda card,* or joker, *he is*) could be a corruption of the Gaelic *caird* (an itinerant tramp). The expression *Put da kibosh on it* (Put an end to it) may derive from *cie bais* (pronounced *bosh*), "the cap of death," a facecloth that was put on a corpse in southwest Ireland.

But it is hard to imagine mellifluous Gaelic or an Irish *brogue* (the word derived perhaps from the heavy *brogan* shoes that Irish peasants wore) becoming rapid-fire guttural Brooklynese, even in the midst of the most manic civilization in history. The Gaelic theory is just that: a theory—and one without sufficient proof. *Put the kibosh on it,* for example, may not derive from *cie bais* at all. One etymologist traces the words to a Yiddish term used in auctions and meaning an increase in a bid so that the bidder's opponents are quashed. Another word-detective suggests the Italian *capuce,* a tin lid used by street vendors of ice cream; to *put the kibosh on,* according to this last version, first meant to put the lid back on the container.

Facts can always be stretched to cover any theory. For instance, in his essay "A Form of Thanks" Cleanth Brooks shows how the King James Version of the Song of Songs would have been pronounced in 1860 Sussex, England:

1. De song of songs, dat is Solomon's.
2. Let him kiss me wud de kisses of his mouth; for yer love is better dan wine.

Brooks is writing about the roots of the folk language of Mississippi and how it sprang from a great lineage; yet these isolated words certainly could be used to make a case for a Brooklynese-Sussex connection as well.

Of the many theories about the origins of Brooklynese or New Yorkese the most startling is the guess that long before Shoiman boined Atlanter, New York entrepreneurs, who for more than a century had a strong trading relationship with the South, picked up the famous Brooklyn accent from the Southern planters of Mobile, New Orleans, and, to some degree, Charleston. These merchants, in turn, passed on the corrupted patrician Southern-ese sounds to the New York lower classes. The ironic suggestion that us bums who moider the language derived our speech habits from Southern aristocrats has been put forth as an hypothesis, "not even a theory, really," by Dr. Marshall D. Berger, a speech professor at New York's City College and a native New Yorker himself. Dr. Berger's best example of Brooklynese as corrupted Southern is the expression *The worm has turned.* Southern planters made that come out *The whum has tuhned,* which eventually arrived in New York as *The whuim has tuined,* and finally became *Da woim has toined* beloved of Williamsburg and Greenpoint. We shouldn't oughta have went South maybe.

While Brooklynese may derive from Southern speech, it is never called a charming dialect like its possible parent, even if it sometimes seems quite as lackadaisical. Brooklynese is clearly not a dialect of the upwardly mobile—not even in New York, as Professor Labov shows in his book *The Social Stratification of English in New York City* (1966). One can hear the differences in speech among personnel in uptown and downtown stores and even within the same store, distinctions that correspond to price and service. The upper class, prep-schooled "honks" of Tom Wolfe speak a different language from that of the "wonks" of the "lower classes"; I've often heard the gentrified *rawther* uptown. Education, economic status, ethnic ties, and age groups have always made a uniform Brooklynese impossible—to which most speech teachers would add, "Thank God!"

But by no means can we moan, "Dose were da days," or "Bon verge (bon voyage), Brooklynese." The thesis that Brooklynese is dead is a lot of *baloney* (Brooklynese that probably derives from the Irish *blarney,* not the German *bologna*). True, one finds few speakers around of the "a nerzy nerse annerz an erster," or "Doity Goity from Bizoity" variety, though the species is far from extinct. True, Brooklyn itself is now more than half nonwhite and filled with the musical sounds of Spanish, the liquid tones of various species of Black English. But Brooklynese is not yet dead and a less exaggerated Brooklyn accent has spread out from Greenpernt more than one hundred miles in every direction; the strains of it won't soon disappear from the land. Columnist Russell Baker, for example, has written a linguistic guide for Yurpeans (Europeans) visiting the United States in which he calls the language spoken here "American" but which strongly resembles Brooklynese, as this sample shows:

Q. *Ahdaya gettuh Rootwun?*
A. *Dake a leffada nexlite, gwate bloxun daycoride tillya kumdooa big facdree, unyul see toorodes. Dake a rodetudda lef unya cantmissit.*

If you hear someone hail a cab in New York, you might well hear him shout *KEE-ab,* according to sociolinguist William Labov, who has been studying changing Northeastern accents at the University of Pennsylvania's Linguistic Laboratory over the past twenty years. As noted in Chapter 1, Professor Labov has predicted the beginnings of an historic realignment in the pronunciation of American English, one that may be as far-reaching as that occurring between Chaucer's and Shakespeare's time. At present this change is most prominent among New York's white lower-middle class. Just as few New Yorkers say *Toity-toid* today (incidentally, my own investigation reveals that many old-time New Yorkers insist this pronunciation was more often *Teydy-teyd*, Thirty-third Street and Third Avenue being *Teydy-teyd n' Teyd*), other features of their dialect may wither away. Especially noticeable, says Labov and his protégés, is the short *a* picking up a long *e* before it. Labov has found that a good number of New Yorkers (he doesn't give a percentage) have adopted this new speech habit, using it in some words (e.g., *cab* and *bad*) but not in others (e.g., *cat, back, pack, bang, bat*).

I'd like to second Professor Labov's findings, but I have never heard the distinct pronunciation *KEE-ab* (said quickly) for *cab,* or *BEE-ag* for *bag* in my extensive, almost daily travels and eavesdropping through the New York City metropolitan area on subway, bus, and foot. Nor was I able to elicit such pronunciations on the twenty or so occasions that I tried to trick people into unselfconsciously saying these words. I did hear *beer* pronounced *BEE-ah,* however, though that is nothing new, and agree with Labov that while *frog* is pronounced *frahg,* the New York *dog* is often (but not always) pronounced *doo-aug,* and while *on* is *ahn* usually, *off* is often *oo-AWF.*

Neither could I find overwhelming support for Professor Labov's contention that *coral,* as in a coral reef, is pronounced *CAH-rel,* while a *choral* group of singers is pronounced *coral.* This is supposed to be some kind of New York shibboleth, but of the ten New Yorkers I questioned, all pronounced both words as *coral,* though I admittedly have heard the *cahrel* pronunciation in the past (only among college-educated people, if I remember correctly). But then my methods are primitive; I mention the results only for the little they are worth. I have noticed the pronunciation of *O.K.* being shortened to a more hurried *K* in the New York City area, and elsewhere; I noted this in *Human Words* (1972) and the pronunciation has become much more common since, though no dialectologist seems to have recorded it. Young people in particular often say *K* in place of *O.K.*, and recently I have heard the expression pronounced even more quickly—like the *k* in *kitty.*

Professor Labov contends that the merger of vowel sounds has tended to cause confusion of meaning, telling of a New York family sharply criticized by neighborhood kids because they gave their son a girl's name—the name was Ian, which the kids all pronounced *Ann.* Again, I've been unable to confirm this (friends with a son named Ian never heard the name pronounced that way), but I am not nearly the scientist the professor is, his methods being truly original and clever, as this admiring account of his field tests indicates: "Labov's method for testing the fate of the final and preconsonantal *r* in speakers of different social levels consisted of choosing three New York City department stores, each oriented to a completely different social stratum. He approached a large number of salesladies, asking each of them about the location of a certain department that he knew to be on the fourth floor. Thus, their answers always contained two words with potential *r*'s—'fourth' and 'floor.' This shortcut enabled Labov to establish in a relatively short time that the salesladies in the store with richer customers clearly tended to use '*r*-full' forms, whereas those in the stores geared to the poorer social strata more commonly used '*r*-less' forms."

Scores of people rich and poor from all over the world have brought words and pronunciations to New York over the last four centuries, many of which have entered the national vocabulary. There is even a theory that the word *gizmo,* for a thingamajig(!), comes from the Arabic *shu ismo* (meaning "the same"), which may have come to New York with Moroccans or been brought back by American soldiers who served in Morocco during World War II. New York has been a world city longer than any other American metropolis and is more so today than at any time in its history. The Magnificent Mongrel has a population of 7.1 million, of whom 2.1 million were born in another country. There are more

Greeks here than any place but Athens, more Russians than any place but in Russia, more Chinese than in any place but China and Taiwan. New York City has more Ethiopians (about 3,000) than several states have black people. Similar statistics could be cited for pages. At P.S. 89 in Elmhurst, Queens, *thirty-eight* different languages are spoken by students, half of whom do not come from English-speaking homes (there are more than 113,000 such children in the New York City school system). People migrate to the city from every part of America and the world, most of them affectionately regarding it as home rather than "a nice place to visit," as the old saw goes. Travel about New York and you will find little neighborhoods of Americans newly arrived from England, France, Germany, Greece, Iran, Israel, Italy, Poland, Portugal, Rumania, the U.S.S.R., Yugoslavia, Puerto Rico, Argentina, Colombia, Cuba, the Dominican Republic, Ecuador, Mexico, Panama, Peru, Barbados, Grenada, Guyana, Haiti, Jamaica, Trinidad, India, Japan, Korea, and the Philippines, among other countries —this in addition to older enclaves like Chinatown, Little Italy, and many, many more. The new immigrants are of all kinds and classes, from those with no aplomb, to those with the most unfazable aplomb, from those who sound like they have potatoes in their mouths to those who sound like they have silver potatoes in their mouths. And all of them are slowly changing the nature of Brooklynese with new words and accents, just as the words and rhythms of Black English and Spanglish (see Chapters 6 and 10) are doing.

New York City is truly "the nest of languages, the bequeathor of poems," as Walt Whitman observed in "A Broadway Pageant." Every year hundreds of new words and expressions are coined in New York, which has long been the communications capital of America. Most of these are obsolete within a few years, but many last. An old one, surprisingly, is *outta sight!* Often regarded as college slang of 1960s, *outta sight* (for something remarkable or wonderful) has been part of the language since the 1840s, in the form of the Bowery expression *out of sight*. Stephen Crane used it in its present form in his first novel *Maggie: A Girl of the Streets* (1896): "I'm stuck on yer shape. It's outa sight."

That many New York coinages don't last is best illustrated by the fate of prolific New York humorist Gelett Burgess, who coined the word *blurb*. When Burgess published his *Burgess Unabridged: A New Dictionary of Words You Have Always Needed* (1914), he wrote the following poem using some of his new words in the preface. The only one of the hundred he coined that we still use is *blurb*.

> *When vorianders seek to huzzlecoo,*
> *When jurpid splooch or vilpous drillig bores,*
> *When cowcats kipe, or moobles wog, or you*
> *Machizzled are by yowfs or xenogores,*
>
> *Remember Burgess Unabridged, and think,*
> *How quisty is his culpid yod and yab!*
> *No fidgeltick, with goigsome jobink,*
> *No varmic orobaldity—his gab!*
>
> *No more tintiddling slubs, like fidgelticks,*
> *Rizgidgeting your speech, shall lallify;*
> *But your jujasm, like vorgid gollohix,*
> *Shall all your woxy meem golobrify!*

Two relatively new New York inventions that seem to have lasted are *Yuppie* and *bag lady*. *Yuppie* is a recent coinage of the last five or so years which originated in the New York City area but already is nationally used. It means and is constructed from "*y*oung *u*rban *p*rofessional." *Bag lady* (short for shopping-bag lady) entered the language in New York in the 1960s. It has nothing to do with the expression *old bag* for an ugly woman (which goes back to the 1920s), or *bagman,* a term for someone (often a policeman) assigned to collect bribe or extortion money, this expression also dating back to the age of the flappers. *Bag* here refers to the shopping bags filled with their possessions that the unfortunate women called *bag ladies* carry as they wander from doorway to alley to abandoned car to park bench through the city. These women, usually dressed in layers of clothing both winter and summer, can be any age, although they are typically in their middle years. Sometimes physically healthy, and rarely alcoholics, they are almost always mentally ill and often refuse all offers of aid. They want nothing of life but for life to leave them alone. The *lady* in their name is both ironic and kind (which New Yorkese is, more frequently than it is given credit for).

Class dialects in New York are generally similar to those in other parts of the country. Middle-class people tend to pronounce their words more carefully, for example, while the rich are supremely sure that whatever they say is right and the poor don't give a good damn. Black English (see Chapter 6) probably has its capital in New York, if this class dialect can be said to have a capital, most new black expressions originating here at any rate. The class dialect Spanglish, in its Puerto Rican form (see Chapter 10), has also contributed local words and expressions to Noo Yawkese. No one seems to have established whether New York's Puerto Rican women favor the white New York dialect and Puerto Rican men lean to the black vernacular—which Professor Labov says is the case in Philadelphia. In any event, individuals of all classes and ethnic and social groups in the city frequently switch from Brooklynese to "network English" depending on the occasion, as has been noted. And in New York, as elsewhere, when members of these classes and groups have specialized occupations they often use words and expressions from the jargons or lingos of the workplace. Thus a New York City police officer speaks of his *rabbi* as his protector, "his influence with the higher-ups" at headquarters, while a New York mugger talks of *doing time* (not of *serving a jail sentence*). A New York waitress might shout *Noah's boy with Murphy carrying a wreath!*, which translates as an order of ham, potatoes and cabbage. New York stockbrokers, lawyers, legislators, garment workers, longshoremen, retail clerks, hotel workers, bartenders, truckers—these and hundreds more professions have their own special expressions that often enter the mainstream of New York talk, as the police term *rabbi* and the lawyer's term *takeover* have. New York printers contributed the national expression *lobster shift* to the language. *Lobster shift* for the newspaper shift commencing at four in the morning is said to have originated at the defunct *New York Journal-American* early in this century. The newspaper's plant was near the East Side docks, and workers on the shift came to work at about the same time lobstermen were putting out to sea in their boats.

Recently a Bronx candidate for head of the Boston public school system was asked by his examiners if he couldn't "get rid of that New York accent"—he didn't get the job, though to what extent his accent played a role in his rejection isn't known. People across the United States often regard Brooklynese as badly as the *click-clack* dialect of the South African Khoi-Khoin tribe, to which the Dutch gave the derogatory name *Hottentot* from their *hateran en tateren* (to stutter and stammer). One Texan Congressman had the noive to say New York City "isn't an English-speaking place," to which a Bronx borough president replied, "Texans speak a language no one understands!" But Americans generally do like Texan speech better if one can judge by a poll conducted by the Linguaphone Institute to ascertain where the best English in America is spoken, from the standpoint of diction. New York City came in dead last, with no votes. New York just *don't never get no breaks* (this *triple* negative, common in the area, is, however, not restricted to New York).

Protest groups have arisen like the Society Against Disparaging Remarks About Brooklyn, which had 40,000 members in the 1950s and replied to 3,000 slurs about Brooklyn speech in the media. But native New Yorkers do often shed whatever Brooklyn accents they possess while climbing the social ladder (even when making the short climb up fashionable Brooklyn Heights), either by emulating the local upper class or by hiring voice coaches to teach them General American. "There is nothing more tarnishing, more cheapening in life than a New York accent," advises one speech consultant. "It's so very *vulgar*. It robs even the most beautiful, intelligent person of any *dignity.*" She is one of some fifty metropolitan area teachers listed by the American Society for Training and Development, who charge from $5 to $100 an hour to make anyone speak as they think everybody should. Television and radio do their bit in homogenizing here, too—as they do everywhere, only more so. The theory is that the Brooklyn or New York accent turns off more people than any other, so that most local media stars who want to become national media stars try to lose it with the help of exercises done in front of mirrors. (Lesson One: "To stop replacing *th* sounds with *d* sounds, as in *my udduh bruddah,* push the tip of the tongue against the cutting edge of the upper teeth and practice saying rapidly: *the, these, them, those, that.*")

A cursory survey reveals no fewer than three courses offered in the metropolitan area teaching "how to lose your New York accent," including a class taught near the garment center on Seventh Avenue. Says one "Professor Henry Higgins," Marilyn Rubinek, who runs a school on East Seventy-sixth Street, where she exterminates New York accents: *"People today want to sound as if they come from nowhere in particular."* People also want good *packaging* of the merchandise in this age of the image—I mean, you got a Ph.D you wanna sound like it. People tell Ms. Rubinek they are passed over for promotion, are discriminated against when traveling. People shudder when they speak, *they are rejected in singles bars!* —all because they say things like *Jeet jet?* (Did you eat yet?), *Skweet* (let's go eat), and *Dere soiving ersters dere* (They're serving oysters there). Or because they answer questions like County Kerry Irishmen do, County Kerry Irishmen who know some Yiddish: "You think the Mets will win the pennant?" "Why shouldn't they?" "What do you think of Reagan's nose?" "What am I, a nose doctor?" Or because they don't believe *pahrmee* is a translation of the French *pardonnez-moi.* Things like that.

New York City's Mayor Ed Koch, no honk himself, recently took teachers and students of the city school system to task because they too often say *axed* instead of *asked,* among other "pronunciation mistakes." *Axed* is actually a regional pronunciation heard in many areas, including the South, and which Noah Webster noted in New England as early as 1789. The reversal of sounds here is called metathesis, one of the oldest processes in the language— in fact, the Old English verb *to ask* existed in the form *acsian* as well as *ascian.*

Out in California Dr. Morton Cooper, a Los Angeles speech pathologist, treats thirty to forty immigrants from da Bronx, Uppuh Manhattan, Toity-toid and Toid, Staten Oi-land, Lunk-Guylan, and Joisey for New Yorkitis, at about a couple of thousand G's a cure. Again we hear the same sinister refrain. "That's what they want," Dr. Cooper says. *"They want to sound like a person who comes from nowhere."* Dr. Cooper rids them of the pain, makes them acceptable to everyone, invisible, plastic, nobody's suspicious of them anymore!

And so they beat on ceaselessly out into the sea of the future borne by the current, using their mirrors, tape recorders, and mouth and throat diagrams. But there are those who swim against it, who like the philological flavor of the polyglot city, who don't think of the New York accent as slurvian, sleazy, monotone, nasal, and staccato (a charge that some Britishers level against all Americans!). Happily there are those who, given the choice, stick to subtler shades of *da, dis, dem, dose,* and *dat.* They may not believe Brooklynese is beautiful, but what dialect really is, and the real choice is whether one is willing to deny one's deepest origins, the very ur-material of the self, by spurning one's native talk. With this, even outlanders agree. "In a country already suffering from terminal blandness, regional accents and dialects should be treasured, not trashed," Carl Grossman wrote in a letter to the editors of *The New York Times* (5/1/84). "As a child growing up in Oklahoma, I relished the chance to hear a New Yorker talk. Every strangely shaped vowel brought pictures to my mind of towering buildings, hot, gritty sidewalks and Ebbets Field. And the fast-clipped speech made me imagine the speeding subways and hurrying pedestrians I had never actually seen. When at age thirteen I arrived in the city on vacation with my parents, my first wish was to hear the banter that was uniquely New York. Now, even after living here for eleven years, I find it is still accent that separates transplants like myself from 'real' New Yorkers. And it is still accent that, for me, helps make New Yawk New York."

Along these same lines linguist Dr. Harold Bender says: "Brooklynese is no upstart. It has a fine tradition going back to the early Dutch burghers. Despite its age, it is still virile and is spreading." Various New York speech defenders also point out that *"goil* is a better rendering than the *gel* or *gairl* of Britain," that "an 'ultimate *r*' gets added to the Oxford and Harvard as well as to the Brooklyn pronunciation of *India* and *law,* and that Brooklyn contractions of the type of *gumnt* for government and *jeet* for did you eat? go *pari passu* with Britain's syncopated Chumley and Lester."

One man who isn't willing to lose his New York accent is John Occhiogrosso, formerly of Brooklyn, whose superb pronunciation of the Kings (County) English won him an expense-paid trip back to Brooklyn in a recent "Best New York Accent in Houston" contest. (A half dozen contestants were eliminated because they didn't know or remember that you play stoop ball with a *Spaldeen,* not a Spalding, in New York.) Mr. Occhiogrosso's test of skill included the proper New York pronunciation of a room-service order from a certain floor of a certain New York hotel, which went: "Oim owan da toidy-toid flohwah, of da Noo Yowak Stadla. Can oi hab a cuppa kowafee an a glazza watta?" Though he has in the past faced some job discrimination on account of his accent, the winner says, in translation: "If people don't like me for what I am, the hell with them. That's the Brooklyn way."

In addition to the peerless Mr. Occhiogrosso, here is a native New Yorker's Hall of Fame for the greatest living practitioners of

Noo Yawkese, admirable speakers one can really loin the language from, a few of whom were accorded similar honors by a New York newspaper several years ago.

BUGS BUNNY, who, says his creator and voice Mel Blanc, has a New York accent combining Brooklyn and Bronx elements.

JIMMY BRESLIN, author, Pulitzer Prize winner, and sometime politician and broadcaster, who hails from Queens and who has been quoted as saying: "You are what you are."

BELLA ABZUG, former Congresswoman, who contends: "Nah, politically, my accent has never been a problem, and I've been all over the country. They loved me in Peoria, and they loved me in Nashville. I think people should be what they are."

ROCKY GRAZIANO, former fighter and television personality, who observes: "Da only reason dey use me on TV is cawsa my accent. I'm outta bizness widout it."

LEO DUROCHER, the "practically Peerless Leader," who when he managed the Brooklyn Dodgers threatened Brooklyn's arch-rivals the New York Giants with: "It's gonna be Poil Hahbuh fuh de Gints."

JACK NICHOLSON, whose portrayal of a New York hood in the film *Prizzi's Honor* won him honors.

JOAN RIVERS, New York comedienne, who explains why she talks so fast: "We [New Yorkers] tawk fast becaws we don't know how long we're gonna *live.* . . . I can do my whole act waiting for the subway doors to close."

HENRY WINKLER as "The Fonz," who could once be found black leather jacket and all hanging out on every Brooklyn street corner and still haunts the borough.

THAT ANONYMOUS BROOKLYN DODGER BROADCASTER, who on a linguistically memorable day at Ebbets Field in the 1930s saw that pitcher Waite Hoyt was knocked down by a line drive and exclaimed: "Oh, no—Hoyt is hoit!"

GERALDINE A. FERRARO, whose New York accent may have lost the Democrats forty-nine states, including New York, when she ran for Vice President in 1984. Do aliens detest the dialect so much? Should Ms. Ferraro go to accent-eradication school? Anyway, Ms. Ferraro, a trial lawyer, hails from Queens, the Borough of Homes, representing Archie Bunker's Ninth Congressional District in Elmhurst (*Ellimheyst,* locally), and should be saluted for her bravery—this stalwart New Yorker didn't try to change a word. She is, one observer notes, "a living example of my entirely unsupported nonscientific probably biased theory that the way people talk often has nothing to do with their education or position in life."

Honorable mention goes to HOWARD COSELL, the DEAD END KIDS (especially LEO GORCEY), early TONY CURTIS, the late NELSON ROCKEFELLER (who mixed a lot of *youses* wid his broad honk *ahs*), MAYOR KOCH, and finally, THAT WELL-REMEMBERED GUY NAMED JERRY with the white blowfish belly sticking out from under his shirt who did those outrageous furniture commercials on local New York TV ("That's the stor-ieeeeee. . . ."). As for the best all-around rendition of the Brooklyn accent I've seen in print, I'd have to vote against Damon Runyon and pick Thomas Wolfe's piece "Only the Dead Know Brooklyn" from his *Death to Morning* (1935), despite the fact that it is somewhat snobbish and the dialect is exaggerated.

A Short Glossary of
Some Cherce Noo Yawk Woids
(No one uses all of them, but almost every New Yorker uses a few)

absoid—absurd
adjern—adjoin
ahn—on
alluh—all the
aniainfoolin!—this is an order
annerz—annoys
Atlanter—Atlanta
avenoo—avenue
awdah—order
awmobile—car

bah—bar, tavern
bawss—boss
becaws—because
BEE-ag—bag (*sometimes*—see text)
beeuh—beer
berl—boil
boids—winged creatures
boin—burn
boip—burp

bon verge—bon voyage
brudda—brother
bunking—bumping
bunk into—bump into
CAH-rel—coral (as in reef)
cherce—choice
chintz—gents (as in "chintz room")
choip—chirp (as in "choip, choip")
coib—curb
coils—ringlets (see *curl*)
counteh—counter
cuppa—cup of
curl—what snakes do when wrapped up
da—the
dare—there (as in "over dare")
dat—what you put over dare
deeuh—dear (as in "Yes, my deeuh")
den—then
dere—there
dey—they
dint—didn't
d'ja—did you
drivah—driver
doity—dirty
doo-AWG—dog (*sometimes*—see text)
dose—those
erl boiner—oil burner
erster—oyster
fadder—male parent
fawk—fork
fayuh—fare (as in "cab fayuh")
feeuh—what muggers inspire
fella—fellow

fergit—forget
finstins—for instance
flahwah—floor
foist—first
frahg—frog
fuh—for
geddin gout—getting out
gint—giant
glazza—glass of
goil—girl
gole joolry—gold jewelry
gotta—got to
guvnah—governor
gwan—go on!
hav—have
hahbuh—harbor (as in "Poil Hahbuh")
hersted—hoisted
hizzonah—his honor (de Mayah)
hoid—heard or herd
housink—housing
howdah—how to
huh—her
idear—idea
jalettum—did you let him
Joisy—Jersey
juhhirmee—did you hear me
KEEab—cab (*sometimes*—see text)
kowafee—coffee
lawbstah—lobster
lemmeawf—let me off
lika—like a
loin—line, learn
Lunk Guylin—Long Island
matta—matter
mayah—mayor (hizzonah)
moida—as in moida da bums!
mout—mouth

mudder—a female parent

nah—no

nerz—noise

neveh—never

noive—nerve

NOO-klee-uh—nuclear

Noo Yawk—New York

no problem—you're welcome

nudge or noodge—pest

numbeh—number

oi—I

oim—I'm

oncet—once

ongana—I'm going to

oveh—over

papah—paper

pernt—point

pleece—law-enforcement officers

pock—a place with trees and muggers

poil—pearl

poiple—purple

riz—risen

secon hand—second hand

seedat—see that

seeyahlatah—see you later

sevent—seventh

shuddah—should have

sliding pond—playground slide

SRO—standing room only or single-room occupancy (in a seedy hotel)

smatter—what's the matter

soupa or soopa—super

soupaficial—superficial

sout—south

Spalding—Spaldeen

sperl—spoil

stoop—porch and front steps

suppah—supper

ta—to

tawk—talk

terlet—toilet

tess—test

ting—thing

toid or thoid—third

toin—turn

toity—the number after 29

Toity-toid and Toid— Thirty-third Street and Third Avenue

troot—truth

true—through

twicet—twice

uddah—other

uf caws—of course

uhparment—apartment

vanella—vanilla

verse—voice

wanna—want to

wantcha—wouldn't you

wateh—water

watta—water, what a

wawk—walk

whaa—what

whatsa—what's the

whudda—what the

wideh—with the

wit—with

woim—worm

wuh—were

youse—you

4 Yawl Spoken Here: The Sounds of the South

✶

Southerners were proud of their accents even before that fiery eunuch John Randolph of Virginia, known for his sharp, biting soprano tongue on the floor of the House and Senate, actually fought a duel over the pronunciation of a word. But then Randolph of Roanoke was widely known for his eccentricity, which deteriorated into dementia in his later years. Better for an alien without the slightest trace of a Southern accent to contend at the outset that South Mouth, despite all the fun made of it, is the most charming of American dialects, in the words of critic Anatole Broyard: "An attempt, at least in part, to find and keep the music in the American language, in some cases almost to sing it"—even if there's a lot of unintentional humor in it, too.

There surely is a "royal sound" to Southern speech at its most eloquent, perhaps because, as one nameless South Georgian says, "It's the closest thang on God's green earth to the King's natchul English." That the rest of the country, not Southerners, are the ones who "talk strange" is an established fact in the South. Linguist Lee A. Pederson of Atlanta's Emory University, who specializes in Southern dialects, agrees that there is truth in the anonymous claim. "The North," he says, "was largely settled by immigrants who learned English as a second language and were heavily dependent on the *written* word. Southerners, on the other hand, have always relied on the *spoken* words. In that respect, Southern speech is closer to the native speech of England, and often to Elizabethan England. It is a much more sensitive and effective medium of communication than Northern speech, for the most part, because it is so rooted in the spoken word."

Some say the Southern accent's close links with the King's English made it possible for British actors Vivien Leigh and Leslie Howard to affect such authentic Southern accents in *Gone with the Wind.* In any case, only American mountain, or hill, dialect (see Chapter 5) preserves old English so well as Southern talk, and the so-called Ozark accent is often considered a variety of Southern dialect, deriving as it doubtlessly does from the dialect of the southern Appalachians, which, in turn, was brought there from Pennsylvania by Scotch-Irish immigrants.

Mountain talk is but one possible form of the Southern accent. Southern dialect is extremely varied, and many linguists divide it into smaller dialects. Some experts call these divisions the *Mountain* (or *Hill*), *Plains,* and *Coastal dialects,* while others opt for the *Mountain dialect* plus the three classifications below.

THE VIRGINIA TIDEWATER, a pleasing soft dialect with little nasalization that is spoken by the most aristocratic of Southerners and which prevails along the coast from the Delaware-Maryland-Virginia Peninsula to South Carolina, with speakers found in Charlottesville and Richmond, Virginia, as well as in some northern sections of the Shenandoah Valley.

SOUTH CAROLINA LOW COUNTRY, extending from northeastern South Carolina's Peedee River to northeastern Florida, but found along the river valleys of the Deep South as far inland as Columbia, South Carolina, and Augusta, Georgia.

GENERAL SOUTHERN LOWLAND, spoken by more than 60 million people in the Southern lowland (outside the mountains, South Carolina and the Tidewater) and including at least parts of sixteen states: Maryland, West Virginia, Delaware, Kentucky, Tennessee, Alabama, Georgia, Florida, Louisiana, Arkansas, Missouri, Mississippi, southern Illinois, southern Ohio, southern Indiana, and all but southeast Texas.

In addition there are the East Texas dialect (see Chapter 10), local dialects with Charleston and New Orleans as focal points, and Southern dialects like Cajun, Creole, and Gullah (see Chapter

10). Dialect subspecies thrive in the South. In the *Linguistic Atlas of the Gulf States,* to be published in four or five volumes over the next four years, some thirteen separate Southern dialects are treated. Elsewhere it has been noted that former President Carter's accent isn't merely Southern, but Gulf Coastal Plain. What's more, it seems that his home state, Georgia, includes not only the Gulf Coastal Plain dialect but smaller dialects called Carolina Mountain, Alabama-Tennessee Low Country, Northern and Southern Piedmont, Atlantic Coastal Plain, and Thomaston-Valdosta.

Charlestonians are particularly proud of their distinctive accent, which they describe as possessing "a smattering of Old English, a sea-island lilt [see Chapter 6] and soft Southern tones." Older Charlestonians are sometimes taken for Britons or Scots. Lord Ashley Cooper, the pen name of Frank Gilbreth, author of *Cheaper by the Dozen* and a columnist for *The News and Courier,* has compiled a *Dictionary of Charlestonese* "to assist sloppy talkers from other sections of the country to understand Charlestonians." He defines *Cholmondely* (pronounced *chumley*) as "the brick thing on a roof that lets out smoke," *ho, ho, ho* as "three ladies of the evening," *poet* as "pour it," *version* as "the kind of queen Elizabeth I was," and *tin sin stow* as "the foive and doyme." When I visited Charleston recently I heard the name of his newspaper pronounced as *The Newsand Korea!*

New Orleans also boasts of its homegrown Southern accent. Shortly after the Civil War a Yankee historian called the town, in prewar days: "the social sink of the Union . . . the bottomless pit . . . [where] a dialect of ingenious and elaborate blasphemy, half-savage slang, and abominable filth was made tolerably intelligible to strangers (who were accustomed only to the ordinary phraseology of the English race) by the occasional introduction of words of which necessity and the idioms of our language compelled the use." New Orleans has, of course, changed drastically since, if it ever really was that way. In *The Earl of Louisiana* (1946) A. J. Liebling told of a New York City accent similar to that spoken by Al Smith, and almost obsolete in New York, living harmoniously in New Orleans alongside a Dixie plantation dialect. John Kennedy Toole's novel *A Confederacy of Dunces* (1983) made the same point.

No matter how many smaller subdialects it is composed of,

Southern dialect is generally heard south and east of an imaginary line traced along the Maryland-Virginia northern boundary, along West Virginia's southern boundary, then along the Ohio River and past the Mississippi (including southern Missouri), and finally down through southeastern Oklahoma and East Texas. Here South Mouth prevails and indeed has held out better than any major dialect against the encroachment of the General-American Middle Western speech that has been the darling of radio and television announcers for the past half century, although large migrations from the North in recent times threaten to homogenize the area.

Southern talk, like that of New England, began as a type of speech basically southeastern English in nature, more than half the colonists in the Virginia colony, for example, hailing from the southern part of England. Puritans, royalists, soldiers, indentured servants, and transported criminals (like Defoe's fictional Moll Flanders, "twelve year a whore . . . twelve year a thief, eight year a transported felon in Virginia") all formed part of this largely uneducated group, whose speech among the religious often had a whine added, possibly to connote a superior piety. Some speech patterns were established early on; for example, the scholar Schele de Vere claimed that Southern disregard for the letter r should be charged to "the guilty forefathers, many of whom came from Suffolk and the districts belonging to the East Anglians."

"Proper" London English of the eighteenth century influenced Tidewater Southern speech more than most American regions for the obvious reason that these Southerners (like Bostonians and New Yorkers) were from earliest times in closer contact with England than other parts of the country, leading the wealthy gentry in the region to ape fashionable Londoners down to their way of talking, a habit that remained long after their days of glory, and one that, in turn, was copied from them by the plainer folk. But while Southern seaport and plantation owner speech was largely modeled on London English, inland speech had little chance of blending into a broad regional usage because of cultural isolation, this resulting in the great diversity of local usages in the area. Nevertheless, the aristocrats of the South made their own (and made a large part of the region's) such upper-class English speech as *jine* for *join, pisen* for *poison, varmint* for *vermin, gwine* for *going, starling* for *sterling, widder* for *widow, piller* for *pillow, winder* for *window,* and *varsity* for *university.*

Other Southern linguistic ties with England included the Scotch-Irish Presbyterian ministers of North Carolina and western Virginia, who were sent back to Scotland for religious training by their congregations, and were responsible for *hae* being used for *have, gin* for *if,* and *wha* for *who* over the course of several generations. Scotch-Irish schoolteachers, who were often indentured servants, also "had no inconsiderable influence . . . upon our pronunciation and language," according to John Pickering, writing in the *American Quarterly Review* for September 1828.

Some critics contend that the Southern accent is distinctive solely because the region was settled from England's Southwest country, but this seems unlikely. While Southwest country dialect has many similarities, Southern speech doesn't possess its most conspicuous feature, the consonant shift of "Did 'e zee the vox?" —for one important difference. Neither is there any strong evidence that the South was settled by people from England's Southwest. It does seem likely that distinctive features of black speech, different from any English dialect, must have influenced the Southern speech to some extent, given the enormous population of blacks in the area and the closeness of blacks and whites on plantations, especially children, who often played together (some black children were indeed designated "play children" for the whites). On the other hand, white speech probably influenced black speech in the area even more.

In general, Southern dialect is best characterized by a slower enunciation than is common in most of the country, combined with the gliding or diphthongization of stressed vowels. This so-called Southern drawl results in pronunciations like *yea-yis* for *yes, ti-ahm* for *time, I-ah* for *I, fi-ahn* for *fine, a-out* for *out, tyune* for *tune,* and *nyu* for *new.* The final consonants following such slow drawling vowel sounds (particularly *d, l, r,* and *t*) are often weakened, resulting in such characteristic Southern pronunciations as *hep* for *help, mo* for *more, yo* for *your, po* for *poor, flo* for *floor, kep* for *kept, nex* for *next, bes* for *best, sof* for *soft,* and *las* for *last.* Southern speech is also noted for being more melodious and various than other dialects because the vowels are long-embraced, like lovely women.

If fully seventy-two human muscles are required in speaking

one word, as physiologists say, it certainly seems that Southerners often employ considerably fewer in tawkin so dif'runt. The Southern drawl, which makes it possible to deliver a sentence in twice as much time as in any other dialect, is most noticeable at the end of a sentence or before a pause, and has been ridiculed on the stage and screen in such phrases as *nice white rice*—lazily pronounced *nigh-yes why-ut rye-is*—something no elegant Southerner would do.

By no means is the Southern drawl found only in the South. Even today it can be heard in parts of New England, of all places, where the "y glide" of the *u* sound after *d, n,* and *t* results in Yankee pronunciations like *dyu* for *due* and *nyu* for *new.* The drawl, in fact, first came to the attention of Americans when Noah Webster enjoined the New England "yeomen" to improve their "drawling nasal way of speaking" in his *Dissertations on the English Language* (1789). As previously noted, Webster believed the New England drawl was the result of a people unaccustomed to commanding slaves and servants and "not possessing that pride and consciousness of superiority" that he thought enabled people to speak in a decisive way. Certainly he did not take into account the drawling Southern slaveowner. In any case, Americans South and North were proud of their drawls. When the gallant Captain Frederick Marryat, British novelist and adventurer, asked an American lady why she drawled, the linguistically patriotic lady replied, "Well, I'd drawl all the way from Maine to Georgia rather than clip my words as you English people do." Nevertheless, Marryat held to his opinion that Americans dwelt upon their words when they spoke "from their cautious, calculating habits."

Southern expressions color the works of our best Southern novelists, ranging from *a rubber-nosed woodpecker in a petrified forest* (an incompetent) and *We've howdied but we ain't shook* (someone one knows but not well) to *as mad as a rooster in an empty henhouse* and *Don't get crosslegged* (Don't lose your temper). Most of these haven't become nationally known despite their charm, often, one guesses, because they are basically too countrified and relaxed for our increasingly urbanized frenetic Republic. "We'll put 'em so far back in jail, you can't shoot peas to 'em," Georgia Governor Marvin Griffin once said of some civil rights protestors.

Other Southernisms are just completely alien to the experience of most Americans. Consider, for example, the expression *a dead cat on the line* for the suspicion that someone is trying to deceive you or something is going on behind your back. This one is downright *bumfuzzling*, as they say in Mississippi for confusing. Twenty-one people interviewed by the *Dictionary of American Regional English (DARE)* used this expression, but not one of them could explain it. When William Safire asked readers of his nationally syndicated word column for help, lots of efforts were made, including "a telephone eavesdropper" and "a stranger in a line dance, whose movements were dead because he didn't know the steps," but they were at best educated guesses. Finally an old man in Louisiana scrawled a letter explaining that the expression has its roots in fishing for catfish, when trotlines with many hooks on them are set in the water. The lines are checked every day, so if a fisherman checks a neighbor's line and there's a *dead* catfish (cat) on it, he knows there's something wrong, something suspicious or fishy. Only a few days later Professor Frederick G. Cassidy, editor in chief of *DARE*, heard a blues singer in a Manhattan club begin a song with the refrain "If a child don't favor his father some way, there's a dead cat on the line."

A Southerner will say *dived* for the past tense of *to dive*, while a Northerner will usually say *dove*. Southerners often call their chickens *gospel birds*, because they're so often served at Sunday dinner, and they have their own local names for things, such as the Floridian *chizzwink* or *blind mosquito* for the crane fly. Cottage cheese in the north is called *creamed cheese* in Louisiana, siding for a house is *boxing* in Mississippi, kids in South Carolina call the big marble or aggie *the bomb,* and the grasshopper is a *hopper grass* in East Virginia. A favorite—given in Roy Wilder Jr.'s *You-All Spoken Here*—is the expression *He's too poor to paint and too proud to whitewash,* describing a proud but impoverished Southern gentleman. I also like the descriptive term *kneewalkin' drunk* and *beating the devil around the stump* for *hemming and hawing.* Southern expressions, like Southern drawls, are often longer and more relaxed than most of the nation's, the dialect indeed filled with what linguists classify as phatic speech, sentences that do little more than make what Anatole Broyard has called "a friendly noise." Certainly, as Mr. Broyard further notes, this is no reason to condemn "You-all" accents, as too proper people often do. Better phatic than frenetic.

You-all is widely considered the *ne plus ultra* of Southern dialect, but this expression, used throughout the South, is much misunderstood. Mainly applied to two or more people, *you-all* can be used when the speaker is addressing one person, but only when the sentence *implies plurality.* Except for some speakers in the Ozarks and rural Texas, only a ham of a stage Southerner would use *you-all* so indiscriminately as to say "That's a pretty dress you-all are wearing." But a Southerner might well say "How you-all?"—the question intended to inquire of the health of you and your entire family or group. Further, the inflection of the phrase is all important. When the *you* (yoo) in *you-all* is accented, as in *"You*-all must come," this means that the group near the speaker is invited, but when the *all* is accented everyone present without exception is invited. The contraction *y'all* is always used in this plural sense. Recently the American Southernism *y'all* (or *yawl*) has been explained, though hardly to the satisfaction of everyone, as a *calque* (a filling in of an African structure with English material) from the West African second person plural *unu,* which is also used in the American black Gullah dialect (see Chapter 6). This interesting theory is advanced in a study by Jay Edwards in Hancock and Decamp's *Pidgins and Creoles* (1972): "In the white plantation English of Louisiana, the form *y'all* functioned precisely as did the *unu* of the slaves. The use of *y'all* (semantically *unu*) was probably learned by white children from black mammies and children in familiar domestic situations." In any case, the closest thing that has been found in English to the collective second-person plurals *you-all* and *you-uns* is the collective second person *you-together* that is sometimes heard in England's East Anglia dialect today.

Though it's hard to generalize about Southern grammatical peculiarities, which vary with a Southerner's education and regional heritage, there are differences from General American that are frequently heard. The familiar and still fashionable use of such verb phrases, or double modals, as *might could* and *used to could* by educated Southerners is practically unique in America. *American Speech* editor Ronald R. Butters has noted a linguistic feature "by which you can always detect a Southerner if you wait long enough" because he or she invariably inserts the word *to* shortly after *have* when asking questions like "Shall I have him to call you?"

I've been knowin him for a long time is a Southernism, as is *he's still in the bed* (for *he's still in bed*). Southerners often use *it* in place of there, saying things like *It's a fly in my soup.* They also often use *a* instead of *an,* as in the sentence "I'll be there in a hour." *Here* and *there* are commonly used superfluously in the South, too ("This here toy's mine" or "That there girl's mine"), and *like to* is as common for *almost* in the South as it was in its Victorian Ireland birthplace ("I like to broke my back"). A few dozen such usages follow, along with the standard English in parenthesis. Many of course are by now heard to a lesser extent outside the South:

"I don't *intend for* (want) her to go out."
"Carry (take) me back to old Virginia."
"I *might could* (be able to) help you."
"I'll *study on* (think about) it."
"I *knows* (know) it."
"We *has* (have) it."
"Didn't nobody go (Nobody went)."
"He ain't got no call (he has no reason) accusing me."
"Ain't got but (I have only) ten cents."
"That's *right* (very) pretty."
"He got *a right smart* (great deal) of work."
"He lives a *piece* (way) up the road."
"He went *this-a-way* (this way) and *that-a-way* (that way)."
"It's a *powerful* (very) long time."
"She cooked *a mess* (a lot) of bread."
"I'd have him *to get it* (get it) for you."
"However you does (no matter how you do it) she don't like it."
"He took it *off'n* (from) him."
"It's *mighty nigh* (almost) used up."
"I'm *fixing* (preparing) to leave."
"Take it *out'n* (out of) the box."
"I'm *a-going* (going) home."
"I *done told* (told) you to stop."
"He's sure *biggety* (a show-off)."
"Stop acting so *feisty* (showing off)."

Southerners have always been able to joke about their drawls and other peculiar linguistic institutions, as former Vice President Alben Barkley did in this limerick:

In New Orleans dwelled a young Creole
Who, when asked if her hair was all reole,
Replied with a shrug,
"Just give it a tug
And decide by the way that I squeole."

Millions of Southerners do *squeole* (instead of *squeal*) like Barkley's Creole. Millions also say *scat* instead of *gesundheit* or *God bless you* after someone sneezes, people in Arkansas preferring *scat* 6–1. A woman who refuses a proposal of marriage from a man *turns him in the cold* or *puts him on the funny side* in Kentucky, *gives him the go-by* in South Carolina, and *rings him off* in Georgia. A South Carolinian will say *outten the light* for *turn off the light*, but *cut off the light* is more generally heard throughout the South. A fussbudget is generally a *fussbox* south of the Mason-Dixon Line and Mom is usually *Mamma*. Older Southerners sometimes say *everwhat* for *whatever* and *everwho* for *whoever*, while their *a gracious plenty* means *enough*. Southerners have their groceries packed in a *sack* or *poke* instead of a bag, call a small stream or brook a *creek* or *run*, and call *laurel* what Northerners generally know as the rhododendron. In West Virginia a big party is a *belling*. Southerners call a jalopy a *rattletrap* and tend to say they are *wore out* or *about to give out* when tired. They often use the conjunctive *which* in a confusing way, according to Ronald Butters, who cites: "The President was not happy with the results of the election, which I couldn't be happier about that."

Southerners wince at the words *Civil War*, which they most often call *The War*, or the *War Between the States*. One can employ such joking terms as *The Uncivil War, The Late Friction, The Schism*, or the *Late Ruction*, but here is a list of the best appellations to use for *The War* when in dedicated Southern company:

The War of Secession
The War for Southern Independence
The Second War of Independence
The Second American Revolution
The War for States Rights
The War of the North and South
The War for Southern Freedom
Mr. Lincoln's War

The War for Constitutional Liberty
The War for Southern Rights
The War for Southern Nationality
The War for Nationality
The Yankee Invasion
The Great Rebellion
The War for Separation
The War of the Sixties
The War for Southern Freedom
The War to Suppress Yankee Arrogance
The Lost Cause

Similarly, the South has different names for important battles of the Civil War. The North's *Bull Run,* for example, is the South's *Manassas,* while *Antietam* to the North is *Sharpsburg* to the South, and the North's *Stone River* is the South's *Murfreesboro.* During *The War* the South used worthless *graybacks* and *bluebacks* in place of the North's *greenback* money.

One persistent old joke has The War to Suppress Yankee Arrogance caused by a dialect difference. It seems that three high-ranking Northern generals stomped into a Washington, D.C., bar and shouted, "We want a bottle right away!" A Southern spy overheard them and breathlessly reported to General P. G. T. Beauregard: "Top Union generals want a bottle right away!" Chivalrous Beauregard obliged, leaving the evening's quadrille in Montgomery and proceeding to Charleston, South Carolina, where he gave them the *bottle* (or battle) of Fort Sumter.

The South is still the home of the chivalrous *Southern Gentleman.* "If you can shoot like a South Carolinian, ride like a Virginian, make love like a Georgian, and be proud of it as an Episcopalian, you're a Southern Gentleman," Clare Boothe Luce said in *Kiss the Boys Goodbye;* but the species has also been defined, by an anonymous Yankee, as "one who rises to his feet when his wife comes in bearing the firewood." The South is also the home of the *redneck, po' white,* and *cracker. Rednecks* are poverty-stricken white tenant farmers and sharecroppers, the backs of their necks reddened and toughened by years of labor in the sun, and though *redneck* has become a derogatory term, as Jonathan Daniels reminded us, both Jackson and Lincoln came from redneck folk. *Po' white* is always a disparaging term for shiftless, lazy white folks, and *cracker,* originally *Georgia cracker,* and possibly named after the cracking whips of slave overseers, means any "low-down Southern white man," according to Mencken, but today seems to be accepted with resignation or good humor by many Georgians and other Southern *good old boys,* who even call themselves *crackers.*

Southern gentlemen, rednecks, po' whites, and crackers are all capable of *rebel yales,* a rebel yell being an untranslatable, peculiarly Southern, peculiarly wordless cry that has been with us at least since The Second War of Independence and may be a corruption of the English fox-hunting cry *Tally-ho,* as has been suggested, but is always "a prolonged high-pitched, bloodcurdling cross between a yell *(yale)* and scream." It is also possible that the *rebel yell* was first the *Texas yell,* borrowed by Texans from an Apache or Comanche war cry that combined the turkey gobbler's cry with a series of yelps.

Virginians, who may have originated the rebel yell, were such great fox hunters that they were nicknamed *beagles* after their hunting hounds in the early days of *Dixie.* As we'll see, Dixie itself may take its name from the 1767 boundary line set between Pennsylvania and Maryland by English surveyors Charles Mason and Jeremiah Dixon, but some etymologists believe that it has its origins in New York City, of all places. This Yankee derivation for among the most Southern of Southern words is explained by the *Charlestown Courier* of June 11, 1885: "When slavery existed in New York, one Mr. Dixie owned a large tract of land on Manhattan Island, and a large number of slaves. The increase of the slaves and of the abolition sentiment caused an emigration of the slaves to more thorough and secure slave sections, and the many Negroes who were thus sent off (many being born there) naturally looked back to their old houses . . . with feelings of regret, as they could not imagine any place like Dixie. Hence it became synonymous with an ideal location."

One is *afeared* to list dialectical words peculiar only to a single region because there is so much traffic between regions today, but *shut my mouth* if *sigogglin, spizzerinctum, catawampus,* and *snollygoster* don't qualify for South Mouth. *Sigogglin (sy-gog-lin)* means "crooked, askew or out of plumb," as in "You sawed that board off a little sigogglin," and has the variant forms *antigodlin, antigogglin,* and *slantigodlin,* all of which may have their origin in the thought that something crooked goes against God's plan for an orderly world. *Spizzerinctum* is a Southern rural term for energy or enthusiasm ("I wish I had his *spizzerinctum*"), while a *snollygoster* is usually a man "who wants office, regardless of party, platform or principles," though President Truman, from Missouri and famous for his use of such terms, defined it as "a man born out of wedlock." *Catawampus* is heard throughout the South for cater-cornerèd (four-cornered), and is often used in such expressions as "He walked catawampus across the street," or "You might call a rhombus a catawampus square."

July is still generally accented on the first syllable in the Southern states (*Ju*ly). Perhaps this will someday become standard pronounciation countrywide. Stranger things have happened. In fact, July—named by Mark Anthony in honor of Julius Caesar because that was Caesar's birth month—was until about 1800 commonly pronounced like the girl's name Julie in English, rhyming with "newly."

If you dare ask for *vittles* in the South, upwardly mobile Southerners may look with contempt upon you, unaware that this backcountry Southern word is a very old, proper English one and that *victuals* is a pedantic misspelling of it. Unaffected Southerners, however, might offer you some *hush puppies,* deep-fried cornmeal batter cakes which may have earned their name in Reconstruction times when black cooks quieted hungry dogs around their outdoor cooking fires by tossing bits of these corn pones to them along with the admonition "Now hush, puppy!" *Hoecakes* in the South are the flat corn bread called *johnnycakes* elsewhere, taking the name because they were once cooked on the business end of a garden hoe. *Frogmore stew* is a seafood dish (without frogs) made on Frogmore, one of the Sea Islands. *Bosum bread* is the large, flat loaf of bread that black stevedores working the Mississippi steamboats carried in their shirtfronts (against their chests, or *bosums*) for snacks throughout the day. *Elberta peaches* are also of Southern origin and may be so named for Elberta Rumph of Marshallville, Georgia, who in 1860 reputedly planted some peach pits in her husband's orchard that by an accidental cross-pollination resulted in the delicious golden variety.

Other interestingly named Southern dishes (for which no etymological explanations have been found) include *limping Susan* (rice and okra); *barefoot bread* (corn pone); *crawdads* (crawfish); *snickerdoodles* (cinnamon sugar cookies); *s'mores* (toasted marshmallows and chocolate); *fandaddies* (fried clams); and *hoppin' John* (black-eyed peas and rice). *Succotash* is often pronounced *circuit hash,* though I haven't seen it spelled that way.

Black slaves awarded cakes for winning dance competitions on Southern plantations are probably responsible for both the dance called the *cakewalk* and the widespread expression *That takes the cake. Root, hog, or die* (to get down to work and shift for oneself) was also originally a Southern expression, first recorded by Davy Crockett and based on the hog's unfailing ability to provide for itself by rooting the ground with its snout, which yields it everything from acorns to truffles. The *catbird seat* (sitting pretty) and *tearing up the peapatch* (going on a rampage)—these expressions popularized nationally by former Brooklyn Dodger announcer Red Barber—are Southernisms, too, as James Thurber makes clear in his short story "The Catbird Seat." *Cat on a Hot Tin Roof,* the title of Tennessee Williams's famous play, does not have its origin in the South, as is widely believed, but derives from the similar British phrase *like a cat on hot bricks.*

Southerners still say such things as "She holp her sister when she was sick," the old preterit *holp* meaning "helped" in this case and being an archaic past tense of the verb *to help* that was used many times by Shakespeare and survives in speech only in eastern Mississippi. *Hassle,* on the other hand, was originally a Southern dialect word (meaning to pant noisily like a dog) that has come to be used nationally as a synonym for quarrel or trouble, perhaps because those involved might be breathing noisily.

A real Southerner will drawl and say *sho-nuff, honeychile,* and *y'all,* and he or she will also tend to accent *only* the first syllable of each word, giving us pronunciations like *po*-lice and *At*-lanta. Despite their *ain'ts,* however, educated Southern speakers often take great care in *not* talking like their compatriots, especially regarding exaggerated speech characteristics that have become the butt of Northern jokes. No *honeychiles* or *sho-nuffs* for them. He or she generally won't use the Southern long *i,* either, except at the ends of syllables, instead using a diphthong similar to the one speakers from other regions use in words like *night, hike,* and *life. Nice rice* is never *nise rise* for the educated unless he or she is putting you on.

When Henry Wallace campaigned with the slogan that this was "the century of the common man," many Southerners had trouble understanding, for *common* is a term of contempt in the South while it is rarely so in the North anymore. Another Southern peculiarity is the use of *ain't* among cultured speakers. Raven I. McDavid, Jr., pointed out in *American Speech* that during *Linguistic Atlas* interviews "nearly every cultured informant . . . in South Carolina and Georgia used *ain't* at some time during the interview. In fact, one of the touchstones often used by Southerners to distinguish the genuine cultured speaker from the pretenders is that the latter are too socially insecure to know the proper occasions for using *ain't,* the double negative and other such folk forms, and hence avoid them altogether." Then again some educated people in other regions use *Ain't I?* in place of *Am I not?*, or use the *Aren't I?* acceptable in England.

In some parts of the South the ladybug beetle is called a *ladybird,* which is also a common nickname (borne by our former first lady, Claudia Taylor Johnson). This is more evidence of the close speech ties of the South with England. The beetles are called ladybirds in England not because the British despise bugs but because the word *bug* is more strongly associated with sodomy there, as in the word *bugger.* Southerners are often a genteel breed much given to euphemisms about sexual matters. Aristocratic Southerners could indeed be quite contemptuous about sex, giving more lip service to chivalrous love. When a fellow Congressman chided the fiery John Randolph about his impotence, he shot back in his shrill voice: "Sir, you boast of an ability in which any slave is your equal and every jackass your superior."

In *Life on the Mississippi* Mark Twain wrote that "The Northern word 'guess' . . . is but little used among Southerners. They say 'reckon.' " But *reckon* as well as such Southern colloquialisms as *right* for *very* ("I'm right sorry") and *heap* for a large quantity ("I'm in a heap of trouble") were present in American speech of the North as well as the South during the early days of the country. Similarly, the *Linguistic Atlas* establishes that Southerners commonly use *bucket* for *pail, raise* for *rear, snap bean* for *string bean, spigot* for *faucet, branch* for *creek* (as in "bourbon and branch water") and *mosquito hawk* for *dragonfly* or *darning needle.* But all of these, too, save for the last expression, are widely and often used throughout the United States today. In the vicinity of Williamston, South Carolina, the cattle call *Chay!* is used (as opposed to *Boss!* in the New York area, or *Cowench!* in other parts of South Carolina). But as one writer has pointed out, this call is duplicated in County Antrim, Ireland, "linking the present residents in a tiny area of the South with their ancestors in the old country."

Two redundancies often heard that illustrate the Southerner's predilection for extravagant language are *in a manner* ("She acts like she's rarin' in a manner to go") and *standin' in need of* ("I'm standin' in need of a stiff drink"). There are hundreds more usages often heard in the South and never or rarely heard in other parts of the country. A *used-to-be* is Southern for a *has-been, dinner* can be the Southern noon (not nightly) meal, *airish* means *drafty, bad to* means *inclined to* ("When he gets drunk he's bad to get in trouble"), *beholden* is frequently used for *indebted to,* and *to break bad* is to behave in a violent manner for no good reason ("He just broke bad today and the *po*-leece got him"). In Southernese *comin' up a cloud* means it's going to rain, to *cut the fool* means to behave in a stupid way, *darest* (the old English contraction of *dare not*) is still used, *draw up* is employed for *to shrink, to fault* means *to blame, to favor* is *to resemble, fixin' to* means *preparing to,* and *give up to be* means *generally conceded to be* ("She's give up to be the prettiest girl in these parts").

Older Southerners might say *swimmy-headed* for *dizzy, sugar* and *Yankee dime* for a *kiss, Yankee shot* for the *navel, Sandy Claus* for *Santa Claus, right smart* for a *goodly amount,* and *quietus* for *to put an abrupt halt to* ("His wife put the quietus on that affair of his"). *Pot likker* is South Mouth for the rich liquid left after boiling vegetables, *play like* means *to pretend* in Southernese, *perked up* means *to have gained weight* and *picayunish* is a synonym for *picky.*

A *good ole boy* is any amiable Southerner of any age (provided he likes guns, hunting, fishing, drinking, football, and women), while *get shed of* means *to get rid of, go to the bad* means *to spoil, gracious plenty* means *more than enough,* a *haint* is a *ghost* or *apparition, hisn* and *hern* can mean *his* and *her, like to* means *almost* ("I like to died"), *mash* means *to press* ("I mashed the doorbell"), *light bread* is store-bought packaged bread, a *lick* is a blow, *the least one* is the smallest child in a family, and *a mess* is a quantity of something. Southerners used *Miz* as a form of address for a woman long before women's lib used Ms. (Miz), *nairn* equals *not any* in Southern talk, *not about to* means having no intention of doing something, *penny one* is nothing at all ("He ain't got penny one"), and *mommocked up* means *damaged* or *defaced.* One author, Hugh Rawson, in *A Dictionary of Euphemisms* (1984), even reports the Southern use of the word *cock* for the *female* sexual organ.

Other common Southern expressions include "I'm plumb tired," "I took sick," "I've got a mind to," and "I aims to get me some of that," yet all but the last of these are often heard in other regions. The list following ain't but a *smidgen* of characteristic phrases available:

"I don't rightly know."
"He's so all-fired lazy."
"Pay her no mind if she cries."
"A parcel of men come by."
"I got shut (rid) of it."
"My health was poorly."
"He took down with a fever."
"I don't know him from Adam's housecat (or pet monkey)."
"It's worth a sight moren that."
"I'm going to law him (sue him) in court."
"That's downright kind of you."
"Every fool thing happens to me."
"I heard tell how he'd gone."
"I've a mind to do it."

Problems can arise from word use variations in the South (although the Southerner might see the problem as variations in the rest of the country). "What in other parts of America is called a sidewalk was and still may be called a *pavement* in my native section of Maryland," wrote Thomas Pyles in *Words and Ways of American English,* "and what is elsewhere called a pavement was in our usage the *street* if in town and the *road* if in the country. Whether the road was paved or not, it would never have been called a pavement; pavements were in towns and cities and were for the use of pedestrians only. Consequently, I step from the pavement to the street; speakers from other sections step from the sidewalk to the pavement. No serious injury has thus far resulted from the ambiguity."

Confusions involving the short *o* sound the way Southerners say it were discussed several years ago in a *National Review* article by Professor S. L. Varnado of the University of South Alabama. "Southerners tend to flatten the short *o* sound so that it sounds like a short *u,*" Professor Varnado pointed out. "The most bizarre example of this is the word *bomb,* which a Southerner invariably pronounces as *bum:*

"Hello, this is President Carter. May I speak to the Russian Ambassador?"

"Spicking, Mr. President."

"Mr. Ambassador, I think we need to sit down and have a nice quiet talk about the number of *bums* in your country and mine."

"The number of *bums.* I do not theenk I understand."

"Simple enough, Mr. Ambassador. I feel that both your country and my country have got too many *bums* around. We must get rid of some of them."

"Correction, pliss, Mr. President. In Russia we haf no *bums.* Also, it is none of your business."

"Do you take me for a fool, Mr. Ambassador? Why, you have as many *bums* as we have. Maybe more."

"Excuse, pliss. That iss capitalist lie. We haf employed our *bums.*"

"Oh, you have employed *your* bums, have you? Well, then, maybe we will have to employ our *bums,* Mr. Ambassador. Think that one over!"

Like all dialects South Talk differs widely within the region. The Southern dialect for *son-of-a-bitch,* for example, can range from *sommumabitch* to *sum bitch,* with infinite variations. A very distinct pronunciation heard nowhere else in the South is heard (if rarely now) among older citizens of Memphis, Tennessee, who will tell you they are from Mimphis, Tinnissee (the distinction is no longer heard among the great majority of Memphians). The differences are not only geographic, and can even extend to Southern nationality groups. In his book *A Highly Ramified Tree* Robert Canzoneri wrote of how his family mixed the lingua franca of Sicily with a Southern accent on settling in Mississippi. This resulted in an invented tongue sometimes all their own with almost incomprehensible rhythms like *July gots?* ("Do you like apricots?") and *Jugo Marilla tax?* ("Did you go by way of Amarillo, Texas?").

Vocabulary is also strikingly different in various parts of the South. Nowhere but in the Deep South is the Indian-derived *bobbasheely,* which William Faulkner employed in *The Reivers,* used for "a very close friend," and only in Northern Maryland does *manniporchia* (from the Latin *mania a potu,* craziness from drink) mean the DTs. Small tomatoes would be called *tommytoes* in the mountains, *salad tomatoes* in the plains area, and *cherry tomatoes* along the coast. Depending upon where you are in the South a *large porch* can be a *veranda, piazza,* or *gallery;* a *burlap bag* can be a *tow sack, crocus sack,* or *grass sack; pancakes* can be *flittercakes, fritters, corncakes,* or *battercakes;* a harmonica can be a *mouth organ* or *French harp;* a closet can be a *closet* or a *locker;* and a wishbone can be a *wishbone* or *pulley bone.* There are some 73 synonyms for a cling peach (*green peach, pickle peach,* etc.), 169 terms for *kindling wood (lightning wood, lighterd knots),* and 222 ways to describe a rural resident *(snuff chewer, kicker, yahoo).*

In Texas the *straight rail fence* of Kentucky that Abe Lincoln split logs for would be a *pole fence,* while in South Carolina it would be a *galloping fence* and in Virginia it would be a *crooked rail fence;* these differences are as great as the differences between the *straight rail fence* and the *snake fence, worm fence,* and *zigzag fence* it is called in other regions of the country. Similarly, a North Carolina *wheel baw* (wheelbarrow) is a *Georgia buggy* in Georgia and a *slip* in Louisiana; a separating area of mall in the middle of a highway is a *medium strip* in Kentucky but *neutral ground* in Mississippi; the attic or space under the roof is a *loft* in Arkansas, a *garret* in Maryland, and the *plunder room* in South Carolina; bacon is *middling* in Maryland and *streaked meat* in North Carolina; kindling wood is *splinters* in Georgia and North Carolina, *lightwood* in South Carolina, and *shavings* in Maryland; and the Eastern earthworm can be a *fishing worm* in the coastal south, a *red worm* in the North Carolina mountains, a *ground worm* along Virginia's eastern shore, and an *earthworm* among uneducated folk in various coastal areas of North Carolina and Virginia.

Notable differences occur in grammar, too. In some Southern dialect areas, for example, uneducated speakers will say *clum* for the past tense of *climb,* while in Virginia many uneducated speakers say *clome* ("He clome the tree"). In this case many Southerners are closer in speech to uneducated speakers in Midland dialect areas, who also use *clum,* than they are to their fellow Southerners in Virginia.

In parts of the Deep South, people pronounce bird *boid,* girl *goil,* word *woid,* earth *oith,* oil *earl (all* is an alternate pronunciation in some Southern parts), and murder *moider*—just as dey do in Brooklyn. The *r*-colored vowel of these words and others is followed by a short *i* sound (which is somewhat inaccurately but traditionally represented as *oi* in dialect writing) and the pronunciation is not considered substandard where it is used.

Of all the major American dialects South Mouth is the most consistently difficult to translate, as will be seen in the pronouncing dictionary given *raht cheer* (right here) toward the end of this chapter. Among the most amusing examples is the expression *a fade barn* that the editors *DARE* tried to track down for a couple of years. The editors knew that the expression existed because field interviews had recorded it in North Carolina without establishing its meaning. When a Raleigh newspaper joined in the search, the answer was quickly apparent. Dozens of correspondents chided the editors for not knowing, in the words of one North Carolinian, that "a fade barn is whar you stow fade (feed) for the livestock."

As a matter of fact, the editors of *DARE* still can't solve some Southern expressions. Up until the early nineteenth century, surveyors in Bourbon County, Kentucky (which does, incidentally, give its name to bourbon whiskey, but was named for the Bourbons of France), used a species of a common tree called the *bettywood* to establish property boundaries. The elusive tree should not have disappeared in little over a century and is probably known by another name today, yet no one has identified it despite extensive etymological, historical, and botanical detective work. The *bettywood* seems doomed to obscurity possibly because the original name was garbled beyond belief into another name bearing not the faintest resemblance to it. (I venture a wild guess: could the *bettywood* possibly be the mispronounced *buttonwood* of the North, which is called the sycamore in the South?)

Some pure South Mouth is becoming widespread. I've often heard the expressions *He's three bricks shy of a load,* and variations on it, for someone not too bright. The term *to fall out* is principally a Southern expression for *to faint* but today is also heard in communities as far north as northern Wisconsin, northern Indiana, and southeastern Pennsylvania. Similarly, *to tote* is a Southernism now heard in all other regions, as is *to carry* in the sense of *to transport* or *escort.* The expression *soft berm* for a soft shoulder on a road is commonly Southern, but is often encountered on road signs in other parts of the country, though one could argue here that *berm* is not a regional dialect term, but a word dating back to the days of knightly chivalry, when in Norman times it meant "the ridge between the edge of the moat around a castle and the fortress wall itself."

Tacky was once an exclusively Southern expression, used mainly by women, for unfashionable or ugly clothes, but recently it has become popular throughout the country. The same can be said for *the spittin' image of*, a strong resemblance, which some say derives from Southern black pronunciation of "spirit and image." The germ of the idea behind this phrase has been traced back to 1400 by Partridge, who cites the early example "He's . . . as like thee as th' hads't spit him." Similarly, in England and the Southern United States, the expression *He's the very spit of his father* is commonly heard. This may mean "He's as like his father as if he had been spit out of his mouth," but could be an American black corruption of "spirit and image," blacks often pronouncing the letter *r* indistinctly. If the last is true it would explain the use of "and image" in the expression since the middle of the last century. *Spittin' image* would then be derived from "He's the very spirit and image of his father"—that is, the child was identical to his parent in both spirit and looks. It's possible that both sources combined to give us our phrase for *exactly alike*, which is also written *spit and image, spitting image, spitten image,* and *spit n' image*.

A genuine Southernism is *She (He) thinks he (she) hung the moon and stars* for someone who loves somebody madly, and blindly, as if that person were a god. According to Professor Cassidy, this pretty Southern expression has been around since at least early in this century, and by now has deservedly spread to other regions of the country. *Well if that don't take the rag off the bush* is a Southern Americanism originating in the late nineteenth century and referring to outrageous behavior as lowdown as stealing the rags or clothes that someone in the ole swimmin' hole has left spread out on a bush. *Gimme a dope* still means *give me a Coca-Cola* in the Southern United States, especially among teenagers. This isn't recent slang, dating back to the late nineteenth century when the fabled soft drink was touted as a tonic and contained a minute amount of cocaine. Coca-Cola's inventor, druggist John S. Pemberton, brewed the stuff in his backyard and knew it was done when he smelled the cooked cocaine—no reactions in the man or among his neighbors are reported.

Another good one is *He looks like he's been eatin' a green 'simmon.*

The *'simmon* in this nineteenth-century Southern Americanism is a persimmon, which takes its name from the Cree *pasiminan* (meaning dried fruit). While the fruit is delicious when dead ripe, a green, unripe persimmon is so sour it can make you whistle. Ripe persimmons suggested *walking off with the persimmons* (walking off with the prize), which also dates back to the 1850s.

Kissin' cousin is a Southern Americanism that originated before the Civil War. The term first implied a distant blood relationship but today more often means a very close friend who is considered family. It still is used in its original sense, however, in the sense of a relative far removed enough to permit marriage, "an eighth cousin" in the North.

One of my favorites is *He's still got some snap left in his garters.* "I really think," Senator Russell B. Long of Louisiana said recently (March 17, 1985), "that's it's better to retire, on Uncle Earl's terms, when you still have some snap left in your garters." Mr. Long was referring to his legendary uncle, former Louisiana Governor Earl Long, who may have used the expression, too. Unable to locate the phrase recorded anywhere else, I'm forced to make the brilliant suggestion that it is a Southern American expression dating back to the late nineteenth century or earlier.

Originally chicken fried in bacon grease, *Southern fried chicken* was brought to America by settlers from the Scottish Highlands and has been popular in the American South since before 1711, when the term *fried chicken* is first recorded there. It became popular throughout the country in the 1930s, when it was first widely sold at roadside restaurants. The rich Southern American stew called *burgoo* probably takes its name from an Arabic word. *Burgoo* was originally a stew that American seamen made, which, in turn, may derive its name from the Arabic *burghul* (bruised grain). The word however, is first recorded out West as *burgou* in 1837, and may be a corruption of *barbecue.* Someone has noted about burgoo: "No two people tell the same story about its origin and no two people will give you the same recipe."

Few people know that *howdy,* a contraction of *how do you do?* and generally regarded as an expression born in the American West, began life as a Southern expression and was taken West by Confederate Civil War veterans. It is first recorded in 1840. Similarly, *Mark twain!* is a slurred Southern mispronunciation of *Mark on the twine, six fathoms!* called out when riverboat leadsmen sounded the

Mississippi River with weighted twine. It is well known that former riverboat pilot Samuel Langhorne Clemens took his pen name from the leadsman's call *Mark twain!*

I'm from Missouri also has Southern origins. During the Civil War, an officer of a Northern army fell upon a body of Confederate troops commanded by a Missourian. The Northerner demanded a surrender, saying he had so many thousand men in his unit. The Confederate commander, game to the core, said he didn't believe the Northerner's boast of numerical superiority and appended the now famous expression *I'm from Missouri; you'll have to show me.* In any case, Dr. Walter B. Stevens recorded this proud derivation of the phrase in *A Colonial History of Missouri* (1921).

The original *fink*— or *ratfink*, for that matter—may have been a cop named Albert Fink, who worked for railroads in the American South. *Finks* and *scissorbills* were anathema to the early labor movement—they adamantly opposed unions—but only the former word survived and is now used to describe not only a strikebreaker but any treacherous, contemptible person or police informer. Mr. Albert Fink could well have inspired the term. The German-born Fink, according to a reliable source, long headed a staff of detectives with the Louisville and Nashville Railroad. He was not involved in railroad labor disputes but his operatives probably policed rates charged on the lines and some of them were likely planted spies who could have come to be known as *finks* in Dixie and points north.

Although *Dixie* may not have been named for the *Mason-Dixon line,* the latter term has come to be used as a figure of speech for an imaginary dividing line between the North and the South. The Mason-Dixon line has an interesting history. Originally the 244-mile boundary line set between Pennsylvania and Maryland in 1763–67 by English surveyors Charles Mason and Jeremiah Dixon, it was extended six years later to include the southern boundary of Pennsylvania and Virginia. The line had been established by English courts to settle a territorial dispute between the Pennsylvania Penns and the Calverts of Maryland, but the use of *Mason-Dixon line* in Congressional debates during the Missouri Compromise (1819–20) gave the expression wide currency as a dividing line between free and slave states. After the Civil War the term was retained as the boundary between North and South, more as a demarcation line of customs and philosophy than geography. Its existence probably did influence the popularity of the word *Dixie* for the South.

A Southern pronunciation becoming more national every year is *vee-hick-el* for *vee-uh-cul,* as most Americans pronounce *vehicle.* I first heard this pronunciation more than thirty years ago in the Army, where it was said to be used to make the word clearer when transmitted over a field radio, but probably the fact that so many noncommissioned officers were Southerners had more to do with this Southern pronunciation. In any case, one agrees with William Safire that the Southern pronunciation makes the word "sound punchier and more authoritative than the vowel-joined VEE-uh-cul." Mr. Safire points out that *DARE* has found the same variation in the word *article (ar-tick-el).*

Despite the increased mobility of Americans and the homogenization of speech by television, it doesn't seem likely that Southern speech will be quietly erased from the American tape, for it is too widespread and deeply rooted in the past. There may be fewer and fewer Senator Claghorns as time goes by, but the sweet sound of the extended *ou* diphthong will be with us for a long time; Southerners who employ one syllable where three or four could be used will be suspect throughout Dixie for many years to come. Anyway, in the event that lazy or relaxed rhythms of Southern speech become the national mode within the next century or so, when temperatures go up due to the greenhouse effect and the whole country gets as hot as Mississippi, following is a final sampling of good South Mouth to git started with.

Sounds of the South:
A South Mouth Pronouncing Dictionary

abode—a wood plant

ahs—sight organs (or as in "The ahs have it")

aigs—as in scrambled or hardboiled

aint—one's father's or mother's sister

air—the organ you hear with

all—a fuel found in allfields

apint—appoint

argy—argue

are—sixty minutes, air

arm—I am

armaggedon—I'm gonna get

Arlen—home of the Irish

arn—instrument for pressing clothes

Arsh—natives of Arlen (q.v.)

ast—as in "Ast me no questions, I'll tell you no lahs."

awf—off

Ay-rabs—Middle Easterners who control more *all* than Texans

bad—bed

bah—not humbug but goodbye

bane—a legume (as in "baked banes")

bard—means poet, borrowed, or bird (as in "The bard bard mah canary bard")

bare—beer

barley—not the grain, but "barely"

barter—butter

bawl—to make water bubble

beg—the opposite of small

belly—proper noun, as in "Belly Cottah, yo ex-Prezdet's brother"

bend—band

beyill—bill or Bill

bidness—like "Mistuh Cottah's paynut bidness"

bile—boil

bleeve—as in "Ah do bleeve"

bubs—the things that burn out in lamps

bucks—books

bum—as in "ahtumic bums" or "Bumminham, Alabama;" "bomb" means palm, as in "bomb tree"

bus—bust

caint—cannot

candit—someone running for public office

case—kiss

cent—a penny or pennies (as in "Ah paid fetty cent fer it")

char—cheer

cheer—chair, here

cist—assist

coal—a cold

Co-Cola—the soft drink invented in Atlanta

con—kind

crap—crab, crop

crine—crying

cuss—curse

dawg—dog

dayum—damn

doc—dark

drank—the present tense of to drink (as in "Have a drank of this")

Dumcrass—Democrats

dunce—dance

et—eaten

Etlanna—capital of Georgia

eyes—ice

Eyetalian—native of Italy

faints—fence

far—fire

favor—fever

feel—field

fem—film

fern—foreign

flares—flowers

foe—four

Frahday—Friday

frawd—fried

fried—afraid

fust—first

gist—just

git—get

glade—glad, happy
goff—golf
gom bee—going to be
goobuhs—peanuts
grain—the color of grass
grind—ground
griuts—grits
gulf—golf
gull—a (generally) young
  woman
hair—air
hale—the nethermost
  regions
har—hair
hard—hired
harth—earth
hate—heat
hawg—hog
heeuh—here, in this heeuh
  place
hep—help
hurt—heart
I.D.—idea
idinit—isn't it
impotent—important
innerdoose—introduce
jew—did you
Joeja—Georgia
keer—care
kin—can
lahf—life
laht—light (as in "Yo laht up
  mah lahf")
libel—label
look—lick
Loosyana—the state
low-law—the PO-lice
madge—marriage
main—man
maize—miss

mast—mask
medal—middle
mere—mirror
mile—mail
mint—meant
mistrayshun—administration
moanin—morning
morn—more than
Mundee—Monday
munts—months
Murkin—American
neck—nick (as "in the neck of
  time"); "necks" means next
New Yoke—New York
nome—no, mam
Nyawlins—city in Loosyana
  (q.v.)
own—on
pahty—party
pain—pin
papal—people
papuh—paper
pare—power
paynuts—peanuts
peg—pig
peony—penny
peyun—pen
phrasin—freezing
pin—pen
piper—paper, newspaper
pitcher—painting or
  photograph
ply—play
po', por—poor
police—please; "PO-lice"
  means police
posed—supposed
prezdet—president
prior—prayer
prod—pride

prolly—probably
puss—purse
quair—strange
raid—read
rail—real
rench—rinse
retch—rich (or to grasp for, as "He retches for it")
rice—race
rifle—raffle
riot—right
rise—rice
rotten—as in "readin', rotten', rithmetic"
rough—roof
Ruh-pub-uh-kins—Republicans
rust—rest
saar—sour
Sahdity—Saturday
sake—seek
salit—salad
sawt—salt
sef—self
sennir—center
shawt—short
shore—sure
shurf—sheriff
sin—sand
skace—scarce
skull—school
small—smile
sneak—snake
sod, sad—side
sot—sight or sat
spear—superior
stars—stairs

steer—stir
stow—store
stud—stood
summers—somewhere
tahm—time
tail—tell
tar—tire
tension—attention
thang—thing
they-uh—there
Thusdee—Thursday
tick—take
toad—told
Toosdee—Tuesday
tuhn—turn
unnuther—one more
Urp—Europe
vampar—vampire
virus—various
wangs—wings
war—wire
Watt House—White House
wawyk—work
winder—window
weary—worry
Wesdee—Wednesday
wheel—whale
whirr—where
wipe—to cry
woek—work
Wretched—Richard
Wushington—Washington
yale—yell
yarbs—herbs
yawl or y'all—see text
year—ear
zackly—exactly

5 Deep Down in the Holler Where the Hoot Owl Hollers at Noon: Hillbilly Tawk

⭐

* Hit was just a small, puny, little old thing.
* He'd skin a flea for hits hide.
* River's so low we'll have to start hawlin' water to it.
* That's the out-doingest (most surprising) thing I ever heerd.
* I wouldn't have her if her head was strung with gold.
* He couldn't hit the ground with his ole hat (he's dead drunk).
* That snow's shoemouth deep.
* She's a half-baked yokum (a fool).
* He arter be bored for the simples (operated on for stupidity).
* She raises hogs to who laid the chunk (does it better than anyone).
* Hit some people woth a sour apple and they get drunk as a biled (boiled) owl.
* He was tarryhootin' (gallivanting) around.
* He's crooked as a barrel of blacksnakes.
* His backbone's rubbin' his belly (he's very hungry).
* They lit a rag fer home (hurried home).
* They'll fight at the drop of a hat and they'll drop it themselves.

These are just a handful of characteristically droll sayings from the hills that I've particularly enjoyed. But my favorite line came from an old mountain woman who had been asked why she had raised "eleven young-uns" herself, why she never remarried after

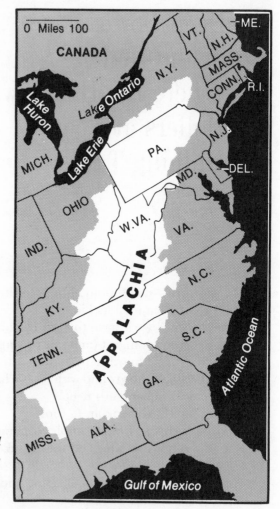

The U.S. area designated as Appalachia, map courtesy The New York Times

her young husband had been "kilt a-felling timber" in the Appalachians many years before. "Because I loved the sweat of his body and the dust of his feet more than any other living man," the old woman replied.

Like her words, mountain dialect, though often humorous, is far more than the caricature it has been made over the years by lazy lanky tobacco-chawin' characters ranging from Lum and Abner and Ma and Pa Kettle to Li'l Abner and the Beverly Hillbillies. Mountain talk, more than any other dialect in America or even England, is the closest relative to the Elizabethan language of

Shakespeare surviving today. Though pronunciation in these mountain areas varies, the Elizabethan English of the Highlanders is virtually the same from place to place and many of their quaint and picturesque words and phrases go back beyond Shakespeare's day to the time of Chaucer and even to the Anglo-Saxon period in England. Mountain dwellers have in fact been called "the purest Anglo-Saxons in the United States" because of their speech, though their ancestry is predominantly Celtic mixed with strong strains of English and German. Neither the mountaineers nor their ancestors speak or spoke true Elizabethan English, of course, since Queen Elizabeth had been dead nearly two centuries when the first mountaineers moved in. But as Mario Pei says, "The speech of the Ozarks comes closer in many respects to Elizabethan English than does the present speech of London" and "is closer to that seventeenth-century speech than any present-day English dialect."

The compound descriptive words characteristic of Anglo-Saxon or Old English are particularly evident in mountain speech. These self-explanatory "kennings," frequently encountered in the Old English narrative poem *Beowulf*—as in "un-living" for the dead, and "bone-box" for the body—are part of everyday hillfolk speech, either carried over from the past or invented in relatively recent times. A baby in the hills can be either a *man-child* or *girl-child,* children's toys are *play-pretties,* an illegitimate child is not a bastard but, much more kindly, a *woods-colt* or *volunteer,* God is the *Good-Man* and Satan the *Bad-Man* or *Booger-Man.* The *spear-side* of the family is the *men-folks* while the *spindle-side* is the *women-folks,* the immediate family is the *home-folks* and all relatives are *kin-folks.* *Horse sense, mother wit, thorough-going,* the *mully-grubs* (the blues), and the *all-overs* (a nervous feeling) are just a few of the many colorful compounds still in use today.

Many *hillbilly* (an Americanism dating back to early 1904) words and phrases thought to be the ignorant speech of Dogpatch are direct survivals of earlier English speech. *Tetchy,* for example, is not an ignorant hick pronunciation of *touchy,* as many people believe, for the word (meaning irritable, testy, or peevish) is nowise related to *touch,* but derives from the Middle English *tecche* (a bad habit), which in turn comes from the Old French *teche* (a blemish). When hillfolks say *et* for *ate,* they are following a precedent that goes back to the 1300s, when Richard Rolle wrote that "men and wimmin ete and drank" and are pronouncing the word close to its accepted British pronunciation; their use of *outen* ("This basket is made *outen* bark") may go back to the Anglo-Saxon *utian;* and their use of *hit* for *it,* though considered illiterate today, derives from the Anglo-Saxon *hit,* the neuter of *he,* which was standard English up until at least the twelfth century. Nor is *hisn* a backwoods Americanism. *Hisn* has a long and respectable lineage, dating back to the early fifteenth century *(Him as prigs what isn't his'n / When he's cotched he goes to prison)* and was used by Richardson in *hisn* novel *Clarissa.* Analogous words are *hern, ourn, yourn,* and *theirn.* Chaucer and others commonly used the *n*-stem or weak declension in words like *housen* for *houses* and *treen* for *trees,* the standard English nouns *children, brethren,* and *oxen* still retaining this form. Even the much ridiculed *you-uns* of mountain speech can be traced to the *ye ones* of Chaucer's time, and the collective second person *you-together* is sometimes still heard in British East Anglia dialect.

"I ain't never seen no men-folks of no kind do no washin' no-how," a mountain woman might say, and her forceful use of the double negative, though considered ignorant today, would have strong links with Elizabethan England, when the double negative was simply employed as a stronger, more effective negative. Shakespeare, in fact, wrote: "Thou hast spoken no word all this while, nor understood none neither."

Mountain people, like Englishmen of Shakespeare's day, have little respect for grammatical categories if a thought is best expressed by interchanging parts of speech. Thus nouns and adjectives often become colorful verbs, as in "It *pleasures* me," "She *prettied* herself up," "I'll *muscle* (lift) it up for you," and "This deer'll *meat* us for a while (provide us with meat for a while)." Hillfolk speech is laced with direct or close descendants of Anglo-Saxon, Chaucerian, and Elizabethan language—from its names for common things, to the use of "educated" words like *dilatory, discern,* and *proferred* by uneducated folk, and old pronunciations such as *ax* for *ask, dar* for *dare, sarvice* for *service, consarn* for *concern,* and *sarten* for *certain.* Some hillbilly sayings can be traced back centuries as well. "Everyone to their liking, as the old woman said when she kissed her cow" was dialogue put into the mouth of a hillbilly girl in a 1925 play. Investigation revealed that the expression dates back to 1562, when it appeared as "Every man as he loveth, quoth the good man, when he kyst his coowe."

That British pronunciation of the word *joined* was *jined,* as it is today in the southern Appalachians, is witnessed by a rhyming couplet in Alexander Pope's *Essay on Man* (1732):

> *In praise so just let every man be joined,*
> *And fill the general chorus of mankind.*

As in other parts of the South, mountain speech often uses *a* before a present participle, as in *I'm a-talking,* or *I'm a-comin'.* This practice, too, has its roots in the distant past, deriving from the Old English prefix *on-* that preceded infinitives such as *onhuntan* (a-huntin'). Shakespeare used *a* like this in *Hamlet* when he wrote: "Now might I do it pat, now he is a-praying."

Afeared is a hill country word that dates back to Middle English (1150–1500). *Clomb, peart, atwixt, up and done it,* and *heap o' folks* have similar ancient histories, while the phrase *back this letter for me* (address it) originated in days when addresses had to be written on the back of the letter itself.

Flummoxed for *upset* or *wrecked* is native to Kentucky mountaineers and may go back to an English dialect word. Another mountain term whose origins have been lost is the expression *wool* (to worry—"The baby wooled that pore little kitten plumb to death"). The Ozarkian *sull* as a verb, however, probably comes from *sullen* ("The old hound's been whupped and he's crawled under the floor and sulled up till he won't come even when you whistle to hie him out").

There are many more examples of what has been called American Anglo-Saxon, American Early English, and American Elizabethan English speech. Such echoes are heard today throughout the Southern mountains, including the Blue Ridge Mountains of Virginia and West Virginia, the Great Smokies of Tennessee and North Carolina, the Cumberlands of Tennessee and Kentucky, and the Ozarks of Arkansas and Missouri. It is also heard sporadically in the mountains of Pennsylvania, in Georgia, Alabama, southern Illinois, and on the Delmarva Peninsula and the islands of Chesapeake Bay. Hill folk working in the cotton mills of the Piedmont took the dialect there, and one investigator found it "well fixed on the Southwestern plains and in cities like Forth Worth and Dallas."

"Our contemporary ancestors," as the hill people have been called, came principally from the British Isles, of course, and were predominantly Scotch-Irish, although they included larger Celtic and Welsh elements than they were thought to contain when the first investigations of their history were made about a century ago. In fact, the "linguistic fossils" that researchers have identified in the Southern mountains are now thought to be in large part inherited not directly from Elizabethan England but from speech brought here by the settlers from along the Scotch-English border, where archaisms such as *afeared* and *argufy* survive to this day. The settlers came first to the western Pennsylvania mountains and spread south from there, so that the hillfolk dialect basically derives from the Scotch-Irish of western Pennsylvania. Immigrants from the Southern Appalachians doubtless took the dialect with them to the Ozarks and other areas.

As recently as forty years ago a writer could observe that the hill people "have changed little" in two centuries. Only over the last seventy-five years or so has "civilization" courted these people, and they still haven't surrendered to its charms. It is true that "many characteristic mountain words" are now unfamiliar in mountain areas, as Raven I. McDavid, Jr., has noted, and perhaps in another generation or two, most mountain folk will be "speaking the general vulgate" spread by the mass media and the automobile. But the isolation of mountain people and their relative poverty—which ensure that their speech will be less affected by education—should guarantee the survival of mountain talk for many years to come, if only in a modified form or in extremely isolated areas. Certainly there is not a large influx of population into the area that will change the dialect any. Despite massive federal aid over the past twenty years, poverty still reigns in Appalachia; the infant mortality rate and unemployment have hardly changed in half of the 397 counties across 13 states (New York, Pennsylvania, Maryland, Ohio, West Virginia, Virginia, Kentucky, Tennessee, North Carolina, South Carolina, Georgia, Alabama, and Mississippi) that are officially designated as Appalachia, and the Census Bureau has noted a recent pattern of migration to other regions that dramatically marked the decades before federal aid was begun on a large scale.

Mountain talk (sometimes called South Midland) has been described by some experts as Southern speech influenced by Midland, and by others as Midland speech influenced by Southern. Whichever came first, mountain talk, typically nasal and high-pitched, but not a whine, is often slower than Southern speech and is frequently stressed very heavily. As Mencken observed: "The dialect preserves many older pronunciations that have fallen out of use elsewhere, and reinforces and exaggerates most of those that remain. The flat *a* appears even in *balm* and *gargle*, but in *narrow* and *barrel* a broad *a* is substituted, so that they become *nahrr'* and *bahr'l*. In other situations the broad *a* is turned into a *u*, as in *fur* and *ruther*, for *far* and *rather*. Brush is *bresh*, such is *sich* and until is *ontil*. The *au* sound is usually changed: *saucy*, as in the general vulgate, becomes *sassy*, and jaundice is *janders*, and aunt is often *ain't*."

The mountain drawl generally comes before a pause in speaking, and is usually reserved for the word or phrase before that pause. But obviously all highlanders do not speak alike and they vary noticeably in different areas. Josiah H. Combs, one of the earliest scholars to examine the dialect or dialects, was aware that there was much variation in the speech of mountain people. "The Elizabethan English of these highlanders varies but little," he wrote. "In other respects their language varies greatly, most noticeably in the substitution of one vowel for another. This divergence in the use of the vowel does not confine itself necessarily to the different states. For example, the hillsman of the Cumberlands in Kentucky says *whut* and *gut*, while the pronunciation further west in the same state, but still in the hills, is *what* and *got*. . . . But in eastern Tennessee one hears *eent* (end) while the usual pronunciation is *eend*."

Generally, the mountaineer drops the *t* in the singular of such nouns as *post* and *nest*, but pronounces the *t* clearly in the plurals of these words, adding an unaccented syllable so that we have *nestes* and *postes*. Words like *salad, ballad, killed, scared,* and *held* are pronounced *salat, ballat, kilt, skeert,* and *helt,* a *t* replacing the final *d* in them. Other general peculiarities are the intrusive *y* in words such as *hear* and *ear*, which change to *hyar* and *yar;* the final *t* pronounced like a *k*, as in *vomick*, for *vomit;* a *t* added to many words, as in *oncet, suddint,* and *clift;* and the use of *hit* for *it* at the beginning of a clause or for emphasis, though not otherwise.

Today the drawl of mountain folk with their close connection to Elizabethan times is characteristic of the pilots of modern airliners, who may affect it to convey a feeling of calmness and reassurance to passengers flying thousands of feet above the earth. In an *Esquire* article on test pilot Chuck Yeager, author Tom Wolfe wrote of "a particular folksiness, a particular down-home calmness that is so exaggerated that it begins to parody itself . . . the voice that tells you, as the airliner is caught in thunderbolts and goes bolting up and down a thousand feet at a single gulp, to check your seat belts because 'it might get a little choppy' " is a drawl that originates in the mountains, Wolfe says, "in the mountains of West Virginia, in the coal country, in Lincoln Country so far up in the hollows that, as the saying went, 'they had to pipe in daylight.' In the late 1940s and early 1950s, this up-hollow voice drifted down . . . down, down from the upper reaches of the flying fraternity to all phases of American aviation. . . . It was *Pygmalion* in reverse . . . pilots from Maine and Massachusetts and the Dakotas and everywhere else began to talk in that poker-hollow West Virginia drawl, or as close to it as they could bend their native accents."

The prudishness of mountain speech has been noted by several writers, especially Vance Randolph. "The truth is that sex is very rarely mentioned save in ribaldry," writes Randolph in his article "Verbal Modesty in the Ozarks," and "is therefore excluded from all polite conversation between men and women. Moreover, this taboo is extended to include a great many words which have no real connection with sex and which are used quite freely in more enlightened sections of the United States. . . . Many mountain women never use the word 'stone' (early English for testicle). . . . Perhaps a century or so of isolation is responsible for an abnormal development of this sort of thing, or it may be that mountain people have simply retained a Pecksniffian attitude once common to the whole country."

Everyday words like *stone, bed, tail, stocking, piece, maiden, bag,* and even *decent* are avoided by mountain people whenever possible because they suggest "lustful ideas," according to Randolph. Completely taboo are words like *bull, ram, stallion, boar, buck, cock, bitch, virgin,* and even *love.* This taboo extends to harmless compounds like *buckshot* or *bullfrog, cockeyed, cocksure,* and even proper names like *Hitchcock* or *Cox.* Ironically, terms like *to give tittie* that would be inappropriate in other areas are freely used (though *heart* is a taboo word). Some of the euphemisms employed for the taboo words are inventive. A cock for example, is a *crower* or a *rooster;* a bull is a *cow brute,* a stallion is a *stable horse;* and a woodpecker is, somewhat confusingly, a *woodchuck. To cut one's foot* means to step in cow dung, as does *to cut one's foot on a Chinese razor.*

"I myself," Randolph relates, "have seen grown men, when women were present, blush and stammer at the mere mention of such commonplace bits of hardware as *stop-cocks* or *pet-cocks,* and avoid describing a gun as *cocked* by some clumsy circumlocution, such as *she's ready t' go,* or *th' hammer's back.*" Since *bull* is also taboo (two Arkansas mountain women clamored for the arrest of a man who mentioned a bull-calf in their presence), as is the word *tail* (a homophone of *tale*), a rare triple euphemism has arisen in the Ozarks for a cock-and-bull tale. There a cock-and-bull tale is called a *rooster story*!

Similarly, a boy is seldom named Peter in the Ozarks, because *peter* is a common euphemism for the penis. "An evangelist from the North shouted something about the church being founded on the rock of Peter," recalled one writer, "and he was puzzled by the flushed cheeks of the young women and the ill-suppressed amusement of the ungodly."

In *Down in the Holler,* Randolph observes some of many interesting vocabulary changes in mountain talk. "A *stew* is not a dish of meat and vegetables in the Ozarks, but a drink made of ginger, hot water and corn whiskey," he writes in *The Ozarks; An American Survival of Primitive Society* (1931). "*Ashamed,* when used with reference to a child or young girl, does not mean ashamed at all, but merely timid or bashful. *Gum* means a rabbit-trap—when the hillman wants chewing gum he calls for *wax. . . .* When he says *several,* he doesn't mean three or four, but a large number. . . . *Judge* or *jedge* is used to mean a fool or clown, and there is even an adjective *jedging. . . . Enjoy* is used in the sense of entertain. *Lavish* is used as a noun, meaning a large quantity. . . . *Portly,* as applied to a man, means handsome. . . . *Out* is used as a verb meaning to defraud. . . . *Fine haired* means aristocratic."

Mountaineers don't mind being called *hillbillies* by other mountaineers, but they do object to flatland *furriners* using the term; they better smile when they say it. Anyway, one of the *outlandish,* or an *outlander* or *foreigner,* as strangers are called in the mountains, would have trouble making sense of much of the highlander's speech and might indeed find it difficult getting someone to translate, as highlanders are slow to *confidence* (trust) an outsider, sometimes distrusting even natives who have *gone abroad*—that is, left the mountains for too long a while. One mountaineer told an interviewer that he didn't speak "the bestest English in the country," not having been "over fattened on book reading," but that he didn't consider his lack of education all-important: "Learning and good words may improve a man's knowings but it hain't nary made a body a better Christian person."

It has been noted that the highlander's speech is rhetorical in the classic sense—that is, in the art of beautiful speech and effective delivery. "Many of the striking figures that seem original to the outsider are traditional ones in the mountains, having been handed down orally from one generation of good talkers to another," James Robert Reese notes in an essay on the language of the mountaineer. "The mountaineer alters, adapts, recombines and uses anew old expressions with a freshness and creativity similar to that of the *Beowulf* poet who called upon his traditional poetic phrasing and word-horde to tell a tale. It is perhaps this large stock of traditional figures, adapted by each speaker in an original manner, that allows the mountaineer to make his everyday talk come alive."

The use of understatement to show humor is a favorite rhetorical device among mountaineers, Professor Reese observes. Once, while sitting with two highlanders, he noticed that one man "kept getting up and walking to a table upon which lay some of the largest green tomatoes ever grown. Too heavy to ripen on the vine, they had been picked and placed on a table to ripen. The man who had grown them kept picking one up, then another, but said nothing as he returned to his seat. His neighbor seemingly took no notice, but as he stood up to leave he said: 'Carl, I'm plumb sorry your garden had such bad growings this year. Those are the sorriest-looking melons I ever did see!' " On another occasion Professor Reese "was sitting with two neighbors, one of whom had given the other garden space after the latter had sold his best land. There was a noticeable difference in the amount of weeds in the garden; the one who owned the land had just finished hoeing his side. Pretty soon, Sam, who had borrowed the garden space, got up, took a few steps toward the garden, looked long at it, turned and said: 'You know I hain't a-going to put out a garden here again next year. That's two year following you given me weedy ground and kept the clean for yourself.' "

Words often have different meanings down in the holler. A wedding celebration can be called a *serenade,* an *infare,* or a *shivaree.* A cemetery is a *burial ground,* a chimney shelf is a *mantel,* and a *grampus* is not a killer whale but a type of fish bait (hellgramite). *Bait,* however, means *a large amount of* in the mountains (as in "We got a bait of 'em"), while steps are called *treads,* a groundhog is a *whistle pig,* and a good writer is a *good scribe.* As for a *fisty* (feisty) woman, she has been defined by one mountaineer as "maybe not fast, but a little too frisky to be nice." In West Virginia a Ph.D is sometimes called a *teacher-doctor,* not a "real doctor." West Virginia, incidentally, is composed of forty western mountain counties that seceded from Virginia at the outbreak of the Civil War, these counties voting not to secede from the Union and forming their own state government. After rejecting *New Virginia, Kanawha,* and *Alleghany,* the new state settled on *West Virginia* for a name, an ironic choice, as Virginia extends ninety-five miles farther west than it does. West Virginia had considered seceding from Virginia several times, due to unequal taxation and representation, and the Civil War provided an excellent excuse. Its constitution was amended to abolish slavery and President Lincoln proclaimed West Virginia the thirty-fifth state in 1862, justifying his action as a war measure. Called the *Panhandle State,* it has an odd outline, leading to the saying that it's "a good state for the shape it's in."

A great number of verbs take irregular forms in mountain talk, especially among the uneducated. *Drug* is the past tense of *drag, fit* the past of *fight, holp* of *help, writ* of *wrote, hurd* of *hear, brung* of *bring, growed* of *grow, het* of *heat,* and *seed* of *see.* The verb *rot* is often replaced by the adjective *rotten* in mountain talk (as in "They 'ull rotten afore they ripens"). Two colorful verbs are *to youth* ("The moon 'ull youth today"—that is, a new moon will appear) and *to big,* to make pregnant ("He's bigged Pernie"). The verb *to smart* means *to hurt* and can be used transitively as in "Hit hain't a-goin' to smart ye more 'an a minute." Some verbs used elsewhere in reference to animals are applied to people in mountain talk, as, for example, *ruttin'* or mating: "Ruttin'-time is over, Buck, fer varmints—but, by God, nor fer you-all."

Blackguard is used as a verb meaning *to abuse* by the hill people, and *to hone* means *to long for* ("I hone for her"), the word deriving from the Middle French *hoigner* (meaning to long for). *Laid-off* in the mountains doesn't mean "fired from a job" but means "planned to," as in "I've been a-layin' off to ketch me a eel." To get *shed* (or *shet*) *of* means *to get rid of* and *go to* can mean *intend*, as in "He didn't go to kill him."

Moonshine for illegally made whiskey wasn't coined in the hills, as one would guess, the word probably originating in England and referring to a colorless brandy smuggled in from France late in the eighteenth century. But a lot of *moonshining* still goes on in the mountains of Kentucky and Tennessee, where the product is known variously as *splo, stump liquor, swamp dew, angel teat, white mule, white lightning, Kentucky fire, squirrel whiskey,* or *pure corn licker.* By any name it can make a man *downcy* or give him the *blind billiards.* Interestingly, the first use of the verb *stash* for hiding something is a 1929 remark about moonshine in the Ozarks: "Billy, he done stashed the jug in th' brash an' now the danged ol' fool can't find hit!"

Like *moonshine,* many mountain expressions have passed into common national use. Though it is hard to tell, these possibly include *cold in the grave* (dead), *just a little piece* (a short distance), *behind the door when brains were passed out* (dumb), *can lick his weight in wildcats, can't hold a candle to* (can't compare to), *dog me if I'll do it, I'll be dogged, faster 'n greased lightning, sharper'n a tack, madder n' a wet hen,* and *plum tuckered out.*

Mountaineers in North Carolina give the name *hells* to the tangles of laurel, rhododendron, and palmia that cover mile after mile of steep mountainsides. The term is first recorded in 1883 but is probably considerably older. Synonyms are *laurel slicks, woolly heads, lettuce beds, yaller patches,* and *blackberry hells.* Sometimes a person's name is attached to a particular hell, such as *Herman's hell,* in remembrance of somebody lost in the mazes of wild vegetation.

Local names for things in the hills aren't widely known, but are often quaint and pretty. Peonies are sometimes called *piney-roses,* dried green beans are *leather britches,* portulaca is *rose-moss,* asters are *star-flowers,* jonquils are *Easter flowers,* violets are *rooster-fights,* the iris is a *flag,* and forsythia is *golden bells.* The serviceberry is called the *sarvice.* This plant (nationally known as the Juneberry, genus *Amelanchier*) was dubbed the *serviceberry* as far back as the eighteenth century and the name has a touching story behind it.

Since its white blossoms appeared almost as soon as the ground thawed in spring, American pioneer families that had kept a body through winter to bury in workable ground used these first flowers to cover the grave.

Oncet and *twicet,* associated with Brooklynese, are also used for *once* and *twice* in the Ozarks, while *ary* and *nary,* which are historically contractions of *ever a* and *never a,* respectively, are still often heard there, especially among older speakers ("I don't have nary a dime to my name"). *Whurr* for *whether* is also heard, as is *allus* for *always, swan,* a form of swear ("I swan!"), and *to study on something,* to think on it.

As noted, *it* is often pronounced *hit* by mountain people, but *hit* isn't used consistently, as many people believe. *Hit* is usually employed at the beginning of a sentence or in a stressed position ("No, hit's too soon"), while *it* is used in an unstressed place ("Glad I've got it to give ye").

Among the oddest pronoun usages among mountain speakers is *where* as a relative *which* or *who.* Though not consistently used in this fashion, *where* is sometimes heard in sentences like "That old water where comes out of a fasset (faucet)." Another strange pronoun usage is the employment of the plural pronoun *them* with several singular verbs that are considered plural, such as "them molasses," "them cheese," and "them lettuce."

Mountain speech sometimes still employs the old form *lief* (prefer), in *as* constructions like "I 'ud as lief to shoot the sorry old critter as no."

The mountaineer also favors negatives, the best ones I've come across being "I didn't aim to put up no bedstid tonight, nohow" and "I ain't never seen no men-folks of no kind do no washing nohow!" Just as beloved is the use of comparative and superlative suffixes, which can be attached to any part of speech. *Curiousist, beautifulest,* and *workin'est* are good examples, but the best is "He was the most moaningestfullest hound I ever did see!"

Mountaineers may be responsible for the common expression *to set a fire under* (to stir someone to action or movement). Mountain people, it is said, sometimes built fires under their mules to get the beasts moving when they were standing four legs spread and refusing to budge despite every other tactic. Palmer Clark, research librarian at the Van Noy Library in Fort Belvoir, Virginia, advises me that relatives of hers in the "chuggy huggy hills of Tennessee" were familiar with the practice. "Aunt Clellie," Mrs. Clark writes, "said when she was a young girl, loads of cedar were transported to Murfreesboro from Hall's Hill Pike. She distinctly remembered that her brother-in-law literally and actually built fires under the mules who hauled the cedar to get them going (this about 1921 or 1922 in Tennessee)."

Common Appalachian exclamations include *'Pon my honor!; Law me! (Lordy me!); The Lord help my time!; This day an' time!; Law, · I reckon!;* and *Laws a mercy!* There are scores more of these and other words, phrases, and pronunciations peculiar to the region. One old story, for example, relates how an old-timer told a visitor of a certain swamp infested with *b'ars.* "You mean *bear,* don't you?" asked the visitor. "No," the old-timer replied. "I mean b'ar. A bear is something without any h'ar on it." For more examples of *b'ars* and *bears* and *dars* see the Mini Mountain Vocabulary following, lest we go on here till it starts *rainin' pitchforks and bull yearlings.* But let's end, as we began, with a larripin good mess of unique and colorful expressions from deep in the holler:

* ★ *Why don't you much me 'stead of faultin' me.*
* ★ *That deer'll meat us for a spell* (provide us with meat).
* ★ *Nary-nary in the seventh, with we uns to bat* (Ozark answer giving the score of a baseball game).
* ★ *It's right airish out* (it's cold and windy).
* ★ *He turkeytailed it for home.*
* ★ *That was real thoughty of you.*
* ★ *He's down in the mullygrubs* (depressed).
* ★ *Let me hotten your coffee.*
* ★ *He daddied that child* (begat the child illegitimately).
* ★ *They're fritter-minded* (frivolous) *people.*
* ★ *I don't care a hate* (give a damn)*!*
* ★ *Greenup's coming* (it's almost springtime).
* ★ *He's jimmy-jawed* (has a projecting lower jaw).
* ★ *I jumped the broom with her years ago* (married her).
* ★ *My shoes ain't fitten to wear.*
* ★ *This pie eats good* (is tasty).
* ★ *He's rode hard and put up wet* (he's overworked).
* ★ *Slick as a peeled onion* (slippery).

★ *He'd fight a circle saw* (he's brave).
★ *He's crooked as a dog's hindleg.*
★ *Fast as skimmed milk through a tow* (burlap) *sack.*
★ *Just a hoot-n-holler from here.*
★ *He lit out like a scalded dog.*
★ *Slow as Christmas* (slow in coming about).
★ *She took her ducks to a pore market* (made a bad marriage).
★ *Slowern' sorghum* (slower than sorghum molasses pours).
★ *He tricked the cat* (became angry).
★ *This house is all yopped up* (messy).
★ *This place is in a mommick* (a mess).
★ *He's always yarnin'* (complaining) *about money.*
★ *There's twinkles* (pine needles) *on the ground.*
★ *He made more noise than a mule in a tin barn.*
★ *He's as tight as the bark on a hickory log* (very cheap).
★ *She's pore as a rail fence* (skinny).
★ *He squalled like a painter* (screamed like a panther).
★ *She is just a layin' there miseryn'* (suffering)*!*
★ *They're mighty clever* (friendly) *folk.*
★ *I got me a sight of redding* (cleaning) *up to do.*
★ *He was just a-spuddying* (ambling) *round.*
★ *Don't you green* (tease) *Sis.*
★ *He sot up to her regular* (he courted her regularly).
★ *That's the beatenest tale I ever heard on* (the biggest lie I ever heard).
★ *I'd sure admire having that car* (I'd like having it).
★ *I'm proud* (glad) *to see you lookin' so well.*
★ *She's high as a Georgia pine* (very drunk).
★ *You're burnin' green wood for kindlin'* (you're performing a futile exercise).
★ *He'll take up with anybody's coon dog that'll hunt with him* (he's so lonesome he'll be friendly with anyone).
★ *That wouldn't pass without pushin'* (it's inferior).
★ *We had dinner on the ground* (a picnic).
★ *He put on a face like a mule eatin' briars* (he frowned painfully).
★ *She's got the dry grins* (she has an embarrassed smile).
★ *I'll try to enjoy you* (entertain you).
★ *Make yourself pleasant* (make yourself at home).

A Mini Mountain Vocabulary

abody—a man or woman
acrost—across
afeared—afraid
afoot—walking
afore—before
agin—against
aig—egg
all deked up—dressed up
argie—argue
atter—after
backards—backwards
the Bad-Man or Booger-Man
 —Satan
beegum—beehive
a belling—a big party
biggity—swollen-headed
biled—boiled
brash—brush
briggoty—haughty
brung—brought
burry—berry
call—reason
c'am—calm
chimney shelf—mantel
chur—chair
church house—church
common—usual
confidenced—trusted, believed
cowcumber—cucumber
crap—crop
deef—deaf
didje—did you?
disremember—forget
drank a water—drink of water
drap—drop
egg coffee—coffee made with
 eggshells in the pot
ezactly—exactly

to fall out—to disagree
fireboard—a mantel
fitten—appropriate
fixin—intending
fur—far
gaint—gaunt
gap—gate
gaumed up—sticky
the Good-Man—God
grannywoman—a midwife
grasswiddy—divorced woman
guvment—government
hern—hers
hesh—hush
hiat—hoist
hisn—his
holler—valley
holp—help
idee—idea
I'd druther—I'd rather
jined—joined
jist—just
juice—electricity
keer—care
kiver—cover
larripin good—very good
lasses—molasses
layin' off—putting off
long handles—long johns
lite bread—commercial white
 bread
low—allow
meetin—church services
mess—prepared dish of food
midlin meat—hog's jowl
to nasty—to dirty
nigh—near
orter—ought to

ourn—ours
overhawls—overalls
passel—amount, parcel
peaked—sick
peers—seems
peert—pert
pie supper—box supper
piney—peony
pizen—poison
a play-pretty—a toy
pleasures me—amuses me
poke—paper bag
pone—corn bread
a power of—a lot
puny feeling—sick
quare—odd, strange, queer
richere—right here
rimptions of—plenty of
rocenears—corn on the cob
set in—start
shacklety—ramshackle
shed of—rid of
shivaree—ceremony after a
  wedding
shore—sure
shortsweetening—sugar
show—movie
sich—such
siddlin', sogodlin, antigodlen,
  antisighidlin—sloping,
  slanting

smidgen—little
the spear-side of a family—the
  men-folks
the spindle-side—the
  women-folks
stout—strong
strange—overly nice
tard—tired
tater—potato
tolable—mediocre
tother—the other
a tread—a step
triflin—lazy
uppity—conceited
vittles—food
vomicket—vomited
war—were
to weather—to storm
whistle pig—groundhog
whup—whip
widder, widdy—widow
winder lites—window panes
workbrickle—a good worker
worser—worse
wrench—rinse
wropped—wrapped
xter—extra
yaller—yellow
year—ear
yourn—yours
zip—molasses

6 "Rappin" Black-Style: Including Pidgin, Plantation Creole, Gullah, and Black English

✦

Black slaves brought to America spoke many African languages and dialects—probably dozens—which is one reason why they weren't harder to control. Slave traders of all colors, as clever as they were brutal, often mixed blacks from different tribes in the barracoons along the African slave coast and aboard the vile slave ships that sailed to America (some so permeated with filth, stink, and pestilence at the end of a voyage that they had to be burned or they would be detected by ships patrolling the seas to prevent the slave trade). Slaves thus found it difficult to conspire and rebel against their oppressors—the lack of a common language was a second set of chains.

But the slave masters did find it necessary to communicate with their "black gold" or "human cattle" and used several simple trade languages or pidgins to do so. Pidgin Portuguese was the first of these *lingua francas,* but Pidgin English (see Chapter 8) replaced it by the seventeenth century, when the slave trade to America began. The small vocabulary and simple syntax of Pidgin English was ideal for ordering the polyglot slaves about, and since when the long voyage ended, most slaves had a rudimentary knowledge of it, its use was reinforced among many of the slaveholders to whom they were sold. Pidgin was spoken on the plantations, along with many varieties of English, and in time it grew into what is called Plantation Creole, a *creole* being a pidgin language that is spoken by members of a second generation, one whose speakers regard it as their native tongue. Slaves were of course forced to make the language their own; they had to learn the language of their masters and their native languages were of little use to them when so many of their fellow slaves spoke different tongues. Plantation Creole was a more sophisticated, expanded pidgin, however, influenced to a large extent by the vocabulary, syntax, and pronunciation of their own African languages and the varying English dialects of their owners and overseers, both educated and uneducated.

Plantation Creole (called *nigger English* or just *nigger* at the time) varied from place to place by the mid-nineteenth century, fairly good examples of it being found in the speech of characters in Joel Chandler Harris's *Uncle Remus* tales, which were modeled on old fables that slaves brought with them from Africa. In the *Uncle Remus* books, old Uncle Remus, a former slave, entertains the young son of his employer with traditional "Negro tales," which, in St. Augustine's words, "spare the lowly and strike down the proud," including the "Tar Baby" stories and other tales of Brer Rabbit (always the hero), Brer Fox, and Brer Wolf. Harris, born a "poor white" or "redneck," a piney-woods "Georgia cracker," collected the authentic tales from numerous former slaves. One who helped him a great deal was an old gardener in Forsyth, Georgia, called Uncle Remus, for whom Harris named his narrator. The tales, however, probably originated with people who spoke the Bantu language and of course no Uncle Remus is among them. Uncle Remus is considered "a servile, groveling Uncle Tom" by some blacks today. Versions of the Brer Rabbit tales without him have been told by the black poets, Anna Bontemps and Langston Hughes.

The author of *Uncle Remus* held that many black usages and pronunciations were not African in origin, as he noted in 1892: "The student of English, if he be willing to search so near the ground, will find matter to interest him in the homely dialect of Uncle Remus, and if his intentions run towards philological investigation, he will pause before he has gone far and ask himself whether this negro dialect is what it purports to be, or whether it is not simply the language of white people of three hundred years ago twisted and modified a little to fit the lingual peculiarities of the negro. Dozens of words, such as *hit* for it, *ax* for ask, *whiles* for while, and *heap* for a large number of people, will open before him the whole field of the philology of the English tongue. He will discover that, when Uncle Remus tells the little boy that he has 'a monstrous weakness fer cake what's got *reezins* in it,' the pronunciation of *reezins* uncovers and rescues from oblivion Shakespeare's pun on *raisins,* where Falstaff tells the Prince, 'If reasons were as plentiful as blackberries, I would give no man a reason on compulsion, I.' "

Nevertheless, even at the time they were for the most part speaking Plantation Creole, blacks made significant contributions to American English; for early in the Plantation Creole period some of the various English words with origins in West African tongues must have entered the language. A number of these words may have been introduced via Swahili, which is composed primarily of Bantu words, but Swahili is not spoken by more Africans than any other language, as is widely believed. This record is held by Hausa, spoken in Nigeria and other parts of West Africa, with some 25 million speakers in all today, many of its words borrowed from Arabic. But Swahili, more correctly called *Kiswahili,* with more than 10 million speakers, is the most important language of Kenya and Tanzania, while spoken fluently in many other countries as a second language. Basically its vocabulary is Bantu (which includes more than *five hundred* languages and dialects), but there are many Arabic borrowings. *Swahili* itself derives from an Arabic word meaning *coastal,* the language having developed in the seventh century among Arabic-speaking settlers of the African coast. Other forms of Bantu spoken by slaves who came to America included Bena, Duala, Jaunde, Kongo, Chuana, Shambala, Suto, Teke, Zulu, Luganda, and Kafir.

Goober for *peanut* originated on plantations in the Southern United States, or, rather, it originated in Africa as the Bantu *nguba* (peanut) and was brought to the American South by African slaves. A Gullah language term for many years, *goober* has achieved wider currency over the past fifty years. *Okra* is also of African origin, the vegetable considered so valuable in ancient Angola that tribes made "sharp knife" raids into neighbors' fields to steal it, killing anyone who stood in their way. *Okra* derives ultimately from the Tshi *nkruman.*

The *poor Joe,* or *po' Joe,* as it is called, is another name for the great blue heron in the American South. No "Joe" is honored by this name. It is probably from the Vai language of Liberia and

Sierra Leone, where *pojo* means "heron." Similarly, both mites and fleas are called *chiggers,* this name deriving from the West African *jigger* for a bloodsucking mite. *Chigger* came to mean a flea as well as a mite because it was confused with the West Indian *chigoe* (flea). Our *jigger* for the small 1½-ounce shot glass used to measure whiskey also comes from this word.

Sweet talk (smooth, unctuous flattery designed to win over a person) possibly came to America with slaves who spoke Krio, an English-based Creole of Sierra Leone, specifically from the expression *swit mot* (sweet mouth) for flattery. To *sweet mouth* someone is the opposite of to *bad mouth* him, another black expression.

There are two theories about the origin of the word *banjo.* One holds that *banjo* was born from a black mispronunciation of *bandore,* an English word of Spanish birth denoting a musical instrument similar to the banjo. The other cites the Angola Kimbundee language *mbanza* for a banjolike instrument. It would be hard to prove or refute either theory.

Enough men to form a good jazz group are credited with lending their names to the word *jazz.* One popular choice is a dancing slave on a plantation near New Orleans, in about 1825. *Jasper* reputedly was often stirred into a fast step by cries of "Come on, Jazz." Another is a Mr. *Razz,* a band conductor in New Orleans. Charles or *Chaz* Washington, "an eminent ragtime drummer of Vicksburg, Miss.," is a third candidate. A variation on the first and last choices seems to be Charles Alexander, who, according to an old account, "down in Vicksburg around 1910, became world famous through the song asking everyone to 'come on and hear Alexander's Ragtime Band.' Alexander's first name was Charles, always abbreviated Chas. and pronounced Chazz; at the hot moments they called, 'Come on, Jazz!', whence the *jazz* music." Few scholars accept any of these hoary etymologies, but no better theory has been offered. Attempts to definitely trace the word *jazz* to an African word meaning *hurry* have failed, but it is possible that it derives from either the Arab *jazib* (one who allures) or the African *jaiza* (the sound of distant drums). It can only be said with certainty that the music was invented by blacks on Southern plantations, the word used by them since pre-Revolutionary days, long before *jazz* came to New Orleans. To complicate matters further, *jazz* was first a verb for sexual intercourse, as it still is today in slang.

Voodoo, mumbo jumbo, and *zombie* are also said to be of African origin. Most authorities believe *voodoo* derives from the African *vodum,* a form of the Ashanti *obosum* (a guardian spirit or fetish), the practice of voodoo, or black magic, having been brought to the New World by slaves as early as the 1600s. *Mumbo jumbo* appears to have come from the name of an African god. *Mama Dyumbo,* the explorer Mungo Park tells us in his *Travels in the Interior of Africa,* was the spirit or god protecting the villages of the Khassonke, a Mandingo African tribe on the Senegal. The name literally means "ancestor with a pompom" or wearing a tuft on his hat. *Mama Dyumbo* was actually more a ploy used by crafty husbands "to silence their noisy wives." He was called upon when one of a man's wives talked too much, causing dissension in his house. The husband or a confederate disguised himself as *Mama Dyumbo* and seized the troublemaker, frightening her with his mask, tufted headdress, and the hideous noises he made. He would then tie the offender to a tree and "whip her silent" amid the jeers of onlookers. Mungo Park called the bogey employed in this ritual *Mandingo,* but he became known as *Mumbo Jumbo,* a corruption of *Mama Dyumbo.* Because the god bewildered offending women, *mumbo jumbo* came to mean confusing talk, nonsense, and meaningless ceremony, or even any technical jargon that could not easily be put into plain English. The *Mumbo Jumbo* custom recalls the ducking-stool procedure employed by early Americans.

As for *zombie,* this originally meant only the snake god worshiped in West Indian voodoo ceremonies based upon the West African worship of the python god. Since dead people were said to be brought to life in these ceremonies, such imagined corpses, shuffling along half-dead and half-alive, were called *zombies.* The word naturally became applied to any oafish "dummy" without much intelligence or spirit. It is also the name of a cocktail that makes one feel that way.

Massa, the American slave word for *master,* could derive from the English *master,* or come from the West African *masa* (chief), or it could be a blend of both. No one knows for sure. The same can be said of *dig* for *to understand* ("You dig, man?"), which may have come from the West African *degu* (understand); and the term *hip* may well be from the Walof *hipicat* (hence *hepcat,* too), meaning "one who has his eyes wide open." African origins are also claimed for *cooter* (turtle); *buckra* (white man); *jitterbug; to bug* (annoy); *jukebox;* and *boogie-woogie.* Likewise, a plausible theory that lacks supporting quotations traces the all-American expression *O.K.* back to American slaves who spoke various West African languages containing words resembling *O.K.* in sound and meaning: the Dogno *o-kay,* the Djabo *o-ke,* the Wolof *waw-kay,* the Mandingo *on-ke,* and the Western Fula *eeyi-kay,* which all mean "yes indeed." The new theory is advanced in David Dalby's essay "The African Element in American English," in Thomas Kochman (ed.), *Rappin' and Stylin' Out* (1972), but most etymologists still believe that *O.K.* derives from the nickname of President Martin Van Buren (*Old K*inderhook, or O.K.).

The first recorded use of the Americanism *every which way* (in all directions) says it was originally an "odd phrase taught by black slaves to the children of Virginia gentry." Similarly, there seems little doubt that the well-known American proverb *Speak softly and carry a big stick* is African in origin. Bartlett's *Familiar Quotations* should at least note that Teddy Roosevelt's biographer H. F. Pringle, in his *Theodore Roosevelt* (1931), quotes Teddy as saying in the first recorded use of the expression: "I have always been fond of the West African proverb 'Speak softly and carry a big stick; you will go far.' " Pringle has T.R. saying this in 1900; in the 1901 speech that *Bartlett's* quotes, Roosevelt prefaces the proverb with "There is a homely adage that runs . . ."

The saddest phrase I know from the days of slavery is *till death or distance do us part.* The marriage vow among American slaves contained this change in the traditional words *till death do us part* because families were often broken up when slaves were *sold down the river.* A close second is the expression *three-fifths compromise.* Under the U.S. Constitution, slaves were considered property and had no vote, but in order to reduce the imbalance of representation between the populous North and the sparsely settled South, the Southern states were allowed by the Founding Fathers to count each slave as three-fifths of a person for their Congressional apportionment. This meant in practice that the more slaves there were, the less power they had and the more power the slaveholders enjoyed.

The Plantation Creole Gullah language introduced the word *yam* to Americans via the Gullah *njam,* which comes from the Sengal *nyami* for the vegetable. *To tote* (to carry) is of less certain African origin but most likely comes from the Konga and Kikonga

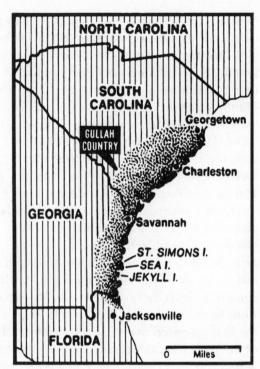

*The U.S. area where Gullah
is spoken, map courtesy*
The New York Times

language *tota* (meaning "to carry") and may also have passed into English through Gullah. Gullah, spoken in its purest form by blacks on the Sea Islands off the Georgia–South Carolina coast, is an example of a kind of Plantation Creole that has survived until today.

The word *Gullah* itself takes its name from either *Ngola* (Angola) or the West African *Gola* tribe. For several centuries the Sea Islands have harbored this language, a tongue foreign to most Americans and one of whose very existence most are still unaware. Because of its geographical isolation Gullah has escaped much of the eroding influence of American English that has afflicted the mainland communities where it is spoken. Although it was once the prevalent black language of the South's great cotton and rice plantations, the language has contracted and thrives only on these few islands that originally provided optimum conditions for its birth and incubation. Possibly arriving in the Sea Islands directly, instead of from Barbados through the Caribbean route, the slaves who first came there had, at any rate, little acquaintance with

English. The heat, dampness, and the inevitable malaria of the islands discouraged white settlement, so that the black population always sharply exceeded the white, and black overseers were commonplace. Unfortunately, today's islands are under siege by those two most formidable foes of tradition, tourist trade and real-estate development. But though Gullah may be doomed to the notebooks and recordings of philologists, it is still spoken to some extent by more than 250,000 people along the southeastern coast from South Carolina to the Florida border, and its vitality echoes from the rhythmic chanting of the flower sellers at Charleston's Four Corners to the rappin' of ghetto youths on the streets of New York. In fact, there are also about a thousand pure Gullah speakers in New York City, most of them living in Brooklyn's Bedford-Stuyvesant section.

In the past, Gullah (more usually called *Geechee* among its speakers) was for some a source of derision and shame, while for others it has always been and continues to be one of ethnic pride. Beyond all else today, Gullah stands as the living testimony of a people's determination to survive and preserve the linguistic bulwark that had shielded them from the most divisive and dehumanizing conditions.

Though we might question the medical wisdom of "Mumps ain't nuttin' if you can get sardine grease to grease em wid," we have little difficulty understanding what is being said. Gullah seems at first glance to be simply a case of "broken," "poor," or "childish" English. Early scholars, misled by the superficial similarities between the languages and perhaps reluctant to credit blacks with any cultural contribution, conceived of Gullah as a corruption of English. One theory described the language as a simplified form of English that arose by necessity when masters had to communicate with their slaves. Relying on sentences shorn of all but uninflected words in the simplest word order and accompanied by extensive gestures, the master would make known his wishes and the slaves would accede to his language as well as his commands. This "baby talk" theory gained wide acceptance because it was plausible and because it made the white man, who had lost his political sovereignty after the Civil War, still the linguistic master of any black. Another theory that would have wholly excluded African influence posited a complex system of geographical references according to which every idiosyncrasy of the language was traced to dialects and localisms within England, Wales, or Scotland.

Not until midway in our own century did scholars recognize the contribution of African languages to Gullah. For the first speakers of Gullah were also its originators. Born speakers of Bantu, Wolof, Fante, Mandingo, Ewe, Twi, Ibo, Yoruba, or another of the hundreds of distinct tongues of West Africa, they forged from this diverse linguistic heritage a unique language. The pioneering studies of the black scholar Lorenzo D. Turner revealed in their comparisons of Gullah and West African languages that the grammatical peculiarities of Gullah are not corruptions of English but an amalgam of forms indigenous to a number of West African dialects. Gullah is not an infant's rendering of English or a random sampling of British dialects, but a language whose structure is the outcome of an historical experience in which select aspects of West African dialects adaptable to an English environment merged to form a common grammar and syntax.

Chief among the twenty-eight or so African languages that influenced the development of Gullah are Wolof, spoken on the coastline closest to the United States; Mandingo, spoken by the largest percentage of first-generation blacks to arrive here; Akan, the language of what was formerly known as the Gold Coast; and Hausa, the geographically extensive language of West Africa's interior and a tongue spoken as a second language by many of the smaller tribes.

Turner in his *Africanisms in the Gullah Dialect* (1949) compiled the first extensive list of African words that were directly loaned to Gullah. Most of these six thousand or so words were personal names and many were descriptive of the African zoological or botanical experience. Mandingo gave its word for turtle, *cooter*, and Wolof yielded *banana*. Turner's etymological investigations of the personal names and nicknames of Gullah (such as *Angku*, boy born on Saturday, or *Betsibi*, mischievous) revealed more than four thousand traceable to African personal or proper names. Other African words used in Gullah include common terms like *dafa* (fat) and *bong* (tooth). Many such terms are convergences, words introduced from Africa that merge with similar-sounding English words, as has been previously noted in the case of *massa* and the slang *dig* (to understand). The vocabulary of Gullah at its inception may have reflected more clearly the pervasive influence of Africa, but as the language expanded it borrowed most of its vocabulary from English. Recent scholarship has enlarged considerably Turner's list of Africanisms in Gullah, but, except for names, the vocabulary of Gullah is nevertheless derived predominantly from English. It is rather the grammar of Gullah that best reflects the defining influence of Africa.

All the distinctive aspects of Gullah's grammatical structure have been identified with West African dialects, though the language is not a pale reflection of one or several of these tongues. In the slave camps awaiting shipment to the New World and during those endless months aboard the slave ships on which death-in-life prevailed, the slaves, bereft of family and friends, were by necessity forced to find some means of communicating their most basic needs to their masters as well as to one another, just as their masters needed to communicate with them. From the mutually unintelligible but linguistically related languages of West Africa and the language of their oppressors, the slaves and their captors developed their own pidgin, a simple language capable of serving only the most essential needs in very restricted linguistic contexts. Finally, on the plantations of the South, this pidgin evolved into a language suited to the slaves' complete needs.

Gullah had to accommodate itself to English, which it did in large part by accepting its vocabulary and certain grammatical categories while retaining those African terms and syntactic rules that were uniquely descriptive of its past. It was never overwhelmed by English. In the segregation of their slave cabins and long halls, in the fields of rice and cotton, slaves reinforced and expanded the uses of their by now native tongue.

The syntactic structure, or underlying grammar, of Gullah is relatively simple and extraordinarily economical, making the language quickly and readily accessible to new learners—an important feature for a language that in its infancy would be exposed to a highly developed, socially preferred, and legally enforced language. If Gullah had not been so easy to learn, it would doubtless not have survived even a generation.

Context is most important in understanding Gullah. Reed Smith, in *The Gullah Dialect,* claims that the Gullah sentence *I yeddy* (hear or heard) *'um but I ain't sh'um* can be interpreted fully sixty-four ways:

hear	it	didn't	it
I heard	her	but I don't	see her
	him		him
	their		them

One certainly can't always assume what pronouns mean in Gullah without knowing the context. As is the case in almost all West African languages, the pronoun form *e'* (as well as its hypercorrected form *he*) in Gullah does not reflect any gender distinction. Under the same African influence, however, Gullah *does* differentiate the second-person singular and plural of the personal pronoun. Gullah's *yu* for the singular and *une* for the plural is probably a direct descendant of the Wolof *yow* and *yeen* converged with the English *you* for the singular and *you* and *one* for the plural. In addition, the objective form *em* does not make any number distinctions (*E' hit em* requires a context for the listener to identify the culprit as man, woman, or horse, and the victim as individual or group), while English requires a context only to fix the referent of the pronoun. A good example of *e*'s use can be seen in a humorous story told by J. Gary Black, the auditor of Beaufort County, South Carolina, from 1920 to 1970, in *My Friend the Gullah* (1974):

"Arthur," I said, "I didn't know you were a carpenter."

"Yes, suh," he said, "Ah bin a carpenter for a long time, many many years."

"Then you must have been one of those who helped build the Ark."

"Oh, no, suh, Ah didn't go back that far. They tell me it tek forty year to build the A'ak."

"I don't believe it took that long," I replied.

"Why not, suh?"

"Well, if it took forty years to build the Ark, when they put the last board on, the first one would be rotten."

"No suh, Mr. Black, dem board bin blessed wid de Holy Spirit. Ah believe if you could find dat A'ak today and put 'em in dis creek, e' would float."

The Gullah *e'* or *he* also functions as a possessive adjective, as it does in various West African languages. This is attested by lines from an interview with a former slave published in *The American Slave Supplement:* "One time they wuz two neighbor—he live close togedder. This lady husband went to he home and get he old police [valise] and get all he clothes and leff home. Leff he little daughter and he wife right dere."

Gullah verbs usually overlook the relative time of an action and its temporal relation to other actions, so that one doesn't hear young speakers struggling over the pluperfect or future perfect tenses. When Gullah does occasionally differentiate between the present and the past, it employs *done* to mark the completion of an action *(Ah done found Moses).* Both the Wolof *doon* and the Mandingo *tun* serve the same function, as does the English *done* with which they probably converged. Gullah also creates a distinction between the continuing and momentary aspects of action by the simple expedient of adding *duh* for the present and *been* for the past of verbs describing continuing action or action over an extended period of time, as in *Tom duh hit e' wife till e' cries and cries.*

Gullah has long maintained African intonation patterns. The intonations of the typical unemphatic declarative sentence *E' gon' away,* for example, rises at its conclusion, ending in a high or middle tone, often with a stressed final syllable. Unlike the falling tone of English questions and the rising one for those presuming a "yes" or "no" response, questions in Gullah are commonly asked in a level tone. Even today, after centuries of decreolization in this most vulnerable aspect of a language's identity, differences in loudness, pitch, and stress still persist.

One could devote a book to Gullah's grammar and, indeed, the world's foremost Gullah authority, Professor William A. Stewart of the City University of New York, plans to do just that; he believes nothing less than a four-volume work on Gullah is needed, one volume each on grammar, vocabulary, evolution, and historic background. He hopes such a work "will affect attitudes toward black children, who are too often thought to be backward when they are instead products of a different though no less complex linguistic and cultural background." Professor Stewart loves the rapid, melodic, almost calypso cadence of drawlless Gullah. "You can't help but fall in love with this language," he says. "When kids speak it, it sounds like a bird song."

Several of Gullah's syntactical peculiarities are found in today's city-based Black English dialect, as we'll see, just as they have influenced black speech in general. An example of the latter is what has been described as "the behind proposition," the use of *at* at the end of sentences (*Where you stay at?*). As for Gullah's vocabulary, it not only used African words such as *okra, cushie* (a cornmeal cake), *yam, cooter, goober, tote, banana,* and *buckra;* it passed these words on to other English speakers. African words used by Gullah speakers that *didn't* pass into general usage include *nyam* (to eat), *ki!* (an exclamation), and *plat-eye* (for an evil spirit). English expressions long common to the language include:

★ *To study on* (think about) *it.*
★ *First fowl crow* (early morning).
★ *'Posit your word* (take an oath).
★ *All two* (both).
★ *Tiel* (stole; *'E tiel um,* He stole it).
★ *Evening* (afternoon).
★ *Peruse* (to stroll).
★ *Wha' fuh ya is fuh ya* (Whatever is for you is for you, *que será, será*).
★ *Up all the windows* (Open the windows).
★ *Great God in Zion, man!* (an exclamation).

The Gullah expression *love come down* refers to the arousal of passion, an intentional stimulation of sexual desire. A woman might have this irresistible power by virtue of the way she walks or talks or sings or smiles, the object of this arousal sometimes reduced to abject pleading: "Ah ain't drunk, Sedalia. Mah love jes come down fer yu, Sugah. Ah'm yu man. Now loose up."

A leg party is an expression used by Gullah speakers on Daufuskie Island off South Carolina, the island so named because it was *da* (the) *fust* (first) *key* (island) north of the Savannah River. "Sometime dancin' be after what we call *a leg party,*" an elderly Daufuskian explained to Alex Haley recently. "All the mens, ol' an' young, in a room with big table full of treatin' plates, a apple, a pigfoot, an' a slice of cake cost fifteen cent. Now the next room be full of womens, separated from us at the door by a long, thick curtain, maybe a blanket. Now, the rules was three, four womens at the time stick out one leg an' foot below that curtain, with all 'em wearin' the same color ol' thick cotton stockin's. An' every man got to bend down, lookin' an' guessin' hard as he can, 'cause pretty young gals back in there, same as plenty they mamas an' them ol' gran'mas, too. Oh, Lord, how you hopin' you can guess a leg of somethin' nice an' fine 'stead of somebody's gran'ma. But all you can do finally is decide which one them three, four ankles just to go 'head an' grab an' squeeze—an' then, Lordy, whoever's hooked onto that ankle, well, out she come, walkin' before everybody! An', buddy, you grabbed somebody's ninety-year-ol' ankle? That's jus' what you got. An' everybody includin' her is fallin' out laughin.' An' rules say you got to buy her one them fifteen-cent apple an' cake an' pig-foot plates."

Eben do a wak tru de daak walley ob de shada ob det, a yent scayd, cuz oona da stay 'long me is a translation of the fourth verse of the Twenty-third Psalm into Gullah. Many Gullah words and expressions are related to religion. No cultural institution underwent so complete a transformation by the black slave community as the Christian Church. The doctrine may have remained orthodox but little else did. The African tradition of emotional ritual dances and songs became the regulated swaying body movements, the controlled vocal chanting and the dramatic emotional conversions of the black Church. Regarding the latter, prospective converts are said to be *seeking,* which is "a distinct, passionate, fervid desire to lose oneself in the community of Christ as represented by His church." Those who enjoy the process of conversion are *coming through* and are often struck with mystic visions, which with simple unadorned eloquence they share with the faithful. As a former slave interviewed for the *Slave Narratives* put it:

"When I been converted I went to Hebben in de sperit an' see wid de eye of fait!"

"How did you feel when you were there?"

"Oh, I 'joicing! I 'joicing! Nebber de lak befor', an' angel tek me an' show me de stars, how dey hang up dere by a silver cord, an' de moon jes a ball ob blood, but I ain't know how it hold up, an' de sun on de rim ob all dese goin' round an' round, an' Christ settin' in a rocking chair obber de sun. Gabriel an' Michael was wid 'em, one on dis side an' on de odder holding de laws. I see eberyt'ing jes lak I say. Sweet Jesus I hope I reach dat place I see."

Two of the most cherished of African linguistic traditions, proverbs and child naming, were preserved in Gullah. The African proverb, with its indirect construction, ambiguous speech, and poetical language, survives in its combination with English vocabulary. The form of these proverbs was rigidly fixed. They were conditionals, rhetorical questions of simple propositions, but the language was anything but rigid. It was ambiguous, allusive, and fashioned with poetical devices ranging from alliteration, repetition, and rhyme to personification and parallelism. Some proverbs defined metaphysical notions: *Hell, det one ditch you cannot jump;* others offered advice: *Work while it is day;* while still others reflected a fatalistic view: *Trouble goin' fall.* In continuing the African tradition of proverbs, Gullah provided for the cultural initiation of the young into a world of beliefs, superstitions, hopes, and fears that was beyond their own degrading American experience. They identified with a culture and its language that were not shackled by the constraints of plantation life.

An example of a practical Gullah proverb that passed into general American use is *Likker'll make you not know your mamma,* which dates back at least to the eighteenth century and probably before this, possibly being adapted from an African proverb brought to America by South Carolina slaves.

The African practice of naming had an almost mystical importance to Gullah speakers. Naming afforded an opportunity of sharing personal and historical experiences, attitudes toward life, and a system of values. Slaves would often have two names: one that the master gave, such as Brutus, and a unique name, such as Sabe, that would be the individual's within the community that really mattered to him, his own. In accordance with African tradition, children were often named after the English equivalents of the days of the week. Sometimes African names themselves ("Sango," "Mingo," "Sambo") or homonyms of African names (such as "Joe," for "Cadjo") were chosen. Finally, the tradition of naming according to prevalent ideas was carried on in the new tongue, so that children were named for the weather: "Bright" or "Rainy"; their appearance: "Curly" or "Noisy"; or their parents' attitude toward their birth: "Welcome." In all, Gullah strove to strengthen the naming traditions, which gave the family a sense of power over their masters, and their children a sense of heritage and pride. The black child was not defenselessly incorporated into the white man's slave society at birth, but entered the inhumane system protected by a sense of self and history—the parents had given the child, and would continue to give the child, everything that it was possible to give.

Black English, an ethnic dialect spoken by a large number of American blacks today, evolved to a great extent from African languages and Plantation Creole languages such as Gullah, but hardly resembles them today. When blacks were freed from slavery and began mingling with whites in all regions of the country, Plantation Creole (except where it was isolated like Gullah) began to weaken, and the language became a dialect—"English with an African accent." Some writers call this Black English a class dialect because it is spoken mostly by poor people with relatively little formal education, but at least echoes of it are certainly heard in the speech of some affluent, highly educated blacks. However, Black English is by no means spoken by all blacks, just as Plantation Creole wasn't the language of all blacks two hundred years ago. Blacks, after all, number more than 20 million in America, more than 10 percent of the population. While J. L. Dillard in his valuable *Black English* (1972) estimates that 80 percent of American blacks use Black English, there is no hard proof of this; that percentage might better describe the number of blacks who use some Black English expressions (as a large number of whites also do!), or who have spoken it to even a limited extent at some point in their lives. No doubt a black person born and raised in an upper-middle-class Boston neighborhood would speak not Black English but the New England dialect spoken there. Hundreds of thousands of American blacks also speak in West Indian dialects (which, in turn, Danish left its stamp upon, and one of which, Dominican, was influenced by Cockney speech!), while many other blacks use Arabic terms in their speech, especially those who have embraced Islam and abandoned their "slave names" for Islamic ones such as Elijah Muhammad or Muhammad Ali. In any case, there is no such thing as uniform black speech throughout the country. In *Say It My Way*, Willard Espy reports that American novelist Ralph Ellison told him there is no one regional black dialect: "At least until the great migration North a generation ago, the dialect changed with the region. Ellison himself was brought up in Oklahoma; his father came from one state, his mother from another. None of the three spoke the same way." Mr. Ellison is right. While Black English, spoken in its purest form by young poor blacks of the ghetto and passed on by schoolchildren from generation to generation, is much the same the country over, the speech of blacks rich and poor is still influenced by the regional dialects wherever they live, the Harlem black speaking

with many New York dialect characteristics and the Middle
Western black affected by General American speech.

The speech of blacks does, however, often have certain similarities from one region to the next, no matter what region the
speaker hails from. In times past, black speech (particularly its
pronunciation) was attributed by so-called scholars to "the thick
lips of blacks" or to their "innate laziness or stupidity." If you
think I exaggerate, listen to A. E. Gonzales, who edited collections
of Gullah folktales in the 1920s. "Slovenly and careless of speech
these Gullahs seized upon the peasant English used by some of
the early settlers," Gonzales wrote. "They wrapped their clumsy
tongues about it, and, enriched with certain expressive African
words, it issued through their flat noses and thick lips as so workable a form of speech, that it was gradually adopted by the other
slaves and became the accepted Negro speech of the lower districts of South Carolina and Georgia. . . . The words are, of course,
not African, for the African brought over or retained only a few
words of his jungle tongue."

Such drivel isn't worthy of comment except to say that black
phonetic characteristics are very similar to those of white Southerners. One of the main reasons black speech is similar everywhere is because it doubtless contains much of Southern
pronunciation and vocabulary, though blacks also contributed to
the Southern way of speech. It doesn't seem reasonable that the
millions of blacks living in the South could have failed to influence
Southern speech to some extent (especially since so many black
mammies brought up white Southerners), but several writers insist
that they did not and that "so-called black speech" is merely
"transplanted Southeastern dialect traits," reflecting the fact that
most American blacks hailed from the Southeastern United States
and retained that dialect to some extent.

One can indeed point out characteristics of black pronunciations that not only have their roots in Southern speech but go back
to various British dialects. *Gwyne* for *going,* to give one example,
is still heard in the British Southern, South Midland, and South
Western dialects, while *haid* for *head* is found in the dialects of
Kent, Norfolk, Devonshire, Lancashire, Northampton, Yorkshire,
Somerset, and Suffolk. On the other hand, African languages may
well have influenced Southern speech in many ways besides the
contributions of new words and expressions such as those already

cited. It has been suggested that the extreme nasalization of almost all African languages may be a basis for the nasalization of Southern white and black speech. What are called the "unstable" sounds of *ay* and *eh* in both Southern and black speech (resulting in pronunciations like either *bayd* or *behd* for *bed,* or either *mayk* or *mehk* for *make*) may derive from the fact that this pair of sounds each belongs to one phoneme in the Zulu African dialect. The same may be true of the Southern and black *oh* and *aw* sounds, among others. The dropping of *l* in words like *self (sef)* is not common in any British dialect that strongly influenced the Southern dialect, and its occurrences in both Southern and black speech may be traceable to there being no *l* in the African Effik, Fante, and Twi dialects. It has also been suggested that black pronunciation of *b* for *v* in words like *river (ribuh)* and *have (hab)* may be due to the fact that there is no *v* sound in any African language, and that blacks substitute *t* and *d* for *th* (*dis* for *this,* etc.) because no African language, excepting Arabic loan words in Swahili, has the *th* sound. It is possible, though far from certain, that this last pronunciation became part of Southern speech, which then contributed it to the *dis, dese,* and *dems* of Brooklynese (see Chapter 3).

Dialectologists have been squabbling about the origins of black and Southern talk for at least several decades now, and there seems to be no end in sight to the argument; a scholar on one side of the question recently spent close to half a book trying to refute criticisms of his previous work. In any event, it seems certain that both Southern and black speech influenced each other—it was not a one-way street—though more research needs to be done on the subject. In the important matter of the syntax of Black English, for example, to my knowledge there have been no studies made comparing this unusual speech syntax to that of Africans.

As noted in Chapter 1, many educated white Southerners have attested that they are often taken for blacks in telephone conversations. Black pronunciation isn't basically different from Southern white pronunciations (see Chapter 4), but in the matter of syntax Black English is quite distinctive. Many of the few verb inflections in other English dialects are eliminated by a large number of speakers of this dialect, *he runs* becoming *he run,* and *he went* replaced by *he go* (if the action occurred in the past), while the verb *to be* is sometimes eliminated entirely, as in *he sick* (instead of *he is sick*). Most important, Black English verbs emphasize aspect rather than tense; in almost all other dialects, verbs always indicate past, present, or future and tell nothing about the kind or aspect of action, but in Black English (as in many African languages) the verb more often shows the kind of action, and the tense has to be learned from the context. Robert Claiborne explains it this way in *Our Marvellous Native Tongue*: "Forms like 'he go' imply a single, completed action; thus 'he go to de sto' may mean 'he went to the store' (yesterday) or 'he will go to the store' (tomorrow). 'He goin' to de sto,' by contrast, implies continuing action—'he is on his way to the store,' or 'he was on his way to the store (when) . . .' Finally, 'he be goin' to de sto' implies repeated or habitual action, meaning 'he used to go the store' (every day) or 'he goes to the store' (every Saturday) or even, conceivably, 'he will go to the store' (any time you ask him). This subtle difference in meaning shows up in the classic ghetto put-down 'You makin' sense, but you don't *be* makin' sense'—literally, 'You're making sense now, but you don't usually make sense,' or, more loosely, 'You're making sense—for a change.' "

Generally, black speech is, if anything, even more lilting, musical, and pleasing to the ear than Southern speech. It is a relaxed speech noted for its indifferent treatment of unstressed syllables (for example, the initial unstressed syllable in *about* is often dropped so that the word sounds like *bahoot*), and the slurring or dropping of consonants (a black contestant on one quiz show reportedly managed to say "I don't know that" with just two consonants: *I o no da*). Poorer, less educated black speakers most often share these tendencies, just as they are associated with innumerable unique phrases, many of which are "grammatical errors," or differences from standard English usage, and have become part of the city-shaped Black English dialect. Among such speakers, for example, the conjugation of *to be* is often as follows: *I's* (I is), *you's* (you is), *he's* (he is), *us's* (us is), *y'all's* (you all is), and *they's* (they is). This leads to expressions like *I's here; you's late;* and *they's fine.* The superfluous *done* is another dialect feature (*I done took it,* or even *I done done it*), as well as the double and even triple negative (*Didn't nobody see it* for *Nobody saw it,* or *Ain't never got no job nohow* for *I never had a job*). The addition of *s* to a plural word is also heard (*feets* for *feet*), as is the adding of *ed* to make a past-tense verb (*I telled him not to come* for *I told him not to come*). Following is a short list of expressions that are fairly common, more frequently among older speakers:

* *You ain't got no call* (reason) *to be mad.*
* *Pay no mind* (attention) *to it.*
* *I'm gonna study on* (think about) *it.*
* *Hush yo' mouth!* (Be quiet!)
* *That's the gospel truth.* (That's the absolute truth.)
* *Ain't that something!*
* *Ain't it the truth!*
* *I like to kill him.* (I almost killed him.)
* *Put it outen* (out of) *my way.*

These expressions and many more, such as *dog my cats!, sho' nuf, Lordy!,* and *I'll be doggoned!* aren't all exclusively black idioms and aren't much heard among younger blacks today, some of them considered to be the vocabulary of the "stereotyped Negro character of yesterday," the "foot-shuffling handkerchief head" that modern blacks try to avoid sounding like, or the Amos 'n Andy types with their "Ain't dat sumpins!" and "Scuse me for protrudin's (intruding)" and dozens more such phrases. Most are rarely heard in the city-based Black English dialect, where even the use of the Southern *y'all* becomes rarer every year (to my ear), possibly because it is considered "Uncle Tomish" by many.

No black wants to be known as an *Uncle Tom* today. In fact, an Akron woman won $32,000 in damages from a Cleveland newspaper several years ago because it called her an Uncle Tom. The derogatory term, applied to toadying black men, mostly by other blacks, can also mean a black *woman* who kowtows to whites or puts up with the status quo, though *Aunt Thomasina* has been used instead. Everyone knows that Uncle Tom comes from the character in Harriet Beecher Stowe's *Uncle Tom's Cabin* (1852), the immensely popular American antislavery novel that caused President Lincoln to say on meeting Mrs. Stowe, "Is this the little woman whose book made such a great war?" Mrs. Stowe depicted Uncle Tom as simple, easygoing, and servile, willing to put up with anything, though it should be remembered that she intended him to be a noble, brave, high-minded, devout Christian and that he is flogged to death by Simon Legree at the end of the book for bravely refusing to reveal the hiding place of Cassie and Emma-

line, two female slaves. Mrs. Stowe's model for Uncle Tom was a
real-life slave named Josiah Henson, born in Maryland in 1789,
who wrote a widely read autobiographical pamphlet. Henson was
far from an Uncle Tom in the term's recent sense. Like many
slaves, he served as the overseer, or manager, of a plantation
before he escaped to Canada. When he journeyed to England on
business, the Archbishop of Canterbury was so impressed with his
speech and learning that he asked him what university he had
studied at. "The University of Adversity," Henson replied. Mrs.
Stowe later told a visitor that she hadn't written her book: "God
wrote it. I merely wrote his dictation." But she almost certainly
got her idea for *Uncle Tom's Cabin* from Henson's seventy-six-page
pamphlet. Her book also gives us the expression *Simon Legree,*
which is still used humorously as a term for a slave driver or a
boss, and which comes from the name of the brutal, drunken
planter—a renegade Northerner—to whom Uncle Tom was sold.
Uncle Tom's Cabin may be unpopular with blacks today, but in its
time it was anathema to slaveowners. One piece of hate mail Mrs.
Stowe received contained the ear of a slave.

Since Uncle Tom's day, Black English has undergone great
changes in American urban areas. Today poor blacks in the inner
city speak the purest Black English, which is often misunderstood
by whites because it depends on syntax and inflection as well as
a unique, constantly changing vocabulary. As we've seen, someone who says *She sad* in Black English means *She is sad all the time.*
The expression *I hear ya* can mean anything from *I agree with you*
to *I understand what you're saying,* or even *Now go away,* depending
on the tone of voice the speaker uses. Tom Kochman, a University
of Illinois sociolinguist, points out that this misunderstanding or
language gulf can extend to the style of speech as well. In a
negotiation, for example, whites often withdraw when they sense
blacks are becoming emotional, "but for blacks showing emotion
is precisely the way to demonstrate they are serious about nego-
tiating."

While it does depend on its distinctive syntax, inflection, and
grammar, the city-based Black English dialect definitely has its
own distinctive vocabulary of slang expressions. Among the latest
slang (which will not be the latest slang when this book is published) is *chill out* for stop acting foolishly, *crib* (instead of *pad*) for
apartment, *tude* for attitude, *to get down* for getting down to essen-

tials, and *serious* for something of the highest merit ("My mother's cooking is serious, man!"). Another interesting one is *Face* as a greeting for someone whose face (but not name) is remembered ("Hey, Face, what's happenin'?"). Older black urban slang includes *the man* for the police or a white employer; *vines* for clothes; *far out*, outlandish; *grays*, white people; *happy shop*, a liquor store; *worriation*, for a big worry; and *pay your dues*, to suffer or serve a hard apprenticeship in anything. But it is often difficult to establish just how contemporary black slang is. I have seen the expression *bad* described as "the most up-to-date" black slang recently, but *bad*, when slowly pronounced *baaaad*, has long been black slang for something or someone *good*. The variation is so old that it is found in Gullah three centuries ago, when *baaaad* was used by slaves "as an expression of admiration for another slave who successfully flouted *Ole Maussa's* rules."

Another fairly recent black slang expression with ancient origins is the term *ace boon coon* for closest or best friend, which is first recorded in Claude Brown's novel *Manchild in the Promised Land* (1965). The word *coon* in this expression is a racial slur meaning a black person when said by a white. It possibly has nothing to do with the animal called a raccoon or coon. *Coon* here may come from the last syllable of the Portuguese *barracões*, which is pronounced like *coon* and meant "buildings especially constructed to hold slaves for sale." The word *coon* is used by blacks, as is the word *nigger*, but is of course considered highly offensive when uttered by whites. Neither has the word become acceptable among most blacks like the formerly offensive word *bwana* has in Africa. The journalist Henry Morton Stanley of Stanley and Livingstone fame first recorded the Swahili *bwana* in 1878. *Bwana* is a title of respect translating as "father of sons," but meaning "sir, Mr., boss, or master." Often applied exclusively to white men in the past, usually in a groveling manner, it is today a common form of address to both Africans and whites in many African countries.

Still another term meaning blacks that is used by blacks is *soul brothers*, which has been around since at least the 1950s. Today it is often abbreviated as *the brothers* (or *sisters*) and further shortened to *bro* when used in a greeting. The meaning here is that blacks are alike in the soul, but in earlier combinations *soul* was used in many ways. *Soul driver* and *soul doctor* were terms abolitionists applied to white men who took indentured servants and slaves from place to place in colonial times to sell them. *Soul sharks* were rapacious preachers, black or white, usually without a pulpit, and *soul butter* was a term for moralizing pap black or white, an expression that Mark Twain popularized. *Soul mate* can be someone much loved, or even a mistress, and a *soul kiss* is a long, open-mouthed "French kiss" during which a lover's tongue explores and caresses the mouth of the beloved. *Soul music* and *soul food* (food like collard greens, black-eyed peas, hog maw, etc., associated with Southern blacks) are also black terms dating back at least to the 1950s.

The word *honkie*, a derisive term for a white, and the direct opposite of *soul brother*, may come from a black pronunciation of *bohunk*, a low expression for a Polish or Hungarian-American that arose at the turn of the century, and is probably a blend of Bohemian or Hungarian (both Poles and Hungarians were called Bohemians). *Bohunks* were also called *hunkies* and black workers in the Chicago meat-packing plants probably pronounced this as *honkie*, soon applying it as a derisive term not just for their Polish and Hungarian co-workers but for all whites. *Honkie,* however, may refer to the nasal tone blacks hear in white voices.

Black Is Beautiful has been a slogan of pride for black Americans since the late 1960s, and may derive from the Song of Solomon in the Old Testament: "I am black but beautiful." Similarly, the expression *Keep the faith, baby* was common among civil rights workers in the 1960s and became a popular slang expression meaning "Don't give up." It is much older than this, however, and has its origins in the Bible (II Timothy 4:7): "I have fought the good fight. I have finished my course. I have kept the faith."

The *dozens* or *dirty dozens,* also called *joinin'* and *sounding,* is a verbal-insult game played by blacks who speak Black English, consisting of streams of insulting words and rhymes used to put down opponents and employing the latest slang.

While black slang changes from year to year, or month to month, or mouth to mouth in the ghetto, many black expressions have become part of general American usage. Besides those already mentioned, these include *kicks* for pleasure; *to make it,* to succeed; *airish,* to put on airs; *cheese-eater,* a toady; *ticky* (probably from *particular*) for exacting; *hang-up,* a problem; *to rap,* to talk; *put on,* to make fun of someone without the person's knowing it; *nitty-gritty; right on! sit-in;* and *tell it like it is!* It could be that many of these terms may well become *standard* English words—as the late, legendary black jazz pianist Fats Waller is reported to have said, "One never knows, do one?" Anyway, considering that I've probably made a few beautiful mistakes, at best, I had better not summarize—as black baseball great Leroy "Satchel" Paige advised: "Don't look back, something might be gaining on you!"

7 Ferhoodled English: Pennsylvania Dutch Talk

✴

"You must go dat road, straight one little way, den you see stable directly—dat road, straight, house directly," a Pennsylvania Dutchman was quoted as saying by English traveler William Ferguson in his *America by River and Road* (1856).

Over a century later another pair of impeccable ears, these belonging to American novelist John O'Hara, heard this Pennsylvania Dutch conversation:

"What did they do with the auto?"

"She got towed in town with a team."

"What for make was she?"

Americans have been recording the Pennsylvania Dutch dialect for well over two centuries now—and there is no sign that they won't be amused and *ferhoodled* (crazy, mixed up) by it for another two centuries or more. This direct descendant of the seventeenth-century Rheno-Franconian dialect of German (the *Dutch* in Pennsylvania Dutch has nothing to do with Holland, being a corruption or Americanization of *Deutsch*, German) has proved "a notable exception to the mortality of immigrant dialects," as one linguist puts it. The theory that among immigrants the first generation speaks "old-country language with heavily accented English," the second generation is "bilingual with a preference for English," and the third generation "is essentially monolingual in English" is exploded by the Pennsylvania Dutch, who have persisted in preserving at least traces of old-country language in their dialect long past the three-generation period—for what amounts to about six or seven generations, in fact. Linguist Mario Pei has written that the dialect seems "destined to go the way of all pidgins" and that though a chair of Pennsylvania German language has been established at Muhlenberg College, Allentown, "the continued vitality of the dialect under modern conditions is doubtful." But no signs of an imminent demise are apparent. One tends to agree with that student of linguistics who grew up among the Pennsylvania Dutch near Reading. Informed that most authorities predicted the dialect would "soon" be dead, she observed, "I vunder vot iss meaning to a linguist 'soon.' "

Pennsylvania Dutch has mainly survived as a pidgin-type dialect in America because of the clannishness of the pious people who speak "Dutch" and the Old World traditions carefully preserved by the strict religious sects to which they belong.

The Pennsylvania Dutch, or "plain people," as they have called themselves since at least 1680 (when they dubbed the more worldly Lutherans and Calvinists *the gay people*), came to America in the seventeenth and eighteenth centuries, fleeing religious persecution in southern Germany, Switzerland, and the Netherlands. They responded to Quaker William Penn's propaganda pamphlets describing the colony named after his father as a rich land of promise free from religious hatreds, and by as early as 1776 they numbered some 100,000, about one third of the colony's population.

The plain people were mostly Palatinate Germans from the country bordering on the Rhine from Switzerland to Koblenz, though they included a large number of Swiss, people from Holland, and even French Huguenots. In fact, the *Mennonites,* who were the first Pennsylvania Dutch to settle in America, founding Germantown, Pennsylvania, only two years after Penn's colony was established, were a Swiss Anabaptist sect who came from Holland and Germany and were originally called the Swiss Brethren. They take their present name from their founder Menno Simons (1496–1561) and are perhaps 250,000 strong throughout the United States today. The *Old Order Amish,* or *Amish,* named after seventeenth-century Mennonite reformer Jacob Ammann, or Amen, are a conservative sect of the Mennonites so noted for

GOOK YUSHT AMOHL DOH!

Monsleit un Weibsleit!!
Buwa un Maed—Yungy un Olty

ATTENTION!

DER EAGLE DRUG SHTORE

Der Besht un der Wholsealsht!

WM. S. SEAGER OBBADEAKER.

In der Dritt Shtrose, Sued Bethlehem.
Alsfort uf hond, olly sorta fun de beshty Drugs un Meditziena, un on de wholsealshty prices. Also, Paint, Oehl, Glaws, Varnish, &c. Mer hen aw an neier article dos gor net gebutta konn waerra; es is de bareemt

"SALTED SODA"

un waerd g'used for seaf kocha. Prowiers amohl—de directions we mers braucht geena mit. Om Eagle Drug Shtore is aw der plotz for

PATENT MEDITZIENA, BITTERS, &C., &C.

Fun olly ort, un on de wholsealshty prices.
    Also, Coal-Oehl, Lompa, Waugha-Schmeer, &c., &c.
Now mind was mer sawya; mer hen olles uf hond was mer denka konn in unser line of bisness. We g'sawt, unser prices sin wholsealer dos in ennichem onnera Drug Shtore in County. Ferges't net der platz,

IN DER DRITT SHTROSE UNICH DER LOCUST

SUED BETHLEHEM

Now is de tseit; macht eich bei, un judg'd for eigh selwer; kummt in foor weasa, uf horseback, uf dem Railroad, odder tsu foos—mer sin gor net particular wie, yusht so dos ker kummt on

DER EAGLE OBBADEAK IN SUED BETHLEHEM

Un bringt eier greenbacks mit. Wholseal for cash—sell is unser style.

WILLIAM S. SEAGER

Obbadeaker[6]

Newspaper ad of a Pennsylvania Dutch drugstore

their quaint customs that Pennsylvania Dutch country is often called *Amishland.* They still regard English as a language to be used only with outsiders. Generally, however, Mennonites have assimilated to a greater degree in language and customs than any of the Pennsylvania Dutch.

Almost as numerous as the Mennonites are the *Dunkers,* who claim about 200,000 members throughout the United States in sects called the *New Dunkers* (arch-conservatives), the *Old Order Dunkers,* and the *Progressive Dunkers.* First emigrating from Germany to America in 1719, they took their name from the German *Tunker,* meaning "dunker or dipper," which refers to their belief in triple immersion during baptism to symbolize death, burial, and resurrection. Their church is called the German Baptist Brethren.

The *Moravians* came from Germany to Georgia and the West Indies, where they were unsuccessful in converting slaves to their religion, before founding Bethlehem, Nazareth, and Lititz, Pennsylvania, beginning in 1740. They did manage to convert a good many local Indians. The Moravian Church, named for Moravia, at various times part of Bohemia and Czechoslovakia, is officially designated the Renewed Church of the Brethren, or Unitas Fratrum.

Least in numbers among the Pennsylvania Dutch are the *Schwenkfelders* of the Schwenkfelder Church, which has some 2,500 members in the Philadelphia area. The Schwenkfelders are followers of Kaspar von Schwenkfeld (1489–1561), a religious reformer, whose middle road between Catholicism and Lutheranism caused his sect to be persecuted by Germans of both religious persuasions. This small group fled to America in 1719.

These Pennsylvania Dutch groups occupy almost the entire southern half of the state of Pennsylvania, where they have established themselves as hardworking, expert, prosperous farmers. Soon after they had sunk roots here they were observed to be speaking a German dialect which, Mario Pei tells us, "with the exception of Alemannic peculiarities in the morphology and vocabulary, and numerous evidence of English influence in the syntax and vocabulary, resembles most closely the dialects spoken in the eastern half of the Rhenish or Lower Palatinate [a German region extending from the left bank of the Rhine bordering in the south on France and in the west on the Saar Territory]." From the beginning there were also references to the "dumb Dutch" and resistance in surprising and quite exalted places to their different ways and language. Even Ben Franklin objected to the "Palatine boors." Why, he wrote, should they be permitted "to swarm into our settlements and by herding together, establish their language and manners to the exclusion of ours? Why should Pennsylvania, founded by the English, become a colony of aliens, who will shortly be so numerous as to germanize us instead of our anglifying them?" (This, however, did not stop him from publishing in 1732 America's first foreign-language newspaper, the Philadelphia *Zeitung,* aimed at the city's German population!)

But more tolerant thinking prevailed, as it usually does in America, in part because the Pennsylvania Dutch never did become so "numerous" as to make Pennsylvania "a colony of aliens." The plain people mostly kept to themselves, wearing clothing based on early-seventeenth-century models, and opposing slavery, public education, the obligation of a citizen to bear arms for his country, and the taking of legal oaths. They lived like the Quakers, abiding by the Bible according to their lights, and like the Quakers they were tolerated and more often admired than scorned.

Clannish in their communal and personal affairs, the Pennsylvania Dutch groups persisted in speaking the *Deitsch* or *Deutsch* (German) of the Rhineland, this language sprinkled with Schweizerdeutsch, and English words and even borrowings from French, Scotch, and Irish. It is somewhat ironic that a Pennsylvania German's vote decided that the official language in Pennsylvania would be English, for the linguistically and socially insular churches of these groups were at first insistent that German be their language; their Bibles were in German, and church authorities decreed that German, and never English, always be used in church services. But this attitude changed with the passage of time. By 1850 some of the Pennsylvania Dutch groups claimed English as their first language and all of the plain people can speak it today. Nevertheless, recent studies show that 300,000 or more Americans "feel more comfortable speaking Pennsylvania Dutch than English" and a "considerably larger number use the language readily." There may be close to a million Pennsylvania Dutch speakers in America and the dialect has remained fairly faithful to its mother tongue over the centuries. It has been reported, for example, that a platoon of Pennsylvania Dutch on patrol in Germany during World War II "were not machine-gunned because the Nazis who heard them talking assumed they were Palatinate German."

Though they have migrated to Ohio and other parts of the country, taking their language and customs with them, most of the plain people still reside in southern Pennsylvania, mainly in the counties of Berks, Lancaster, Lebanon, Lehigh, Northampton, and York. Their Palatinate dialect mixed with High German and English does vary a bit from county to county, but the differences are few and almost all "Dutchmen" can understand each other. The dialect seems to be here to stay for a long time. Not only are the plain people still clannish (though the strict sects are taking more liberal attitudes, and younger people are more frequently leaving the fold), but the Pennsylvania Dutch are a very practical people who clearly see the economic benefits of their quaint ways. One observer is of the opinion that "they probably regard the dialect as being as obsolescent as the hex signs on their barns, but if there's one thing these people are notable for it's hard-headed pragmatism—chances are they'll go on speaking Pennsylvania Dutch as long as it attracts the free-spending 'outlanders.' "

The free-spending outlanders have made "Pennsylvania Dutch Country" a favorite American vacationland, and tourists flock there by the millions each year to see the quaintly dressed plain people clopping along the roads in their canopied, side-curtained rockaway wagons (named for Rockaway, New Jersey, their first place of manufacture) and to eat home-style "good and plenty" communal suppers at dozens of tourist restaurants in towns like Intercourse and Blue Balls (neither, incidentally, named by the plain people). The visitor hears virtually no Pennsylvania Dutch spoken in the usual tourist traps, but in out-of-the-way markets, in country stores, at auction sales, and at other places where Dutchmen gather, the good listener is rewarded, and often with humorous linguistic gems.

Pennsylvania Dutch is widely regarded as a humorous dialect because of the extraordinary lengths it goes to force English words into German word order or syntactical constructions. "A combination of broken-English, bad grammar, and grotesque construction accounts for most of the humor in their speech," says one local expert. The results are gaffes like "Come in and eat yourself" (an invitation to dinner) or "Throw the body out the window his blanket." Following is a sampler of humorous sayings heard in the area:

* "I can't go to the party because I have nothing to wear on me."
* "Miller will pay me two dollars a day if I eat myself—but chust one dollar if he eats me (if he provides meals)."
* "What does it give for dinner?" (What's for dinner?)
* "Sally, you chew your mouth empty before you say." (Finish eating before you speak.)
* "His eating went away." (He lost his appetite.)
* Sister calling her brother to dinner: "Amos, come from the woodpile in; Mom's on the table and Poppa's et himself done already."
* "Aunt Emma's shoo-fly pie sure eats wonderful good."
* "Lizzie, go in the house and smear Jakie all over with jam a piece of bread."
* "Eli stung his foot with a bee."
* "There's two roads to Hinkletown. They're both the same for far—but the south road is more the hill up."
* "Rachel is a big bobble-mouth; she don't think before she says."
* "Now don't horn the machine so much, Jake—you'll blow the baby awake."
* "The paper wants rain." (Predicts rain.)
* "It's making down hard." (Raining hard.)
* "It ain't right—he don't use his wife so good all the time." (He mistreats her.)
* "You look good in the face." (You look healthy and happy.)
* "Aunt Min is wonderful heavy—she sits broad."
* "Sara's tooth ouches her something wonderful."
* "Keep the paint off!" (Wet paint!)
* Mother to child at a swimming pool: "Don't dive there—come up here where the water is thicker."
* "Go out and tie the dog loose." (Untie him.)
* "Cousin Sarah ain't good—she's been with the doctor all winter." (She's very ill.)

The proverbs of the Pennsylvania Dutch people have been publicized so long and often in tourist publications that many have become nationally known, including:

* *Ve get too soon oldt—und too late schmart.*
* *Kissin' wears out—cookin' don't.*
* *Borrowing makes for sorrowing.*
* *Them what works hard eats hearty.*
* *Other people's bread tastes better.*
* *Half a loaf or half a ton / each is better by far than none.*
* *May your friends be many, your troubles few, and your sausages long.*
* *The hurrier I go, the behinder I get.*

Other sayings are notably sexist, such as:

* *He who has a secret dare not tell it to his wife.*
* *No woman can be happy with less than seven to cook for.*
* *A plump wife and a big barn / never did any man harm.*
* *Better it is single to live / than to the wife the britches give.*

Unique and colorful Pennsylvania Dutch idioms include *hands-in-the-pocket weather* for very cold weather; the *onion snow* for the last snow of the year; *sneaky weather* for snowy weather; *hoechnawsyich* or *high-nosed* for a conceited person; a *blutkup* for a bald-headed man; and a *finger hut* or *finger hat* for a thimble. *Full of misht* means full of manure, or worse, while *the skitters* is the runs, and *yarixed* means vomited; *himmerdale* means rear end, and a no-good is a *shite-poke*.

Store-boughten food isn't common in Amish homes. Special words for special dishes include *dippy* for gravy; *coffee soup* (bread with coffee poured over it); *butter bread* (bread and butter); and *fastnach,* a doughnut. In the middle of the morning, Dutch farmers are *hongerich* (hungry) and ready to eat a second breakfast, so the womenfolk bring a basketful of food, called the *ten o'clock piece,* to them in the fields.

Big bugs are aristocrats in Pennsylvania Dutch; *bodderation* is bother; *kerflommixed* is excited; *ferhext* is bewitched; *lippy* is smart-aleck talk; *booghered up* means mixed up; and to *rift* means to belch. April first in Dutch country is traditionally moving day, which is called *flittin' day.* At the time a big *friendschaft* (a lot of relatives) usually help and the *haus* is all *butzed up* (cleaned) and *redded up* (tidied) without any *grexin'* (complaining).

Conservative Amish won't have electricity on their farms because it's considered *worldly.* They worship at home instead of churches, unlike the *church Amish,* also called the *Black Bumpers* because they do own automobiles but paint the bumpers and all the chrome black as soon as they buy their cars.

Hugging and kissing in Pennsylvania German is *knoatching und schmutzing,* and when a young girl marries outside her religion she is said to have *gone gay.* Courting is called *settin' up,* falling in love is *falling in luff, diddling* is sexual intercourse, and *up a stump* means pregnant. A century ago, American poet Charles Leland wrote the following "Pennsylvania Dutch Love Story," skillfully blending the English and German words and forms of the curious dialect:

> *O vere mine lofe a sugar-powl,*
> *De fery shmallest loomp*
> *Vouldt shveet de seas, from pole to pole,*
> *Und make de children shoomp.*
> *Und if she vere a clofer-field,*
> *I'd bet my only pence,*
> *It vouldn't pe no dime at all*
> *Before I'd shoomp the fence.*
>
> *Her heafenly foice, it drill me so,*
> *If oft-dimes seems to hoort,*
> *She is de holiest animale*
> *Dat rooms oopon de dirt.*
> *De renpow rises vhen she sings,*
> *De sonnshine vhen she dalk;*
> *De angels crow und flop deir wings*
> *Vhen she goes out to valk.*
>
> *So livin white, so carnadine,*
> *Mine lofe's gomblexion show;*
> *It's shoost like Abendcarmosine,*
> *Rich gleamin on de shnow.*
> *Her soul makes plushes in her sheeck*
> *Ash sommer reds de wein,*
> *Or sonnlight sends a fire life troo*
> *An blank Karfunkelstein.*

De uberschwengliche idees
Dis lofe poot in my mind,
Vouldt make a foost-rate philosoph
Of any human kind.
'Tis schudderin schveet on eart to meet
An himmlisch-hoellisch Qual;
Und treat mitwhiles to Kummel Schnapps
De Schoenheitsideal.

Dein Fuss seind weiss wie Kreiden,
Dein Ermleon Helfenbein,
Dein ganzer Leib ist Seiden,
Dein Brust wie Marmelstein—
Ja—vot de older boet sang,
I sing of dee—dou Fine!
Dou'rt soul und pody, heart und life:
Glatt, zart, gelind, und rein.

Pennsylvania Dutch pronunciation often stays with a person despite one's education. In one story a boy returns home after graduation from college. "John, I'm so proud of you; you're a college graduate now, ain't?" his proud mother says. "Ya, Mom, I'm one of them," the boy replies. "Why, Mom, you know'd when I went away to college I couldn't say norse (north) or souse (south), and now I can say bose (both) of them."

The pronunciation of *v* like *w* has been called the Pennsylvania Dutch's shibboleth. (*Shibboleth*, for "password," derives from the Hebrew for "ear of corn," and the Gileadites used it to distinguish the sons of Ephraim from the members of other tribes, the Bible relating that they slew 42,000 Ephraimites who couldn't pronounce the *sh* in the password *shibboleth* and had to say it *sibboleth*.) The plain people, unless well educated, often pronounce *valley* as *walley*, and *volume* becomes *wollum*, etc. *W*, on the other hand, is generally pronounced *vf*, as in *UHvfAY* (away), and *vfll* (will). The dialect features an excessive elongation of heavily stressed vowels, but is affected more by consonant variants like *w* for *v* than it is by vowel changes. These consonant changes include, among others, the heavy pronunciation of *b* so that a weak *p* seems to be added to it, as in *gkri:bp* (crib); *f* with a *v* coloring as in *vfl:vf* (five); *g* with a weak *k* flavor to it, as in *hAWgk* (hog); r pronounced as the German guttural *r;* *th* pronounced as *d* or *dt,* as in *dtOH:s* (those); and *z* pronounced as *s.*

The following chart translating Pennsylvania Dutch pronunciations into standard American ones shows consonant changes in the dialect better than any technical explanations:

boghie—buggy	ice—eyes
bortsch—porch	Maple—Mable
britches—bridges	mate—made
bull—pull	ret—red
bush—push	rite—ride
cham—jam	sank you—thank you
chaw—jaw	sing—thing
Cherry—Jerry	sink—think
chob—job	some—thumb
choin—chain	sought—thought
choose—juice	vistle—whistle
Chorge—George	walley—valley
chudge—judge	wisit—visit
colt—cold	woted—voted
crotch—garage	zis—this

Scholars have pointed out likenesses between Pennsylvania German and both Yiddish and Plantation Creole. With Yiddish there is a similar German-English idiomatic pattern in answers such as "Why not?" in response to the question "Why did you do that?"; in identical words like *foggel,* "a light fog"; in the inverted word order of sentences ("Throw your father down the stairs his hat"); and in the use of *already* in the final position of sentences ("Let's go, already"). The similarities probably "reflect the importance of German in the formation of both Yiddish and Pennsylvania German," as Professor J. L. Dillard suggests in his *All-American English.*

As for the Plantation Creole connection, Professor Dillard points out that nineteenth-century writer John H. Beadle reported a "Hoosier dialect" which he believed was "the result of union between the rude translations of 'Pennsylvania Dutch,' the 'Negroisms' of Kentucky and Virginia, and certain phrases native to the Ohio Valley." According to Dillard, the forms cited in Beadle's *Western Wilds and the Men Who Redeem Them* (1878) "do look like Plantation Creole (and are thus 'Negroisms' in some sense)," but "it would take considerable research to determine whether his more general statement is true . . . [though] many such things were going on on the border."

As would be expected, older Pennsylvania Dutch speakers use a broader dialect speech than the younger generation, who have become more assimilated or at least acclimated. But the lilt and stress of the dialect, with its unique German inflections, has even "infiltrated into the talk of non–Pennsylvania Dutch speakers," being called the "Berks County Accent" by Pennsylvanians.

In addition to the lilting "Berks County Accent," Pennsylvania Dutch has made a small, picturesque contribution to the American language. From the dialect came the word *sauerkraut,* the German for "sour cabbage." The term was first recorded in 1776; later, in 1869, General Joseph Heister ran for governor of Pennsylvania and was dubbed "Old Sauerkraut" because he was of German extraction, his sobriquet perhaps contributing to the use of *kraut* for a German in years to come. Other Pennsylvania Dutch contributions to the American dinner table were *pretzel* and *noodle* (from the German *nudal*), which came into the language early in the nineteenth century. *Mashed potatoes,* too, was introduced as a Pennsylvania Dutch dish in the eighteenth century and was, in fact, called *Dutch* or *German potatoes* before being dubbed *mashed potatoes.*

Philadelphia scrapple, an American breakfast dish for almost two centuries now, is an invention of the plain people. *Scrapple,* literally meaning "little scraps," is made of scraps from hog butchering, cornmeal, onions, and spices chilled into a loaf and then fried in slices. *Snit* (a slice of dried apple) is also a Pennsylvania Dutch word. So may be the soul-food dish *chitterlins'. Chitterlins'* possibly derives from the German *Kutteln* (entrails, tripe), a deep-fried dish the plain people make from batter-dipped small intestines. The word may not be a black or Southern one at all.

When you *dunk* your doughnuts you are using a Pennsylvania Dutch word, just as you are when you put a *hex* on someone or buy a good-luck *hex sign* or *hex mark* that the plain people put on their barns. The important *Conestoga wagon,* which helped settle the West, and the *flatboat* were introduced by the Pennsylvania Dutch. So was the *German fireplace* or *stove,* a five-sided stove placed in a fireplace and using its chimney as a smoke pipe. It takes its name from the tradition the plain people had of decorating such stoves with pictures of Biblical scenes described in German, the *German stove* named for the German words on it, not after the people of German descent who invented it. It was introduced in the early eighteenth century, and its design was widely copied.

The plain people were also the first to grow *zinnias* and *fuchsias* in Pennsylvania, introducing these beautiful flowers and the words for them to American gardens, both flowers having been named for German botanists. The flowers, however, were native to the New World.

Mario Pei has observed that "there is no perceptible influence from German in the speech sounds of American English, save insofar as German has given rise to a new mixed language like Pennsylvania Dutch." A number of Pennsylvania German words have limited use in English today. *Toot* or *tut* for a paper bag is sometimes heard, as are *spritzen* (to sprinkle), *Belsnickel* (for Santa Claus), *wunnerfitisch* (inquisitive), and *strubbly* (disheveled). Typical Pennsylvania Dutch usages have also spread to a limited extent, especially (because *lasen* is both *leave* and *let* in German) the use of *leave* for *let* ("Leave her have it"), *that* for *so that* ("Heat the water that it boils"), and *all* for *all gone* ("The cheese is all") or *dead* ("Papa is all," which phrase, incidentally, was the title of a popular Broadway comedy).

Other common Pennsylvania Dutch peculiarities include using the word *make* for *go* ("Make down the road") or *close* ("Make the window shut"); *ain't* for *won't* ("Ain't she will?"—that is, "Won't she?"); and *It wonders me* for *I wonder* ("It wonders me where he went").

Ain't is used in several ways by the plain people—often as an oral question mark like the German *nicht wahr* or the French *n'est-ce pas*. Frequently heard are constructions such as *Nice day, ain't?* ("It's a nice day, isn't it?"), *Nice evening tonight, ain't it is?* ("It's a nice evening, isn't it?"), and *You're coming, ain't?* ("You're coming, aren't you?").

Listen closely when among the Pennsylvania Dutch and you'll certainly hear some of these typical expressions:

★ *Outen the light.* (Put it out.)
★ *My off is on.* (I've begun my vacation.)

★ *Make the fire finish.* (Extinguish it.)
★ *It will make down soon.* (It will rain.)
★ *I want out.* (I want to go out.)
★ *He made out to come.* (He planned to come.)
★ *Come here, oncet!* (Come here!)
★ *Does he sing yet?* (Does he still sing?)
★ *Nice crop of wheat, say not?* (It's a nice crop of wheat, isn't it?)
★ *I mind of the time.* (I remember the time.)
★ *It's going to give a storm.* (There's going to be a storm.)
★ *She doesn't want for to go.* (She doesn't want to go.)
★ *I don't want for to see him.* (I don't want to see him.)
★ *He doesn't know what for.* (He doesn't know what it's all about.)
★ *What's the matter of you?* (What's the matter with you?)
★ *Ain't you ready maybe, yet?* (Aren't you ready?)

Few people are aware that the Pennsylvania Dutch dialect is composed of rural pioneer pronunciation and vocabulary as well as German words and pronunciation. Backwoods loan words and pronunciations are still found in the speech of the plain people, including *plumb* (very), *buss* (kiss), *flitch* (bacon), *younguns, mebbe, nuther, hitch* (marry), *sech* (such), *a coon's age* (a long time), *kever* (cover), *Old Harry* (the Devil), *datter* (daughter), *dander* (temper), *yonder, tother* (the other), *elbow grease,* and *purty.* German words that hang on include *schnell* (quickly), *dumkopf* (fool), *sitz* (seat), *fress* (eat), *spossich* (funny), *genoonk* (enough), *greisslech* (sick), *dutchie* (tramp), and *lobbisch* (silly). (See also the long list at the end of this chapter.)

Finally, it should be noted that Pennsylvania Dutch has strongly influenced what is called the Pennsylvania accent spoken by almost all Pennsylvanians except those living in Erie, Warren, McKean, Potter, Tioga, Bradford, Pike, and Susquehanna counties—these people speaking a dialect modified by the speech of upstate New York. The Pennsylvania accent is sometimes called the Philadelphia accent, but "Philadelphian" (see also Chapter 10) features the Eastern habit of dropping the consonant *r* in words, while most Pennsylvanians pronounce it, though not as strongly as Midwesterners. Among other vocabulary differences, Philadelphians more frequently use *square* instead of *block* ("It's two squares away") and *anymore* to indicate a positive continuing action or emotion ("She loves it anymore") than most Pennsylvanians. Pennsylvania Dutch accounts for the elongation of the so-called long vowels in the Pennsylvania dialect and for the rising or falling intonation these vowels receive when stressed; for example, *say* is pronounced *sAY* or *sAH*, and *mile* is pronounced *mAH:l*. Philadelphia speakers, like New Yorkers and unlike most Americans, do not distinguish in pronunciation between *for* and *four, morning* and *mourning,* and *hoarse* and *horse.*

A Glossary of German-Based Terms Common in Pennsylvania Dutch

abedit—appetite
aesal—jackass
airlich—honest
alend—trouble, bother
alter—old man
amer—bucket
amohl—once
bauch—belly
beddlar—beggar
bendle—string
biscotza—skunk
blabbermaul—talkative
blaid—bashful
bleib—stay
blut-kup—bald head
bobbagoy—parrot
bobbeer—newspaper
bobbelmaul—gabbler
bodderation—bother, trouble
bree—gravy, juice
brill—glasses
bubbely—baby
butz—clean off
corrisser—to court
crittlich—crabby
croosht—crust
crotz—scratch, rub
divel's dreck—devil's manure

dobbich—awkward
donkbawr—thankful
dormlich—giddy
dummkup—dumb
dunk—dip
fahoongart—starved
farrichterlich—frightful, fearful
fartzoon'd—cross
fedder—pen
feeish—beastly
feraikled—disgusted
ferdail—divide
ferdarva—spoiled
ferfowl'd—rotten
fergesslich—forgetful
ferhext—bewitched
ferhoodled—tangled, mixed up
ferlooched—cursed
ferricked—deranged
fershitt—spilled
fershmeerd—bespatted
fershteckle—hide
fershticked—smothered
fersooch—taste
freindlich—friendly, affectionate

fress—eat
gabootzt—cleaned
gabut—exhausted
gadonka—loud cry
ganoonk—enough
garooch—odor
geitsich—stingy
gichtra—convulsions
gleedich-hase—red hot
glutzkupp—dumbhead
gounsh—swing, a swing
gowtz—bark
greisles—sickens
greislich—horrible
grex—grunt
g'shnorrix'd—snored
hase-wasser—hot water
hausich—row
hechsed—hexed
hesslich—hateful
hinnerdale—hinder part
hinnersfeddersht—ass
  backwards
hinnersich—backward
honswarsht—clown
hoongerich—hungry
hootchelly—colt
ivvernooma—overtaken
jonijumbubs—pansies
kedreck—cow dung
kenn—knowledge
k'noatsha—hugging
koos—kiss
kreftich—vigorous
kreisch—cry
kintish—childish
kretz—itch
kronk—sick
krottle—crawl
krotz—scratch

lavendich—alive
lecherich—laughable
leddich—unmarried
ligner—liar
lobbich—silly
looshtich—jolly
luftich—airy
marickaerdich—remarkable
nixnootzich—good-for-
  nothing
nochcoomer—offspring
nodeerlich—natural
nookich—naked
obbadit—appetite
obgawaned—weaned
ousgabootz'd—cleaned out
plesseer—pleasure
plesseerlich—delightful
roontzel—crease
rootsh—crawl, squirm
roppled—rattled
ruich—quiet
schlafferich—sleepy
schlaig—whipping
du schlecht'r—you dirty
  so-and-so
schmear—fat, grease
schmecklich—tasty, wet, and
  luscious
schmootzich—greasy-looking
schnoop-dooch—handkerchief
schooslich—one who pokes
  along
schrooching—twisting or
  squirming
schtaerkeppich—stubborn
sei-ish—hoggish
shaidlich—harmful
shendlich—disgraceful
shlipperich—slippery

shlook'd—swallowed
shloomers—nap
shlooxa—hiccups
shlovverich—slobbery
shmartzlich—painful
shnorrix's—snores
shnovvel—beak, nose
shpawrsom—frugal
shputta—sneer
shrecklich—frightful
shteddle—town
shtroovelich—uncombed
shtuvverich—stubborn
sitz—seat
sopperlut—zounds!
spossich—funny
stroobly—tousled
tzooker—candy
ufreerish—worked-up, stubborn
ufroorish—big commotion, riot
unfershtendich—absurd
unglicklich—unlucky
unnersheed—difference
vendue—public sale, auction
weesht—nasty
weetich—enraged
windla—diapers
wonnernaus—an inquisitive person
wutz—pig

8 Da Kine Talk

✦

The Hawaiian Creole dialect called *da kine* or *da Hawaii kine talk* and spoken through the *Poi Belt* has its basis in Pidgin English or Beach-la-Mar. Pidgin English is a *lingua franca,* a hybrid language that is a combination of various tongues. The earliest pidgin recorded is *lingua franca* itself, these words Italian for "the Frankish tongue." Lingua franca arose along the Mediterranean, a medley or babble of Italian, French, Spanish, Greek, Turkish, and Arabic common to many seamen in the ninth century or earlier. A Frank was any West European at the time, for the tribe ruled over most of Europe. The trade language enabled Muslims to conduct business dealings with Europeans, and Mediterranean traders still find it useful in the Levant. *Pidgin English,* originally developed by British traders in China, takes its name from the way the Chinese pronounced "business"—*bijin.* It combines English and Portuguese, as well as German, Bengali, French, and Malayan. There is even a magazine, *Frend Belong Me (My Friend),* published in pidgin by the Catholic Mission in New Guinea. One estimate has 30 to 50 million people speaking some variety of pidgin and it ranks at least twentieth among the world's most common tongues. Pidgin usually contains some 300–400 nouns, 40–50 verbs, possibly 100 modifiers and a few dozen native terms. In it, whiskers are *grass belong face,* a pocket is *basket belong pants,* and the sun is *lamp belong Jesus.* Lascar seamen employed as stokers on nineteenth-century British steamers used the apt pidgin expression *shit belong-um fire* for ashes. Here is an example of pidgin taken from a handbook issued to American Pacific area troops during World War II:

Guard: "You fella you stand fast. You no can walkabout. Suppose you fella walkabout me kill im.

Translation: Halt or I'll shoot!

The Twenty-third Psalm in pidgin would go something like this:

Big Name watchem sheepy-sheep. Watchum fella. No more belly cry fella hab. Big Name makum camp alonga grass. Takum fella walkabout longa, no fightem no more hurry wata. Big Boss longa sky makum inside glad; takim walkabout longa, too much goodfella . . .

Among the various Chinese pidgins was *chowchow pidgin,* with cooking and eating terms; *joss pidgin,* the language of religion; *sword pidgin,* used in fencing; and even *love pidgin,* with its phrases of love and courtship. One early Chinese pidgin booklet was entitled *A Vocabulary of Words in Use Among The Red-Haired People* (Caucasians).

Chinese pidgin came to Hawaii with Chinese immigrants hired to work in the Islands. *Beach-la-mar,* or *Bêche-de-mer,* is pidgin or lingua franca known only in the Pacific, a conglomeration of English and native dialects. (The *bêche-de-mer* was a staple of trade, the natives prizing it for food, and the language takes its name from the sea slug or sea cucumber.) *Beach-la-mar,* which even then contained a number of Americanisms, such as *boss* and *schooner,* was used in Hawaii for many years, at least since 1818. Richard Henry Dana called it "the Sandwich Island language" in *Two Years Before the Mast* and quoted several examples ("By-'em-by money *pau-*gone; then Kanaka work plenty"). Among the pidgin expressions still heard in the Islands is the humorous *to kill one's neck* for *to break one's neck* ("He fall into the hole and kill his neck"), and *brokum-up* for *demolish.* But pidgin began to be creolized in Hawaii at about the time English was first taught in the Hawaiian schools in 1853, developing into the *da kine* dialect used by the contract laborers from many countries who came to work the Hawaiian cane and pineapple fields.

The term *da kine* used in *da kine talk* is a shibboleth, a popular phrase distinctive of Hawaiian talk that is employed many ways and which can mean "this kind of." Because the words *da kine*—believed to have their origins in Japanese—are used so often, they have become the name of Hawaiian talk in general. One hears them in such varied expressions as "Take da kine (broom) and sweep the floor." "Where da kine (it) going to be?", and "He da kine (crazy) about her."

Da kine speakers, according to authority Elizabeth Ball Carr, "have a habit of prolonging stressed vowels and of clipping unstressed vowels and all consonants. Sometimes it is difficult for an ear trained to Mainland American speech to catch words because of the comparative rapidity of utterance. There is little drawling, even where there is hesitation; the speed and pitch of utterance remind us more of the British norm than the American."

Several Hawaiians I talked to during a recent visit to the Islands denied that such a dialect existed, apparently ashamed of it for some reason, but there is no doubt that da kine is alive and thriving. Da kine draws its vocabulary and some of its pronunciations from the many languages of the laborers who came to work in Hawaii, these including Chinese, Korean, Japanese, Samoan, Filipino languages, Portuguese, and Spanish—all of them and more mixing with Hawaiian and the English of whites and blacks.

Bagoong, a popular shrimp sauce, is one of the many cooking-term loan words da kine borrowed from Tagalog, which, along with Visayan and Ilocano, was one of the languages Filipino laborers brought to Hawaii when they came to work on the sugar plantations. An open-necked men's shirt made of pineapple fiber is called the *barong tagalong.* Hawaiian Filipinos are humorously nicknamed *bayaws,* from the Ilocano and Tagalog *bayaw* for brother-in-law, and the da kine term *bayaw style* refers to the supposed Filipino habit of segregating men and women at social gatherings —the men sitting on one side of the room and the women on the other. Most Hawaiians are familiar with the Filipino's enthusiastic shout of joy and approval: *Mabuhay!*

Portuguese first influenced Hawaiian English through bits of pidgin with a Portuguese base that came to the Islands via explorers and traders only a decade or so after Captain Cook and his men touched land on Kauai in 1778. The first such word recorded was *piquinini,* meaning "a small thing," which comes from the Portuguese *pequenino,* "small child." In 1820 Lucia Holman, a Christian missionary's wife, recorded in her diary that three huge, rotund Hawaiian women cast a critical eye upon the slender missionary wives who had just landed in Hawaii and laughingly called them *piccaninny,* which other Hawaiians translated for Mrs. Holman as "too little." The ample Hawaiian ladies went on to advise Mrs. Holman to "eat and grow big."

When Portuguese workers came in great numbers to Hawaii during the late 1870s, more loan words were introduced. Over the years many gastronomic terms have entered Hawaiian English from Portuguese, including the popular *pão doce* (sweet bread). Portuguese themselves were dubbed *baccaliaos* because of the many codfish (Portuguese *bacalhau*) they consumed. It has been suggested that the "Portuguese lilt" from Madeira and the Azores is the source of some Hawaiian intonation patterns. Portuguese also contributed terms like *stay* (from *estar*) for *is,* as when Hawaiians speaking da kine say, "Where you stay go?" (Where are you going?). *Bobora head* is a da kine blendword for a Japanese citizen, not a Japanese-American, that is used jokingly by Americans of Japanese ancestry and derives from the Portuguese *abóbora* (gourd) and the English *head,* having the literal meaning "pumpkin head." (Americans of Japanese ancestry from the mainland sometimes call Japanese-Americans born in Hawaii *Buddaheads.*)

The use of *already* for *yet* in da kine expressions such as "I called you up but you weren't there already" probably stems from a similar Portuguese practice, as does the use of *for* instead of *to* ("We don't know what for do"), that of *for why* instead of *why* ("For why you tell lies?"), and that of *what* instead of *that* ("Eat all what you can"). The use of *sabe* in place of *understand* by Hawaiians is said to derive from the Chinese pidgin *savvy,* which came from the Portuguese *sabe* (he knows).

The Japanese language has influenced spoken Hawaiian English both semantically and phonologically. Japanese immigrants gave da kine words like *jabon* (the shaddock) and *hikka* (a stew). It was in Hawaii that the Japanese *hibachi,* primarily a hand warmer in Japan, became exclusively a brazier for cooking. The Japanese word for tidal wave, *tsunami,* entered English in Hawaii, as did a number of other terms. All in all, close to a hundred Japanese words and phrases (which are much easier to pronounce and remember than Chinese) are heard in the everyday speech of Hawaii, and even in the English phrases of Hawaiian speakers one can hear the typical syllable-timed rhythm of Japanese.

An interesting Japanese expression is the word *kibei* for "a Japanese person returning to the United States (Hawaii) from

Japan." This is formed from the morpheme *bei,* the abbreviation of *beikoku,* "the United States of America," and the morpheme *ki,* "the act of returning."

Japanese words blended with those of English and other languages also form part of the da kine vocabulary. These include the *bon dance,* not a barn dance but a popular folk dance; *a chawan cut,* a haircut that looks as if it had been done with a bowl (Japanese *chawan*) placed on the head; *mama-san,* a respectful form of address to an elderly woman (*san* is a well-known Japanese honorific); and *tamago head* for an egg (Japanese *tamgo*) head or stupid person, this term having no connotation of "intellectual" as does its American counterpart.

When Hawaiian da kine speakers say, "My name begins with the alphabet B" (instead of "the letter B"), they are following a Japanese practice, the Japanese word for *letter* being the same as that for *alphabet.* The typical Hawaiian use of *attend to* instead of *attend* ("I attend to Honolulu High School") also has Japanese roots, as does the use of *eyeglass,* in the singular, for *eyeglasses, glass cup* for *glass,* and *throw out* for *throw up* ("The baby throw out his milk").

John Reinecke, a linguist who pioneered in the study of Hawaiian dialect, tells the story of the Japanese evangelist in Honolulu who never mastered the Japanese trouble with *l* and sang "Jesus Rub Me" to his audiences. But then just as Asiatic immigrants to Hawaii had their troubles with English, Americans and Britishers had their own troubles with the languages of the South Seas. Few people know, for example, that *Pango Pango* should really be the name of the Pacific island of Pago Pago, the chief harbor of American Samoa. *Pango Pango,* in fact, is the way the locals still pronounce the name. An old story, which may be true, explains that the island is called Pago Pago because missionaries transliterating the local speech into the Latin alphabet found that there were many sounds that had to be "represented by *n* in combination with a following consonant." So many, in fact, that there weren't enough *n*'s in their type fonts to enable them to set all such words in type. So they quite arbitrarily eliminated the *n* from some words, leaving us with Pago Pago instead of *Pango Pango* (the proper pronunciation).

Chinese contributed few loan words to Hawaiian English because its phonetics differ too radically from those of the other languages, words in Chinese often altering in meaning when a vowel is pitched differently. The Chinese pidgin *chowchow* (for food or to eat) did become the still widely used da kine word *kaukau,* which many people mistakenly believe is a pure Hawaiian term because *chowchow* became Hawaiianized as early as 1791. Chinese restaurants are responsible for popularizing the Hawaiian word *pupu,* which means hors d'oeuvre or appetizer and was formerly fish, chicken, or banana served with kava. This is familiar throughout the United States in the form of *pupu platter,* a Chinese restaurant hot plate of various appetizers, though no major dictionary records the term.

A *pake mu'u,* pidgin Chinese plus Hawaiian, is a Chinese-style Hawaiian *mu'u* (pronounced *mu*) dress, *pake* being pidgin for "Chinese"; while a *driving hui* is a car pool that takes children to school, the Chinese *hui* meaning "club." Chinese is also responsible for a good number of da kine expressions. When Hawaiians say *half* for *and a half* ("We stay here eight years half, no?") they are imitating a Chinese usage, as they are when they *burn* firecrackers instead of shooting or setting them off. The employment of *borrow* instead of *use* in such expressions as "May I borrow your telephone?" corresponds to a similar practice in Chinese. *Bumbye* or *bymby* for *in a while* ("Bumbye we go beach") means "later" in Chinese pidgin. Chinese pidgin also contributed the use of:

★ *Catch* for *get* (as in "Us go beach—catch da tan"), *catch* here deriving from the Chinese pidgin *catchee.*
★ *Look-see* for *look* ("I take one look-see").
★ *More better* for *better,* as in "Leela bitch drunko, kaukau first, moah betta" ("It's better to have a little bit to drink and some food first").
★ *No can* for *can't* ("He no can open the door").
★ *Number one* for *the best* ("Him number one").
★ *One* for *a* or for *each* ("I drink jus' like one horse"), due probably to the absence of an indefinite article in Chinese.
★ *Plenty* for *many* ("I got plenny place stay," meaning "I have many places to live").

Spanish contributions to da kine began back in the early 1830s when cowboys of Spanish origin were recruited from California to deal with wild cattle that were destroying the country around Waimea. These cattle, descendants of a bull and several cows that explorer Captain George Vancouver had left in 1783 and which had been protected previously under a strict taboo by Kamehameha I, were eventually controlled by the vaqueros, who were called *paniola* by the Hawaiians from the word *espagnol* (Spanish); the Hawaiian word for cowboy is still *paniolo* today. Other Spanish words came to Hawaii with the Filipinos and the Puerto Ricans, who immigrated there later in the century. The term *calabash cousins* is a familiar da kine blend from Spanish and English, meaning two close friends, so close they drink from the same calabash. A *ratoon crop* is a second crop of shoots growing from a ratoon mother plant and is used metaphorically to mean a child born late in the life of its parents. Among the da kine expressions that have their origins in Spanish is *close the light* instead of turn out the light and, conversely, *open the light* used in place of turn on the light. Hawaiians call a pineapple a *pine* because the first name for the fruit in the islands was the Spanish *piña*, which was anglicized to *pine*.

The last of the large immigrant groups contributing to da kine talk is the Koreans, who arrived in the Islands at the turn of the century, though not in such great numbers as the Chinese and Japanese. Korean names for various foods, such as *kimchee*, are well known in Hawaii, as are respectful loan words such as *abuje* for father. The haunting folk song "Arirang," which takes its title from a hill path in Seoul and describes the sadness of two parting lovers, is often played and is the name of a famous Korean restaurant in Honolulu. The use of *get down* instead of *get out* ("We all get down from the car and walk") is one of a number of da kine talk expressions with its roots in Korean.

Various other languages, including German, Russian, Samoan, and similar Pacific Island languages have also made contributions to da kine talk, minor though they may be. *Lavalava*, for a rectangular cloth worn by men or women, is an interesting Samoan loan word that is recorded in *Webster's*.

Hawaiian, fast disappearing as a language, has of course contributed the most words and expressions to da kine talk, aside from English. Hawaiian, with a vocabulary of only 20,000 words, didn't become a written language until missionaries developed a written form of it in 1822. "Poor in sounds," it has but seven consonants (*h, k, l, m, n, p,* and *w*), and these can't be used without a following vowel, so that Merry Christmas, for example, comes out "Mele Kalilimaka." Hawaiian has the distinction of having the word with the most consecutive vowels in any language—*hooiaioia* (certified), with eight in a row. In this language, related to Tahitian, Samoan, and Maori, words can mean different things depending on the speaker's inflection—*kaus,* for example, can mean "rain," "two people," "a class of slave people in old Hawaii," "a war," or "a battle."

Some scholars fear Hawaiian may gradually become as dead as Latin, a language that only specialists can read or speak. There are only 1,000–2,000 native speakers of Hawaiian in the Islands, out of the 130,000 or so people who identify themselves as Hawaiians, and some 300 of these live on the private island of Niihau, where Hawaiian is spoken exclusively. Though the next generation must keep up the language, a recent study shows that enrollment in high school and college Hawaiian courses has dropped more than 40 percent since the 1978 school year. On the other hand, a few experts feel that the language is going through a consolidation rather than a decline, that new words such as *bicycle* and *747* are coming into it and it is being brought into the twentieth century.

Though its twenty letters combine into only forty possible syllables, Hawaiian has contributed numerous words and expressions to da kine, and many of these have become standard English words as well. *Aloha,* meaning either "hello" or "goodbye," is probably the best-known of these. *Aloha* literally means "love" in Hawaii and can mean "I love you" if *mi loa* is added to it—*Mi loa aloha.* It has been called "the world's loveliest greeting or farewell." Hawaii is of course the *Aloha State,* its anthem "Aloha 'Oe" (Farewell to Thee) written by Queen Liliuokalani.

Muumuu, for a long, loose dress, is another Hawaiian word that had been adopted into English. The style of dress, fashionable from time to time in America, was modeled on the Mother Hubbard missionaries introduced to cover up "immodest" Hawaiian maidens.

The *ukelele* may take its name from the Hawaiian word for flea, in reference to the way a player's fingers "jumped like fleas" over the instrument's strings. On the other hand, "Ukelele" or "Flea" was the nickname of Edward Purvis, a short, frail British Army officer attached to King Kalakaua's court who loved to play the Portuguese instrument and helped popularize it in Hawaii. The ukelele may have been named for him.

Americans are quite familiar with the hula-hula, too, though the Hawaiian name for this pantomine story-dance is simply *hula,* the dance noted for its highly stylized hand imagery, which uses many of the 700,000 "distinctive movements of the hands, arms, fingers, and face" we've mentioned "by which information can be transferred without speech."

Hawaiian is also responsible for the world's "littlest fish with the longest name": the *humuhumunukunukuapuaa,* though the tiny reef fish is also more appropriately called the *O.* By popular vote this little creature became Hawaii's state fish in 1984. The fish won fame in the 1930s song "My Little Grass Shack in Kealakekua," which has a verse that mentions it.

Pau, for "pow, finished, exhausted," has wide currency in English, at least in Hawaii, as do the directional terms *makai* (toward the sea), and *mauka* (toward the mountains), invaluable directions in the Islands, where everything is either more toward the mountains or toward the sea. Hawaiian weather forecasts commonly make predictions like "Mostly sunny, with a few mauka showers in the afternoon." Incidentally, Hawaiian has no word for "weather" in general.

In all, more than 250 Hawaiian words are commonly heard in Hawaii's English. A listing of some of these not included here follows this chapter, along with more interesting blends of Hawaiian and English, of which there are hundreds. One Hawaiian word that would have to lead off any complete dictionary is *'a'a,* which is now Hawaiian English, meaning a kind of rough lava. *Luna* for a foreman is very well known, too, as is *wikiwiki* (hurry up). Humorous blends of Hawaiian and English include *aku head pupule* ("crazy fishhead"), which was long the nickname of a popular Honolulu radio announcer; *business wahine* for a prostitute; and *wikiwiki burger,* a fast-food hamburger. *Hapa haole* means a person who is half-white, *hapa* here the English word *half* assimilated phonologically into Hawaiian with the *f* replaced by *p* and the final vowel added. *Wowie Maui* or *Maui Wowie* means a variety of Hawaiian marijuana grown on the island of Maui, much higher priced because it's said to contain a higher percentage of the substance in marijuana that gives the high.

No huhu! is a popular da kine expression meaning "Don't get angry," so popular that it became the basis for a hit song ten years or so ago. *No pau yet!* means "I'm not finished!"; *No pilika* means

"It's no trouble"; and *pio the light* is da kine for "Turn out the light." *Cool head main thing* means "Don't panic"; *Geev um* is "Give 'em hell" (the cry often heard at sporting events); *That's O.K.* is short for "Thank you"; and *Wassa madda you?* or *Assa madda you?* means "What's the matter with you?" *Ain't no big thing* ("It's not important") derives from a song popularized by Hawaiian singer Don Ho, and *Go for broke* ("Make your greatest effort"), now widely used in the United States, is a Hawaiian expression that began life as the World War II slogan of the 442nd Regimental Combat Team. Besides the typical examples already mentioned, da kine speakers will often say, among scores of distinctive expressions:

★ *Across* instead of *across from* ("I sat across you at school").
★ *Anybody* for *everybody* ("Anybody go to beach today").
★ *Bedclothes* instead of *pajamas.*
★ *Broke* for *tore* ("My shirt broke on the nail").
★ *Bla* for *brother* (a term of address, like *bro* in Black English, used by Island-born men).
★ *Corns* for *corn on the cob.*
★ *Cousin* as a common term of address for anyone.
★ *Fire* for *burn* ("Volcano fire us").
★ *Hot tea* for what most Americans call *tea* (though this term is used in South Carolina, too).
★ *Much* for *many* ("I didn't get much days off").
★ *Package* for *bag* ("Put the groceries in one brown paper package").
★ *Pull down* for *lose weight* ("Didn't you pull down since last year?").
★ *Small-little* for *small* ("When I was small-little I lived here").
★ *Make soft* for *be careful* ("Make soft with the eggs in that package").
★ *Mails* for *letters* ("Did I get a mail today?").
★ *Slangs* for *slang words* ("We don't like to use slangs").

The "more-or-less English" that provides the framework for da kine talk is said by Mencken to resemble "vulgar American in its disregard of grammatical niceties," but he points out that its vocabulary differs from that of the mainland. Common words that have changed in meaning include *meat,* which signifies only beef in Hawaii, *bogus,* which means boastful, and *lab* which has come (by a confusion of *laboratory* and *lavatory*) to mean bathroom.

Da kine is said to be "coming closer and closer to everyday vulgar American," but this dialect of American English still holds its own, being spoken to some degree by anywhere from two thirds to almost all the people who have lived in Hawaii for any length of time, according to various estimates. There is no sure indication that it has declined in use since Hawaii became our fiftieth state ("The Overseas State") in 1959. It seems likely that Hawaii's polyglot population (only 2 percent are pure Hawaiian) will go on speaking it and conducting business in it for years to come.

A Hawaiian Glossary

These Hawaiian and Hawaiian-English words and expressions, not including those mentioned previously, are commonly used in the da kine dialect. Hundreds more can be found in Elizabeth Ball Carr's scholarly and comprehensive *Da Kine Talk* (University of Hawaii, 1972).

'ae—yes
ahana!—shame on you!
akamai—smart
aloha—hello, goodbye, love
aloha shirt—the typical
  short-sleeved,
  bright-colored print shirt of
  Hawaii
'a 'ole—no
auwē!—oh!
'ele 'ele—black
hana—work
hanahana man—plantation
  laborer
he aha?—what?
hilahila—shy
ho'olu' olu—please

hoomalimali—baloney, bull
huhu—angry
huli stomach—upset stomach
  (stemming from the belief
  that babies suffering from
  colic "had their stomachs
  turned upside down by a
  jealous, evil-eyed person")
I make die-dead—an
  expression used by children
  in games like cops and
  robbers, when one "shoots"
  another
ipo—lover
kala mai ia'u—excuse me
kamaiina—old-timer
kanaka—human being

kane—man
kapa—cloth made from bark
kapu—taboo, forbidden
kea—white
koa—brave, warrior
kōku—help
kola—money
lani—sky, Heaven
lei—flower wreath
lōlō—stupid
luau—feast
mahalo—thank you
mai ka'i no—good, fine
malahini—tourist, greenhorn
malo—loincloth
manine-looking—starved, thin,
    like the common marine
    reef fish
manu—bird
manuahi man—an "extra"
    man, hence a lover of a
    married woman
menehune—legendary good
    elves of Hawaii who work at
    night
moemoe—sleep (a
    reduplication of moe, sleep)
mokeu—ship
moku—island
nani—beautiful
nēnē—the Hawaiian goose,
    the official state bird
niu—coconut

nui—large
number one luna—the head
    boss on a plantation
one-finger poi—poi (q.v.)
    thick enough to be scooped
    up with one finger, as
    opposed to thinner,
    two-finger poi
ono—delicious
ono-looking—good-looking
pa'ani—play
pali—cliff
pa'u—sarong
pau—finished, over
pehea 'oe?—How are you?
pilau—rotten
pilikia—trouble
poho—out of luck
poi—native dish made of taro
    root (see one-finger poi)
poi dog—typical Hawaiian
    dog, formerly fed on poi
    and used to hunt wild pigs
pōpoki—cat
pua—flower
pua'a—pig
'uku bla—ugly boy (literally
    "flea brother," from
    Hawaiian uku, flea, and
    pidgin English bla, brother)
'ulu—breadfruit
wahine—woman

9 Harpin' in Boont

✦

Boontling is dying, almost dead. This remarkable lingo of Boonville, California—its name a telescoping of "Boonville lingo"—is spoken fluently today by only a small handful of the town's older residents and several enthusiasts enchanted by its history.

At one time almost all the residents of the coastal town of Boonville understood Boontling, and perhaps a thousand people spoke this enlarged family language or lingo fluently. Boontling might strictly be called an "American English jargon," as its best scholar, Charles C. Adams, has termed it, but it is more often dubbed a *lingo* (Adams even entitled his book *Boontling, an American Lingo*), lingoes being languages similar to family languages with private expressions, nicknames, words used by children, and the like. In any case, its unique lexicon qualifies it as a dialect under our loose definition of the term.

Boontling was born about a century ago in the beautiful backwoods country around Boonville, whose steep hills and lush fields, were first settled in 1850. It thrived in the isolation of the valley, some one hundred miles north of San Francisco, enjoying its heyday from around 1890 to 1930. One story has the lingo originating in 1892 at the Anytime Saloon, where the four Burger and Duff brothers concocted a vocabulary composed of old Scotch dialect words (the area was settled by Scotch-Irish pioneers) and freshly minted expressions into a code that children, womenfolk, and their rivals could not understand. More likely, according to one old-timer, or *codgy,* the lingo began in the hop fields of Bell Valley, "where children worked alongside their parents, and adult harvesters invented a jargon as a medium for private group gossip deemed unfit for young ears."

In any case, the rural dialect or argot was nurtured by Boonville's relative isolation and self-sufficiency up until the 1930s. *Boonters* liked to *shark* (fool) the *brightlighters* (city dwellers) and each other by coining new words. One favorite amusement was to hang around the stagecoach depot and talk about strangers in Boontling. Boontling seems to be the one bona-fide American dialect we know of that originated as a kind of word game, the only other notable example, Pig Latin (or Igpay Atinlay), which gives us the English word *amscray* (scram), having originated in seventeenth-century England.

This is not to say that secret languages or dialects are rare phenomena. Secret languages range from Cockney rhyming slang ("trouble and strife" means "wife"; "I'm so frisky" is "whiskey," etc.) to stock exchange phrases like the now obsolete *fourteen hundred!*—for many years, starting in about 1870, the London Stock Exchange had only 1,399 members and to ensure secrecy in the Exchange, the words *fourteen hundred!* were cried as a warning whenever a stranger came onto the floor. Similarly, in early American country stores there was often a complicated code system for marking goods so that the merchant could tell what every piece of merchandise cost him without the customer's knowing, which gave the storekeeper an advantage when bargaining. A merchant, for instance, might make the phrase NOW BE SHARP represent 12345678910 (an *N* would equal the numeral 1, an *O* the numeral 2, a *W* the numeral 3, and so on). Every trusted clerk would be given this equation, and if a piece of merchandise was marked, say, *NWW* on the back, anyone with the formula would know its cost was $1.33.

One of the most interesting secret languages was the female language developed by the women of Arawak, an island in the Lesser Antilles. This language was invented when fierce South American Caribs invaded the island before the time of Columbus, butchering and eating all the relatively peaceful Arawak male inhabitants and claiming their women. In retaliation, the women devised a separate female language based on Arawak, refusing to speak Carib and maintaining silence in the presence of all males, a revenge that was practiced for generations afterward.

No one knows how the secret whistle language of Kuskoy or Bird Village in Turkey evolved, although it might have begun as a warning signal for Black Sea smugglers or others engaged in illegal activity. Bird Village, about eighty miles southwest of Trebizond, takes its name from the birdlike whistling that the villagers often used in place of words. Voices don't carry far in this mountainous region, but the shrill whistles can be heard for miles, the high-pitched sounds carrying news of births and deaths, love affairs, and all the latest gossip. The whistling serves as a kind of house-to-house telegraph system. In order to get the power to "transmit," the whistler curls his tongue around his teeth so that the air is forced through his lips. No pucker is made, as in most whistling. To amplify the sound, the palm is cupped around the mouth and the whistling "words" come out with a great blast. It's said that the language is so powerful and complex that lovers can even romance each other with tender whistles from as far away as five miles. A similar whistling language is "spoken" by villagers in the Canary Islands, though a Kuskoyite wouldn't be understood if he whistled to someone there.

Boontling has a vocabulary far exceeding that of any other secret language. As one old-time speaker boasted, "Almost anything can be said in Boontling." Another man claimed that when he was drafted during World War I Boontling was so much his language that he "had to learn English all over again" on leaving home.

Over the years Boontling acquired about 1,200 unique words and phrases. Its vocabulary consists of twenty or so different types of terms: Scotch-Irish dialect words; other foreign language words; American dialect and slang words; American Indian words; telescoped or reshaped words from English; Biblical allusions; metaphors; coinages; references to local people, places, and happenings; and *nonch harpin's,* or taboo speech.

Scotch-Irish dialect terms include *tweed* for young man, *deck* for look at, and *wee* for little. The local Pomo Indian *bishe* for deer was transformed into the Boontling word *boshe* for to hunt deer and the *bosher's* (deerhunter's) *boshe barl* (barrel), meaning deer rifle. California Spanish of a earlier day yielded the Boontling *doolsey,* sugar or candy (from *dulce,* sweet), as well as *layche,* milk (from *leche*), and *breggo,* sheep (from *borrego,* yearling lamb). The French *gourmand* became the Boontling *gorm,* to eat, as did the Old English dialect term *chiggle,* while the Old English verb *harp* (which Shakespeare put into the mouth of Polonius—"Still harping on my daughter!") came to mean to talk.

Local characters gave their names to a great many Boontling words—perhaps 15 percent of the vocabulary. These eponyms include a camp cook called Z.C. whose thick, potent coffee inspired Boonters to name all coffee *zeese* in his honor. *Charlie ball* means to embarrass in Boontling because a local Indian named Charlie Ball was quick to blush. A telephone is called a *buckeywalter* because in the old days one Walter Levi was the only person in town who had a phone at home. Working was called *ottin'* after an industrious German logger named Otto. A big fire in the fireplace is designated a *jeffer,* since old Jeff Vester always had such a blaze going. Pie became *charlie brown* because logger Charlie Brown ate pie with every meal. Because clothes horse Nettie Wallace always wore lace, Boonters call anyone who affects fancy dress *nettied.* A retarded boy named Tudd inspired *tuddish* for all similarly handicapped people. *To joe mack* (to defeat in a fist fight) came from the name of Joe McGrinsey, a brawler who never lost a battle. Boontling itself, of course, takes its name from Boonville, the largest community in Anderson Valley and named for W. W. Boone, an early storekeeper and relative of Daniel Boone.

Outsiders also qualify as eponyms. A *booker,* for example, is any black man, after Booker T. Washington. *Trilbies* are small feet, honoring the heroine of George Du Maurier's novel *Trilby* (1894), who was noted for her beautiful feet.

Boontling telescoped words (or, to be more accurate, "phonemic reshapings") from English are more numerous, including *bourp* (a contraction of boar-pig) for bacon; *forbes* for four bits; *toobs,* two bits; *haireem,* "hairy-mouth," for a shaggy-muzzled dog like an Airedale; and *nonch* for bad, or inferior, from *non* plus "much," hence the term *nonch harpin',* dirty talk.

Metaphors in Boontling include the poetic *white spots,* meaning dead lambs in a field, *peerls* (pearls) for rain, *milky* for foggy, *mink,* "a girl with expensive tastes," and *bulrusher,* an illegitimate child, from the Biblical story of Moses found in the bulrushes. One visiting politician from Sacramento was dubbed *a pottager from the*

Gold Dome, a Biblical allusion to Esau, who sold his birthright for a mess of pottage.

When the Hippies came to Mendicino County in the 1960s, the Boonters dubbed them *posey tweeds,* a translation of "flower children." The language can adapt itself colorfully to modern circumstances. For another example, the action of the *Apollo II* moon landing was summarized by a Boonter as "Thribs kimmies piked to the green-teesle region" (Three men traveled to the green-cheese region).

Other interesting Boontling expressions are *applehead* for a woman, *tonguecuppy* for sick, *strung* for dead, *book* for place, *sluggin nook* for a sleeping place, and *croppies* for sheep, because sheep crop the grass when grazing.

Nonch harpin', "or dirty talk," is said to comprise about fifteen percent of Boontling's vocabulary. These are, in reality, kind of rough-hewn pioneer euphemisms for sensitive subjects and a necessity for the speech of a lusty yarn-spinning people who indulged in much *hootin', hornin',* an' *fisterin'* (laughing, drinking, and fighting). *Madge,* for example, meant a whore, after the name of the local madam, and one went *madgin'* at a *madge house.* According to legend, *burlapin'* means to make love or fornication because a local youngster spied the owner of a local store and a customer making love on a pile of burlap sacks in the back room of the store. The boy ran out into the street shouting, "They're burlapin' in there!"

Several sources, including Dr. Adams's authoritative book, conclude that Boontling was probably spoken by almost everyone in Boonville at the height of its popularity, the language something of a local sport. It may not strictly qualify as a genuine dialect, its pronunciation (except for the Scotch-Irish and foreign loan words) and its grammar like that of the Midland dialect of American English, but had it lasted in an isolated valley longer than the century or so that it thrived, Boontling might have developed into a bona-fide dialect. As it was, perhaps its base was not solid enough. In any case, by the 1930s the Great Depression migration from the Dust Bowl to California had flooded the valley with non-speakers of Boontling who diluted the town's "tight little society." A logging boon during the war years added to the watering down, as did television with its "Standard Network English," and, finally, the dude ranches that opened in the area brought in even more outsiders. The town's phone booths are still marked *Buckywalter,* men's rest rooms are marked *Kimmies* and there is a gift shop called the *Eeble Heelch,* which means "eyeball everything." But as the original Boonts grow older and pass from the scene and their descendants marry outsiders, there's "nobody left to harp to," as one old-timer puts it. Boontling is already a curiosity and will by the end of the century be only an historical curiosity. Descriptions like this recorded one will probably never be heard again:

The hob started with the apple-heads all nettied, and the seekers active. But the hig-heeler got teetlipped when he decked that raggin was going on, and harped to the raggers to either shy or pike. Then came the midnight chiggrel. Two of the kimneys, Punk and Spring Knee, got into a fister and knocked the chiggrel on the floor. Punk was high-heeled and kept in branding irons until his apple-head, Em, could get the higs for bail.

Translation:

The dance started with the women all fancy-dressed and the ladies' men active. But the man in charge got angry when he noticed that indecent dancing was going on, and ordered the dancers to either quit or leave. Then came the midnight supper. Two of the men, Punk and Spring Knee, got into a fight and knocked all the food onto the floor. Punk was arrested and kept in handcuffs until his wife, Em, could get the money for bail.

A Boontling Dictionary

Following are more than a hundred colorful samples of the thousand or so Boontling words and phrases, these including examples from the various Boontling word sources, ranging from Indian terms to invented ones. Words and phrases recorded in the text aren't repeated here.

ab—to push someone into line (possibly deriving from the name of someone called Ab who did this, or from a pejorative use of *ab chaser,* following).

ab chaser—a resident of the coast (an abbreviation of *abalone chaser,* a fisherman).

afe—to fart (a reshaping of *a fart*).

almitty—a burp (a local woman named Almitty was renowned for her loud belching).

apple-head—girlfriend, wife, or woman (after some anonymous man's girlfriend, said to have an apple-shaped head).

ark—to wreck (perhaps a reshaping of the English word *wreck*).

barl—to shoot a rifle (said to imitate the sound of a rifle shot in the local mountains).

barlow—a pocketknife (after the Barlow brand of knife).

barney—to hug or kiss (a local named Barney was very affectionate to women, hugging and kissing them at every opportunity).

bat—to masturbate (said to be a back formation of *bachelor*, bachelors thought by locals to be prone to the practice).

beartrack—berry pie (berries in pie were thought to resemble the berries or seeds in bear manure).

bee'n—the buttocks (a reshaping of *behind*).

belhoon—a dollar (origin unknown, even young languages having their mysteries).

belkeek—a rabbit (a reshaping of *Belgium*, as in *Belgian hare*).

big book—the Bible.

big end—to strike out in baseball (because the big, fat end of the bat misses the ball when a hitter swings for a strike and after a third strike the hitter has nothing but the big end left).

bill nunn—pancake syrup (local trencherman Bill Nunn poured syrup on everything he ate).

billy ryan—a goatee (because one Billy Ryan wore such a beard).

blevins—a poor carpenter (after the local Blevins family, which had several inept carpenters in it).

blooch—to chatter aimlessly (a reshaping of *bluejay*, a noisy bird).

blood 'n hair—an auto accident.

boo—a potato (from the Pomo Indian *bu*, potato).

breggo—a sheep (from the Spanish *borrego*, lamb).

briney—the sea; also a home run in baseball (because a local player once hit a home run into the ocean).

buck pasture—a man with a pregnant wife (the man is thus fenced off from sexual contact with women, out in the pasture with the other bucks).

burt stork—a man with a large family (after a man named Burt with a very large family, plus the stork who brought them!).

candeel—a government worker (because a local once complained to a county worker, "We eat sowbelly while you eat canned eel," eel considered a delicacy locally).

can kicky—very angry (so angry as to kick an empty tin can in the street).

cassie—a sloppy housekeeper (a local woman named Cassie kept house so poorly that her name came to describe her inefficiency).

chapport—to challenge to a fight (as Charles Porter often did by shedding his fancy clothes, which had previously been dubbed *Chapports*).

chipmunk—to hoard (as the chipmunk does nuts).

chucklehead—a dumb, naive person (from Southern dialect).

chuck robinson—a late riser always behind schedule (after a local with this name of similar habits).

cock—to get angry (perhaps from the cocking of a gun during a violent argument, or from the belligerent behavior of certain male wild birds).

collar—jumpy, nervous, and irritable (like a jumpy horse in a collar).

combs gittin' red—a youngster's coming of sexual age (when roosters mature, their combs redden).

croakins—a funeral (from the slang *to croak,* or die).

cy miller—a wild-goose chase (when a fire alarm call came, the firemen thought it came from Cy Miller's house instead of Similia, where the fire raged, and rushed to Cy's house on a wild-goose chase).

daylighter—the sexual act performed during the day.

deeble—to castrate (a reshaping of to *deball*).

deejir—a degenerate (from *degenerate*).

dick—to cheat or crowd out (a local Dick ruined the seduction plans of another man by tricking him and then moved in to make the seduction himself).

diddle—a bottle of bootleg whiskey (a Dr. Diddle dispensed whiskey as medicine during Prohibition in the area, c.1906).

dinklehonk—a cowbell, a cow (said to be imitative of the sound of a cowbell in the local hills).

dirty neck—a bum, someone just above a *deejir* (q.v.)

dissies—metal-buckled shoes (a man called Dissie, because he said *dis* for *this,* wore such shoes, which were soon named for him).

dreef—a married man suspected of being impotent (a distortion of *dry fuck*).

dusties—a grave or cemetery.

dwight's flagpole—the largest flagpole in town (named after a local drunk who slept at its base).

ear-settin'—a scolding (from the practice of twisting the ears of sheep dogs to punish them).

earth—truth (because earth is regarded as plain and fundamental).

eelk—an old cow (a reshaping of *old cow*).

eelstig—an old man (a reshaping of *old stag*).

eesle—an asshole (a reshaping of *asshole*).

fairbs—a dirty person (after a local man who never bathed).

fence-jumpin'—adultery (after animals leaping a pasture fence to graze elsewhere).

flories—biscuits (for the excellent biscuits a local woman named Flora made).

floyd hutsell—a lantern (after a local man, Floyd Hutsell, who always carried one because he was afraid of the dark).

frish—San Francisco.

glowworm—a lantern.

golden eagles—women's panties (because these were often made from Golden Eagle flour sacks in the old days).

greeley—a newspaper or newspaperman (after nineteenth-century American newspaper editor Horace Greeley).

gray-matter kimmie—a college professor (see *kimmie*).

haines-crispin—a feud (after a feud between men named Haines and Crispin that ended in their death in a shootout).

hairk—haircut (an alteration of *haircut*).

halvers—a condom (from the request "Go halvers with me" young men made when asking others to share their supply of contraceptives).

heefus—a small-hipped person (a reshaping of *half-ass*).

heelch—everything (a reshaping of the idiom *the whole cheese*, meaning *the same*).

hens' eggs n' ovals—writing (from a local who used to excuse himself to practice his penmanship by saying, "I've gotta get to my hens' eggs n' ovals").

higher n' a billy—to be very drunk (after billygoats, who climb to the highest crags of mountains).

high heel—a police officer (after an early sheriff who wore an elevated shoe because of a leg deformity).

hood—an odd, eccentric person (after a strange family from the Valley who wore hoods on their coats).

husk—to masturbate (analogous with husking an ear of corn).

ite vault—a bank (the Ite, for Italian, refers to the *Italian* Giannini family of the Bank of America).

jay esser—a lawsuit (from the initials of a local man who had been involved in a long lawsuit).

jeanship—a black sheep (*jean* for a local black family named Jeans).

joe ride—a fast, furious ride (after a driver named Joe whose wild rides were legendary).

kaishbook—pregnant (a Pomo Indian word).

kimmie—a man (probably from the Scotch *kimmer,* a man).

kraisey—a mix-up (coined after two very religious local girls who met a vagabond in the mountains and took him to be a vision of *Christ*).

ling—language, lingo.

log-lifter—a very heavy rainstorm.

moldunes, mollies—large breasts (after a big-breasted woman named Moldune).

mouse ear—a narrow vagina.

neebles—a eunuch (a distortion of *no balls*).

ose wipin's—toilet paper (*ose,* ass, plus *wipings*).

pinchy—stingy (from *pinching pennies*).

pottager—a government worker (after the Biblical Esau, who sold his birthright for a mess of pottage).

ricky chow—sexual intercourse (said to be "imitative of the sound of bedsprings").

ridge—an old man (after an old man nicknamed Ridge, because his house stood on a prominent ridge; he lived to be almost a hundred).

rookyto—a local quail (imitative of the bird's call).

roopey—a cowboy (a mispronunciation of *whoopee,* a cowboy yell).

rosy—red wine (said to be named after Rosy, the wife of a local winemaker, but probably influenced by *rosé*).

rout the kimmie in the boat—to get a woman pregnant (from the American slang expression *rock the little boy in the boat,* meaning the same; see *kimmie*).

rudy nebs—a well with good water (after a well featured in the once-popular Rudy Nebs comic strip).

schoolch—a schoolteacher.

scotty—a big eater (after Scotty, the insatiable dog of a local hunter).

she-booker—a black woman.

shoveltooth—a doctor (after a local physician with protruding teeth).

skee—whiskey.

stiff hat—a boxer (because boxers in the area formerly wore hard high hats in the ring).

string—to kill (from string up, hang).

a stringy-hair-'n'-wrinkle-socks—a disheveled, unkempt woman.

suck—an infant.

sucks—female breasts.

taikelf—manual stimulation of the clitoris (a reshaping of *tickle finger,* the long middle finger).

taish—to defecate (a distortion of *take a shit*).

tally whacker—the penis (a Southern expression).

teep—to urinate (a distortion of *take a piss*).

tom bacon—handlebar mustache (a local named Tom Bacon had a long mustache, the tips of which he could curl about his ears).

trashmover—a heavy storm (like the one that once moved the accumulated trash from Anderson Creek).

visalia—a roping saddle (from a brand name).

wee—small (from the Scottish).

white oak—to work hard (because the white oak is hard and difficult to cut).

yeast-powdery—a woman sexually aroused (the analogy is to a yeast-powder biscuit rising and the female pudenda swollen by erotic stimulation).

10 More Discombobulating Twists in the Way Americans Talk

By various estimates anywhere from three to twenty-seven major dialects are spoken in America, Professor Hans Kurath's *Linguistic Atlas of the United States and Canada* recognizing at least twenty-four well-defined regional ways of speech. But there are many more local dialects, or subdialects, that are spoken by relatively few people, several of them confined to certain towns or islands. Actually, the dialect number could be increased myriad times, depending on how loosely one uses the term *dialect.* James Thurber, for instance, claimed that there was a nasal, rapidly spoken dialect called Gudda in his hometown of Columbus, Ohio. He named the dialect for the "verb of possession" *gudda* (got a) "that most frequently pops up in it"—*I gudda house; I gudda horse; I gudda barn,* etc. It might be said that all American cities, towns, and villages have their peculiarities of speech, shibboleths that distinguish the natives from visitors, like the pronunciation of Boise as *Boysee* by Idahoans (outsiders call it *Boyzee*), or the employment of distinctive expressions like the use of *you're driving me to Poughkeepsie* (where there is a famous mental hospital) for "you're driving me crazy" by people who live in small towns near that New York city on the Hudson.

Dahntahn (downtown) in busy Pittsburgh, for another example, most two syllable words lose a syllable: "Howard is hired" sounds like *Howard is Howard* (Howd is howd). Also, the sounds of hard *i* and *ow* are merged in the Smoky City, as Michael McGough of the *Pittsburgh Post Gazette* has demonstrated by writing a Pittsburghian poem in which the words *I'll, towel, owl, cow,* and *how* all rhyme.

There is, incidentally, no marine influence accounting for the name of the Pittsburgh baseball team. The team takes its name from the nickname of its first president, J. Palmer "Pirate" O'Neill, who was so called because he signed a player from another club, pirating him away rather unscrupulously.

Pittsburgh is just one of the 176 cities in America with a population of more than 100,000 that has its own dialect. If that old Hindu proverb is right, then dialect changes every eighteen to twenty miles in America, as it does everywhere else, and, strictly speaking, almost every American hamlet has what could be called a dialect, even if its speech is essentially the same as that of its region and the only variations are the use of a few words differently or the different pronunciation of a word or two. Philadelphia (see also Chapter 7) is another big Pennsylvania city with its own special pronunciation and vocabulary. Unlike many Pennsylvanians, Philadelphians, bordered by the New York Metropolitan area, disdain the *r* in words, preferring the New York habit of dropping it. Typical Philadelphian pronunciations include *oys* for *always; bounce* for *balance; kore* for *car; kear* for *care; DAY-un* for *down; GLEE-ad* for *glad; GEH-oh* for *go; HAY-us* for *house;* and *Ful-UFF-yuh* for *Philadelphia.* The changing Northeastern pronunciations reported by William Labov (see Chapter 1) are particularly noticeable in this city, where it is possible to hear a sentence like the following: "He left his HAY-us in Northeast Ful-UFF-yuh and got into his kore to GEH-oh DAY-un to Shpring GOR-den Shtreet like he oys does. But on the way he got into a FUH-eet with another driver. It was BEE-ad."

Translation: "He left his house in Northeast Philadelphia and got into his car to go down to Spring Garden Street like he always does. But on the way he got into a fight with another driver. It was bad."

It would, of course, be impossible to include all the U.S. city, town, and village dialect variations in this small space. It is said that Basque sheepherders in the western United States "have created a new language or dialect based on English words adapted to Basque flections." As for the speech of Chicagoans, one might quote Agatha Christie's butler in *Murder on the Orient*

Express. "Does he speak English?" Hercule Poirot asks, referring to another character. "A kind of English," the butler replies. "I think he learned it in a place called Chicago." Then there is the speech of Minnesota Swedes, Brighton Beach Russians, New England's Portuguese fishermen, Vietnamese in Boston, Laotians in Louisiana, Puerto Ricans in the Bronx, Arabs, Cubans, Jamaicans, and many, many more specific populations. One could even include the dialects of Eskimo tribes in Alaska, which have some truly odd pronunciations. Mario Pei, observing that the sounds of all animals are imitated and remembered wherever the animals can be closely observed, reports that there are actually words for the speech of a whale in Eskimo. Some Eskimo tribes use *peu-wu* for the whale's sound, while the Alaskan Nutka Indians say *Çhw* ("constriction of the throat, strongly uttered *h*, sound of *w*").

As noted, lingoes like Boontling (see Chapter 9), and Marin Countyese, the laidback talk of the affluent in Marin County, near San Francisco, qualify as dialects under a liberal definition. Walt Whitman's forgotten poem "Song of the Answerer" puts it this way: "Every existence has its idiom, every thing has an idiom and tongue." In point of fact, *every American* might be said to have a dialect of his own by which his family and friends can identify him, such dialects of individual speakers of a language called *idiolects.* While there isn't nearly time or space enough to examine even most such "subdialects" here, following is a representative sample of conspicuous ones.

Bawlamerese in Murlin

Baltimore, Maryland, named for the British Baltimore family so prominent in its history, and famous nationally for such diverse things as the *Baltimore oriole,* the *Baltimore clipper,* the *Baltimore Flyer,* the *Baltimore beauty,* the *Baltimore belle,* the *Baltimore heater,* the *Baltimore & Ohio Railroad (B&O)* and even baseball's *Baltimore chop,* is also noted for its local *Baltimore dialect*—called *Bawlamerese* because the place is locally pronounced *Bawlamer, Murlin.* According to an official guide published for *torsts,* Bawlamer is forty miles from *Warshnin,* the nation's capital. Among other linguistic curiosities, Bawlamer men cut (not mow) their lawns with a *paramour* (power mower), while their wives do the *warsh* (wash), *wrenching* (rinsing) the clothes and *arning* (ironing) them on an *arnin board*. Little Bawlamer kids like the zoo's *elfin* (elephant) and *draff* (giraffe), and teenagers hang out at the local *drucksterer* (drug- store) after *hoskull* (high school) lets out. Crabs are their favorite but most Bawlamerins like a *cole race beef sanwich* (cold roast beef sandwich). Basically, Bawlamerese is part of the Delmarva Penin- sula dialect, this Southern dialect spoken in sections of Delaware, Maryland, and Virginia, but Baltimore's proximity to Washington, D.C., makes it a cosmopolitan city with a language character all its own.

The term *plug-ugly*, describing a city ruffian or rowdy, or any such disreputable character, seems to have been born in Balti- more. First recorded as an Americanism in 1856, "it derived in Baltimore . . . from a short spike fastened in the toe of [such rowdies'] boots, with which they kicked their opponents in a dense crowd, or as they elegantly expressed it, 'plugged them ugly.' "

In 1981, when the *Bawlamer Aurioles* were playing the *Pittsburgh Parrots* in the World Series, TV newscaster Howard K. Smith, who hails from Louisiana, twitted the locals about their twang. "They call their city Bawlamer, Murlin," Smith said. "They call garbage *gobbidge*. Legal is pronounced *liggle*. *Paramour* is their word for power mower and if you ever ask directions, remember that *Droo- dle Avenue* means Druid Hill Avenue. *Clays* means clothes. *Doll* means dial—the phone. *Cancel* means council, as in town council. *Council* means cancel, as with a check." Soon Baltimore officials drafted a reply to *Harrid K. Smiff*, this reading, in part: "You get the pixture, but what's so funny about a paramour to cut the grass, we'd like to ax?"

An *aig* in Bawlamerese is an egg, while *arnjuice* is orange juice, the *Arsh* (Irish) come from *Arlin* (Ireland), *awl* (oil) goes into the crankcase, *arspern* is what you take for a headache, the *Beeno* (B&O) is a railroad, a *bleef* is what you believe in, and *blow* is the opposite of above. Down is pronounced *day-on*, shore is *sure*, food is *feud*, and fight is *fat*. With these principles in mind anyone should be able to translate the preamble of the "Livelier Balti- more Committee" in their guide to the city:

We've been watching Bawlamer and its gubmint for over thirty-five years and we're not tarred yet! We don't work all over Murlin, though. You won't find us in Anna Runnel, or Habberdy Grace, or Downey Ashin, the Allamic, that is. We are busy, however, making sure you can get a mortgage whether you live in Hollandtaydn or Dundock. And we're concerned how they'll deed the Patapsico. And how to get help if your landlord won't fix a broken bawler or a leaky fawcit in your baffroon. . . . Whether rapid transit goes down Harrid Street, or across Norf Abnew, or on to the old Beeno tracks concerns us too. And we'll call the gubmint in Naplis or Warshin to get things done. So while we know little of Drooslin, Arlin, or Yerp, ax us a question about Bawlamer and we're lobble to be less ignernt.

Bonac for "Foreigners"

Less than a hundred miles from Times Square a community of Long Island fishermen called the Bonackers speak a dialect that retains the sound of Shakespeare's England and has rarely, if ever, been recorded in any language book. The Bonackers reside in East Hampton, a town they helped settle in the mid-seventeenth century when East Hampton was founded as a whaling port by settlers from Connecticut across Long Island Sound. They were not the affluent among these settlers; they were, in fact, often their servants, and at first they built shacks along *Accabonac Creek,* the richer citizens disparagingly calling them *Bonackers* after the place where most of them lived.

Some one thousand Bonackers live in the Hamptons today, many of them speaking the old English dialect called Bonac that retains much of the vocabulary and the same vowel sounds the original settlers employed. Many of the families are closely related. There are, for example, Posey Lesters and Devon Lesters and Roundswamp Lesters and Pantigo Lesters. The Posey Lesters take their name from a nineteenth-century ancestor who always walked the streets with a flower in his lapel, while the Roundswamp Lesters are named for the place where this branch of the family originated. Anyone born outside the East End of Long Island is called a *foreigner* by a Bonacker and the entire world outside the area is known as *away.* "Even my wife's a foreigner, she came from away," one old fisherman says.

The salty dialect spoken by the Bonackers is often related to fishing, still the main livelihood of the people. "What you got *finnin'* over there?" a fisherman might shout to someone else pulling in a catch a hundred yards away. "This spring I *caught* pretty good," says a fisherman in relating his luck, "but I couldn't get a price for the *stock.*"

A harbor is a *hobboh* in Bonac, its *r* melting away as *r*'s often do in this dialect, the word *farmer,* for another example, becoming *fammah.* One also hears words like *awchit* for *orchard, op'm* for *open, eebn* for *even, yit* for *yet, nawthin'* for *nothing,* and *winnuhry* for *wintry.* In Bonacker homes *durst* often takes the place of *dare not,* and *cattywumper* means "crooked" or "disorderly."

No matter what your name is, Bonackers reply, "Yes, yes, bobby," or "Yes, yes, bub," when you ask a question. About the nearest similarity to the vocabulary of another area in Bonac are a few nautical phrases also heard in Massachusetts, these including *cutter,* a command to turn sharply, and *finestkind,* which means "A-OK."

Bonackers, who speak with something resembling an Irish brogue, try not to converse in Bonac when strangers are around, and it is seldom heard in the summer season when the population of this community made famous in *Jaws* increases threefold from its 55,000 winter population. Yet these people cling to their dialect, which one of them calls "The King's English, only we come under an earlier king." They are "a stubborn bunch," in the words of another Bonacker fisherman, and resist all attempts by teachers to "get the Bonac out of their speech." They still live modestly, as their ancestors did, often on the same land, maintaining their dialect as a badge of pride. If Bonac dies, it will only be because the Bonackers have been forced from their land by rising prices and real-estate development in this summer playground of the rich, which is fast becoming a year-round suburb of Manhattan.

Getting Boobleated on Isleboro, Maine, or on Martha's Vineyard, Massachusetts

That folks on islands like Isleboro, Maine, don't talk like people in the region around them has been noted in many areas. To take another New England example, sociolinguist William Labov has studied the famous resort island of Martha's Vineyard off Massachusetts and found interesting connections between the ages of speakers there and their pronunciation of the *ow* diphthong (the common pronunciation of the vowel in *cow*). The longer a speaker had lived on the island the less likely he or she was to pronounce *cow* (or *crowd* or *house*) this way, Labov found. *Foreigners* (summer visitors), on the other hand, almost always used this "proper" pronunciation recommended by elocutionists, rarely ever using the "lazier" pronunciation *RAoo* (with the long *oo* of *good*) that had long ago been introduced by Yankee fishermen. Martha's Vineyard, incidentally, got its name, according to an apocryphal tale, from an old Yankee sea captain who owned the island group it was part of. To his favorite daughter he gave his most productive island, Martha's Vineyard; to his next he gave the islands closest to home, Elizabeth's Islands; and to his last daughter, Nan, he just offered what remained, and Nantuck-it. More likely the island's name has a more prosaic origin. The Indians called it *Noe-pe* ("Amid the Waters"), while the Norsemen who landed there named it Staumey ("Isle of Currents"). It was probably christened *Martin's Vineyard* by English navigator Bartholomew Gosnold in 1602, for no reason that we know. After a century it took the name *Martha's Vineyard,* probably because its name was confused with that of a little neighboring island to the southwest called Martha's Vineyard that had also been named by Gosnold. (*That* little island is now called *No Man's Land,* after an Indian named Teque*noman.*)

There are other idiosyncrasies in native Martha's Vineyard speech, but not so many as on Isleboro, off the Maine coast. These islanders, like the Bonackers in the Hamptons, call summer people and tourists *foreigners,* though they have the kindlier designation an *over homer* for someone from just across the bay. So strange is their idiom that outsiders often can't understand a thing they say, and the islanders generally wouldn't have it any other way.

Strange names for things abound here. A sea-urchin, for example, is called a *whore's egg,* a term which is also used in Newfoundland. Similarly, long strands of seaweed or kelp are called *devil's aprons* and clay holes on the beach that someone could sink in are called *honeypots.* Weather is divided into *weather overhead* (how the sky appears) and *weather underfoot* (the condition of roads, etc.). *Weather overhead* brings *so'thad winds* and *no'thad winds,* the last especially disliked by those who are *spleeny* (can't take the cold) or have arthritis so badly they can barely *stiver and go.*

Islanders here are a *pretty kipper* (exhilaratingly healthy) people, however. Maybe it's because of the *dundefunk* (fried pork served with homemade bread and molasses) they eat, or the *joe floggers* (hard molasses cookies), or the homemade *duff* (pudding), or the *dropped* (poached) eggs, or the *blackjack* (gingerbread), or even the *smother* (pot pie). The islanders like to eat turnips, too, and in the old days they used to hold gatherings, similar to corn huskings, that were called *turnip scrapes,* where people got together and scraped turnips while eating turnips that were served for refreshments.

Don't strain your pooper, people who work too hard are told on Iseleboro, don't *pucker* (hurry) too much or *conk yourself out* (get dead tired) *heftin'* (lifting) things. But someone too prolific with such advice might be told *hawl your jaw* (shut up) or *stop dinging* (nagging) me. There wouldn't be many curses in the presence of strangers, though. Isleboro men have vocabularies that could *titrify* (mortify) you, but are reserved people in public, where the closest they'd come to a curse would be *Gawdfrediamonds!* The closest Isleboro women would come to a curse, in public or private, would be *twink!*

Isleboro natives do use words and phrases common to other areas of the country, including *hot spells, cold spells, worn to a frazzle, laugh like loons, too many irons in the fire, fly into a tirade, hobnob, put upon, a bone to pick, an ax to grind, set a spell, lummox, not by a damn sight,* and *spider* for a frying pan. But a disproportionate number are unusual ones. *Get a wiggle on it* means hurry up, for example; *doss over more often* means come again; to have *no commux* with someone means not to associate with him; to *muckle a hold* on something means to get hold of it; *pint!* is an order telling somebody to leave quickly, and *to be in a tickle* is to be in a good mood. *Trump* is an unusual Isleboro word for a youngster, *stern* means the rear end, and *skiver!* is the local cry to scatter chickens. In Isleboro dialect, *deer* is pronounced *de-ah, youngster* is *your'n, hist* is *hoist, calculate* is *calate,* and *shocking clams* is *shucking clams.*

Another Isleboro word I've heard nowhere else is *upstropolis,* meaning confused or *discombobulated,* also used here, though not so rarely, not even so rarely as *boobleated,* meaning the same to a greater degree! Then there is *hot-me-tot,* which, like *pucker,* means to be in a hurry—islanders don't like to be in a hurry and have a lot of terms warning against it, *don't ram the roads* being still another. *Hot-me-tot* is supposed to be a corruption of *hot-to-trot*. The islanders also use colorful expressions like *hoary-eyed* and *resuscitating fire* (used by someone who claimed he had a run-in with Satan). But one could go on and on. An excellent collection of Isleboroisms is given by Darrel A. Roberson in *Yankee Magazine* (January 1977).

Louisiana Language:
Bougalie (Cajun), Creole, and Gumbo

Cajun and Creole constitute the two French dialects of the American language spoken in Louisiana *(Loozeeanna)*. A third type, Gumbo, is a dialect of the French language rather than English; it was the pidgin French of the blacks who came as slaves to New Orleans from Senegal in colonial times and is spoken by relatively few people today.

Cajun takes its name from *Acadia,* the former French province centering on Nova Scotia, from which the British expelled the Acadians, or Cajuns, in 1755, deporting those who did not pledge allegiance to Britain, about 4,000 of whom settled in the region around St. Martinville in southwestern Louisiana. The sufferings of the expulsion are described by Longfellow in *Evangeline* (1847), familiar to generations of American schoolchildren. But the Cajuns endured and soon were maintaining a separate folk culture, including their own dialect, which has been declining in use since the end of World War I, although it is still heard in the area. Deportees were officially designated French neutrals, but they were usually called *Acadians,* this word pronounced *Cadian* by 1868 and finally *Cajun.* Their name for the Cajun dialect they speak is *Bougalie* (bogue talk). *Bogue* and, of course, *bayou* come ultimately from the Choctaw word *bayuk* (creek), which the Creoles and Cajuns got from the local Indians.

The picturesque Cajun dialect retains archaic French forms, and the Cajuns use a great number of French words in their speech, including the common and very useful *oui* (yes), *mais* (but), *mais mon!* (no!), *bien* (good), *grand* (tall), *m'sieu* (mister), *demoiselle* (miss), *comment?* (how?), *pardon* (pardon me), *adieu* (goodbye), and *chérie* (dear). Common French phrases heard among these people include *c'est vrai* (it's true), *comme ça* (like that), *là bas* (down there), *il dit* (he said), and *qu'est-ce que c'est?* (what is it?).

To such words and phrases are added English, Spanish, German, Indian, and American black expressions and inflections accumulated over the years in Cajun country, which primarily includes the Louisiana parishes of Acadia, Allen, Beauregard, Calcasieu, Cameron, Evangeline, Iberia, Jefferson Davis, Lafayette, St. Landry, St. Martin, and St. Mary—though Cajun is also spoken in a good number of other parish towns from New Orleans to the French Settlement east of the Mississippi in Livingston Parish.

Cajun food and music have a national following in America today. The music derives from Celtic and country tunes and is very popular on the *crawfish circuit* from New Orleans to Houston. Cajun cooking features dishes like *jambalaya,* the word deriving from the Spanish *jamón* (ham), this dish originally made with ham. *Gumbos, crawfish étouffé,* and other peppery delights are also part of the cuisine, which has been making a big hit in Eastern cities recently.

The original Cajuns were isolated in the south Louisiana bayous, fishing and hunting in their *bateaux,* shallow craft well suited to navigate such backwaters. There the Cajun language developed, from a mixture of old Breton French, English, Spanish, American Indian words, and at least to some extent from the language of freed black slaves and black Caribbean immigrants who came to work in the area as laborers and sharecroppers.

American black pronunciation is notable in Cajun speech in such words as *aks* (ask), *shoh-nuf* (sure enough), *ehf* (if), *jis* (just), *haw* (horror), *git* (get), *yoh* (your), *uh* (of), *ayg* (egg), and *uh mehs uh* (a mess of). In this respect Cajun differs from Creole speech, which shows little black influence. The Creoles, descendants of the French who first colonized New Orleans, did not at first associate with blacks and Indians as the more democratic Cajuns did, their speech owing no debt to these groups. The word *Creole* comes from the French *créole* meaning "a native." By the end of the eighteenth century, however, Creole began to be applied to black slaves of the Creoles as well as to themselves, was next applied to a black person with any French or Spanish blood, then came to mean a native-born black as opposed to a black born in Africa, and by the middle of the nineteenth century described any

Louisianan, the state of Louisiana dubbed *the Creole State*. The word is a confusing one which can be defined only in the context it is being used in, for Creole also means a pidgin language spoken by a second generation of speakers, and in Alaska of the late 1860s it even meant a native of mixed Russian and Indian blood!

There are a great many vowel and consonant changes in Cajun. The *ay* of words like *break* or *make*, for example, is pronounced *eh*, yielding *brehg* and *mehg*. On the other hand *eh*, as in *get*, is pronounced *ay*, yielding *gaydth*. The final consonant *d* is pronounced so forcibly at times that it assumes a *t* quality, *kid* becoming *keet*. Final syllables in Cajun words tend to be given heavier stress, as in *meh-BEE* (maybe), though prefixes are also frequently stressed (before = *BI-foh*).

Cajun French words are often more colorful than their French counterparts. The French, for example, call the hummingbird an *oiseau-mouche* (bird-fly). Good enough, but hardly comparable to the poetic Cajun *susfleur* (upon flower). The French have no name for the white perch, a fish not known in France; the Cajuns call it by the descriptive name *sac-à-lait* (bag of milk).

Cajuns sometimes take American words and make them into something new, imitating the sound of *bacon* with the French *béquine*, for example. A Saturday-night dance in Cajun county is called *fais-dodas*, a rough approximation of one of the calls in a square dance.

Cajun speakers tend to repeat proper names in sentences, as in "He bring Paul, but Paul, Paul he drown, Paul." What a standard English speaker would call "grammatical errors" also enhance Cajun speech, probably giving it its peculiar flavor more than any other single feature, as these common expressions show:

★ *For why you ask me?*
★ *He been try make me mad.*
★ *You see ma cow down by bayou, you push him home, yes.*
★ *What for she call?*
★ *He be gone tree day now—yesterday, today, and tomorrow.*
★ *I don't got but ten cents, me.*
★ *His horse more better as that.*
★ *She the bestest child.*
★ *Us, we can go.*
★ *I don't see those girl.*

★ *I ain't got noplace to go.*
★ *He don't got no more better boat.*
★ *I go five time.*
★ *Where's at the place?*
★ *He used to couldn't smoke* (he wasn't able to smoke).

Creole speakers traditionally had more education than Cajuns, and Creole doesn't contain as many grammatical "errors" as Cajun, though there is a tendency to omit auxiliary verbs, as in *She going fall soon* (She is going to fall soon), to use the present tense instead of the past *(Who tell you that?),* and to use plural for singular verbs *(Those man are coming),* among other peculiarities. Generally, Creole vowel and consonant differences approximate those of Cajun, with several important differences (such as the soft pronunciation of *r*), and the French words and phrases Creole uses are very similar to those used in Cajun. The French accent is heard among some Creole speakers, especially in New Orleans, but Southern-type speakers in Louisiana are mostly free of French influence.

Cajun seems to have given us the local pronunciation of many Louisiana town names, as well as the word *shivaree* for an elaborate noisy celebration, *shivaree* being an alteration of the French *charivari*—a word Cajuns brought to America—which meant a mock celebration with pots, pans, and other noisemakers that was originally held in medieval times to express disapproval of widows who didn't wait long enough to remarry. Creole has also contributed several words to the English vocabulary, including *lagniappe* (lan-yap), meaning a gift or bonus, the word borrowed from the Spanish *la ñapa* (gift), and used by New Orleans' Creole merchants for the gifts they gave to customers.

Today, Cajun is spoken fluently by few young people, and many of the young speak very little Cajun or none at all. Traditionally a spoken language and not a written one, it has in recent years become a language of the old, Cajun culture and language steadily eroding. A Cajun textbook published in 1977 by James Donald Faulk of Abbeville, Louisiana, set out to help correct this situation and its good sales have indicated that there is a widespread interest among Cajuns to preserve their language and way of life, which has so long resisted assimilation.

Monsignor Jules Daigle, an eighty-five-year-old Roman Catholic priest from Welsh, Louisiana, in late 1984 published the first Cajun dictionary, a 650-page volume that reflects a lifetime of studying the language in the Cajun community he serves. He insists that Cajun is not a poor linguistic relation of French and "is no more a broken language because it contains so much English" than the Romance languages, which combined Latin and other tongues. He seems to feel it his mission to revive the Cajun dialect or language, and while this may not be possible, he will at least have preserved a great part of it that might have been lost. "In my day, when everybody spoke Cajun, you made a mistake and were corrected," he says. "But when people became ashamed to speak Cajun and it was forbidden in the schools, there were fewer and fewer people able to do the correcting. . . . It would be a crime against history to let a language that has existed for 220 years, that has been spoken by millions of Cajuns, to let that language die. The Cajun people fused beautifully with the American culture. Because we were so cooperative, our language is almost gone."

America's Cockneys: Conversing in Key West Conch

The Conchs (pronounced *Conks*) of the Florida Keys speak a Southern American subdialect that is notably different from the rest of the speech of the South and even differs from the dialect of south Floridians, who were called *fly-up-the-creeks* in the mid-nineteenth century (after the popular nickname of the small green heron, *Butorides virescens,* native to Florida).

The Conchs are so named because as the first English fishermen to settle in the Keys they depended on the conch (*Strombus alatus,* a spiral-shelled gastropod) for food and even used its giant shell as a trumpet to communicate from shore to ship and from key to key. The descendants of a band of Cockney Englishmen called the Eleutherian Adventurers who migrated from London to Bermuda in about 1649 in search of religious and political freedom, they came to the Florida Keys early in the nineteenth century from Eleuthera in the Bahamas. Once in the Keys they made their livelihood from fishing, wrecking, and gathering sponges. From the beginning, the Conchs built homes on both sides of Key West and tried to keep separate from other settlers, their close family ties binding them together. Their aloofness helped the Conch dialect last as long as it has. Influenced by Bahamian English, Cuban Spanish, and Cockney as well as Southern American and General American dialects, their speech contains words and expressions found nowhere else in the area. A dishcloth, for example, is called a *natural sponge* by the Conchs. Their umbrella is a *bumbershoot,* and a closet in their homes is a *locker.* A Conch stove is a *grits box,* and they regard the pantry as the *kitchen safe.* Conchs call any native of Nassau a *saw.*

In Conch speech, as in Cockney speech, the *w* and *v* are confused, a *vest* becoming a *west* and *visit* becoming *wisit.* An *a* before *g* is pronounced like short *i,* so that *rag* is transformed into *rig* and *bag* into *big.*

The Conchs treat the *h* in the Cockney way, saying *orse* instead of *horse* and pronouncing *hell* as the letter *l.* Other special characteristics are the frequent use of *ain't* instead of *haven't* or *won't,* and the omission of *ed* from verb past-tense forms ("The orse jump the fence yesterday").

Spanish idioms tend to be translated literally by the Conchs; *"Cuántos años tiene?"* for example, becomes "How many years you got?" not "How old are you?" They pronounce *i* in the Spanish manner, particularly in the names of people—Olivia becomes *Oleevia* when addressed by a Conch.

Among other British dialect features in Conch talk is the use of the *i* (as in *pit*) in unstressed suffixes spelled *ace, ain, ate, ed, en, es, ess, et, ice, id, in, ip, is, ist, it, ite,* and *uce. Palace* is thus pronounced *palis* and actress pronounced *actris.* The same *i* is often used, in the British way, in medial syllables spelled with *e, i,* or *y,* including words like *seventy, furniture, anywhere,* and *Florida.*

Conchs use the *a* of *father* for *ar* in words such as *cigar, park,* and *car,* just as Southern Americans characteristically do, but which is also a characteristic of British speech. There are a number of other similarities to Southern talk, just as there are to British and General American dialect features.

Conch talk lives on in the Florida Keys, but appears to be slowly disappearing, as is the case with other island languages, including the Ocracoke dialect of the Outer Banks of North Carolina and the island dialects of Bonac and Isleboro examined above. Recent studies have shown that among younger people it is giving way to Southern and General American English, but that it will be around for a long while in the speech of old and middle-aged Conchs, with the older inhabitants using the British or Cockney dialect much more than all the others.

Speaking Spanglish

Spanglish is a linguistic paella of English and Spanish that is also known as Tex-Mex and Texican, though it is not confined to the state of Texas. While Spanglish is most audible in the American Southwest, where a theatrical company called the Bilingual Foundation of the Arts presents plays in Spanish, English, and Spanglish, it is heard in all regions where there are large concentrations of Hispanic people, notably California, Miami, the Gulf Coast, Puerto Rico, and the New York City area. Using both English and Spanish words, it is generally pronounced as if it were Spanish.

Because the term *Hispanic* is a catchall one applying to many different peoples, including whites, blacks, and Indians, from many different countries, the Spanish contribution to the dialect is hardly uniform. One language teacher has pointed out, for example, that "the translation by someone from a country bordering the Caribbean for 'I am waiting for a bus' might be taken by a native of South America's Andes region to signify 'I am waiting for a small child.' " Hispanics in America came mainly from Mexico (60 percent), and most live in Texas or California (51 percent), but large numbers also hail from Puerto Rico, Cuba, the Dominican Republic, El Salvador, Colombia, Venezuela, and other Central and South American countries. There are more similarities linguistically between these 17.5 million Hispanics than there are differences and the Spanglish they often speak is understood by them all.

It seems inevitable that the new linguistic amalgam called Spanglish will be around for a long time, if only because America's Hispanic population is growing more rapidly than any other segment of the population, leading some analysts to believe that Hispanics will replace blacks as the nation's largest minority group by the year 2000—with some 35 million people, about 12 percent of the total of all U.S. residents.

It is true that many Spanglish words—for example, *lonche* (lunch)—are neither standard English nor Spanish, prompting several observers to call the dialect "a debasement of both tongues." But other experts suggest that the borrowing of words from English and the transformation of some of them into Spanish verb forms—Spanglish verbs are conjugated in the Spanish fashion—are proof of the strength of both tongues. "To be able to take an American word and conjugate it in Spanish takes a facility that attests to the speaker's knowledge of the languages," says Dr. Guadalupe Valdes, a New Mexico State University linguist.

Some see Spanglish as a developing language or a regional dialect, but it is more likely a kind of class dialect, like Black English, that transcends regions. There is a lot of alternating between Spanish and English in the dialect. A speaker might say, for example, *Fuí al cine last night* for "I went to a movie last night," or *¿Dónde está el vacuum cleaner?* for "Where is the vacuum cleaner?" Or, leaning more to the English side, a speaker might ask *Do you have cold cerveza?* instead of "Do you have cold beer?" In any case many Anglo storekeepers in many large U.S. cities barely miss a beat in replying to inquiries from customers like *¿Dónde está la pantyhose?*

Often the easier word to say wins out in the contest between English and Spanish in Spanglish; dates, for example, are usually said in English, a date like 1945 much less cumbersome to say than *mil novecientos cuarenta y cinco*. Sometimes English words are so common in Spanglish that Hispanic speakers believe the words *are* Spanish. "I've heard of Puerto Rican kids asking their parents, "How do you say 'ice cream' in English?" says the head of an Hispanic studies program in New York City.

In the past, American English alone has borrowed more than five hundred words from Spanish, these including *filibuster, buffalo, vigilante, bronco, rodeo,* and *cinch* (see the long list following Chapter 1). Contrary to popular belief, *spic,* an offensive, derogatory word often applied to Spanish Americans, is not a corruption of the word *Spanish;* first recorded in 1915, it is thought to be a shortening of *spaghetti,* reinforced by the phrase *No spika da English* often spoken by Italian immigrants and mocked by bigots.

In any case, the Spanish of the mostly poor and uneducated people who speak Spanglish may also enrichen the English language. Spanish terms already adopted into Spanglish include *la ley* (the law) for the police and *lechuga* (which literally translates as "lettuce") for money. Among the many assimilated English loan words in the dialect are *jonrón* for home run (and its verb form *jonronear,* to hit a home run); *noquear,* to knock out (in boxing); *daime* (dime); *ganga* (gang); *fullar* (to fool); *troca* (trunk); *kiklar* (to kick); and *bikla* (bicycle). *Bombo* means a drunk, from the idiom *to be bombed,* or very drunk. Some of these adaptations, especially those from sports, have a long history in Latin American countries.

The new verb forms found in Spanglish are often obvious ones like *shopear* (to shop) and *mopear* (to mop up), but can be clever constructions such as *gorileando* (to bully), from the American slang *gorilla* (thug). *¿Quieres monkear?* is Spanglish for "Do you want to hang out?" *monkear* borrowed from the American slang "to monkey around." Sometimes, however, a borrowing can cause confusion. *Embarrassar,* for instance, from the American *embarrass,* means to embarass in Spanglish, but sounds the same as the Spanish *embarazar* (to become pregnant).

An ancient slang called Caló, from the argot of Andalusian Gypsies but transferred over the years to the barrios of Mexico and the American Southwest, is among the older influences on Spanglish. But new forms dominate the dialect, and these are added to every day. *Simon,* pronounced *see mon,* and meaning "see, man," is a good example; it comes from the West Indian black dialect *see, mon* meaning the same. Another recent one is *Tio Taco,* literally an "Uncle Taco" but the Spanglish equivalent of the black dialect term Uncle Tom, for someone who kowtows to whites.

Though grammarians argue that Spanglish is "corrupt" and "illiterate" and fear of it has spread even to other countries—Mexico, for one nation, has initiated a campaign to discourage its use—the dialect is very much a reality that cannot be avoided. Variations of it are increasingly used as a common conversational mode in areas with heavy concentrations of Hispanics, and America will certainly be hearing a lot more of it in years to come—whether reading it on signs like *El Super Taco* and *Hamburguesa Doble con Queso* (a double cheeseburger), or hearing hybrid expressions like *croseando la calle* for "crossing the street" and *muy star wars* for "very modern."

Talkin' Texian

"Texian" is another variety of Southern speech (see Chapter 4), no matter what most Texans may tell you—at least that variety of Texian spoken in the eastern half of the state. Western Texian, featuring the Western drawl, is, like other Southwestern and Far Western speech, more strongly influenced by General American. The Western Texas drawl extends the slight *uh* glide of General American speech (where *uh* is added before *l* and *r* in a stressed syllable, as in *shoo-UHr*, sure) to many more sounds. School, for example, is *skool* in the Middle West but pronounced *SkOOuuhl* in the Western drawl. This same *uh* drawl is added after, among other letters, *a, ow,* and *eh,* examples being *Auhlbert* (Albert), *fowahl* (fowl), and *Eauhlmer* (Elmer). The Western drawl of West Texas is more restrained and not so musical as the Southern drawl of East Texas. While it is an unhurried speech, the Western drawl doesn't suggest "relaxed laziness," suggesting cogitation, or weighing one's words, rather than mere indolence. Many ranching terms enrich this dialect and one hears remarks like "It's such a fur piece you've got to ride a pregnant mare to get back."

Technically, the Southern dialect of East Texas is of both the twangy lilting South Midland variety of Northeast Texas and the Southern plantation variety heard in Southeast Texas. Of course these two dialects, and that of West Texas, mingle throughout the state, but the East Texas dialect influenced by Southern and Mountain speech (see Chapters 4 and 5), and to a much smaller extent by General American, is the typical speech of Texas. Nowhere in America is there a more effortless speech, one more relaxed in delivery. East Texian is distinctly nasalized with a slow tempo and is intoned almost monotonously. Its vowels are held long, and the first syllables of words are often accented, especially in short words. Speakers are apt to speak rather too loud, for aliens, throughout the great breadth of the Lone Star State.

"There is something good and something bad of every land"

in Texas, as an old saying puts it, for the state was settled by immigrants from many lands, including Mexicans, Germans, Czechs, and Northerners, as well as people from the Southern states, while recently there has been a massive invasion of Yankees. Spanish ways and words are common in a state founded by Spaniards; even something as basic as the famous *ten-gallon hat* that Texas cowboys wore in days past has its roots in the Spanish word for braid, *galón*—because the wide-brimmed hats worn by cowboys were originally decorated with a number of braids at the base of the crown. The nearest thing in Texas today to a ten-gallon hat is called a *Stetson,* every red-blooded male Texan owning at least one of these. This basic Texan hat shows Yankee influence. The *Stetson* was invented by Philadelphian John Batterson Stetson, who had to travel west because of poor health at the time of the Civil War. While out West it occurred to him that no one was manufacturing hats suited to the cowboy, and on his return to Philadelphia in 1865 he went into the hat business, specializing in Western-style headgear. The wide-brimmed, ten-gallon felt hats he manufactured immediately became popular with cowboys. They have been called *Stetsons* or *John Bs* ever since, and the John B. Stetson Company is today one of the world's largest hat manufacturers.

In more recent times Spanglish, a lively combination of Spanish and English, has become so prominent a way of speech throughout Texas that it is also known as Tex-Mex and Texican. From one end of the state to the other there are so many slight variations in ways of speaking that Texans can't even agree on the pronunciation of Texas—the leading contenders are *Tex-siz* and *Tex-sis,* with the Yankee *Tex-suhs* a distant third. Dyed-in-the-wool Texans hold stubbornly to their pronunciations, too. A visiting Britisher told one rancher: "The Hereford bull, who comes originally from my own part of the world, does not pronounce himself Hearford, as you seem to suppose, but Herreford." "Is that right?" the rancher replied. "Wal, he pronounces himself Hearford on my ranch."

Hospitable Texans *do* still say *Y'all all come!* Stetson tipped over his eyes, the typical Texan will say things like *Kin ah carry you home?* for "Can I give you a ride (or lift)?"; *Ah need to visit with you,* when he means he wants to chat with you on the phone; and *Kin ah hep you* for "Can I help you?" One lady who worked for Air France and was taught to say *France* like a Frenchwoman habitually answered the phone, "Air Frawnce, kin ah hep you?"

Texans particularly like to pronounce the *en* sound their own way. They don't cotton to it being pronounced *en,* so when they talk about the *awl bidness* they might mention the *innerjy crunch* or the *free interprise system.* By the same system *ten* becomes *tin, twenty* is *twinny, cent* is *cint, went* is *wint, friendship* becomes *frinship, tennis* becomes *tinnis, temperatures* are *timperatures, entertainment* is *innertainment, Wednesday* is *Winsdy* and—to put an *inding* to this— *Kennedy* Airport is *Kinnidy* Airport.

The rule in Texas is to say *heidi* (howdy) to anyone who says *heidi* to you. *Thank you* is pronounced *thang cue.* Other *wards* with pronunciation unique to the *airs* (ears) of most *Markins* (Americans) include *watt* for *while, hem* for *him, blond* for *blind, aint* for *aunt, main* for *mean, day-ins* for *dance, rum* for *room, drouth* for *drought, suede* for *sweet, bob wahr* for *barbed wire, prod* for *proud* and *small* for *smile.* The *Lard* only knows how many more such specimens there are from Hico (pronounced *Hy-co*) to Houston.

Many common words with the *ay* vowel sound are pronounced with *eh* in Texian, including *nehkid* (naked) and *eht* (ate). The *aw* sound is heard in words like *dawg* (dog) and *cawst* (cost); the long *i* is generally pronounced as *ah,* as in *fahuh* (fire) and *hahuh* (hire); and many Texans pronounce the *oo* sound as *oh,* as in *poh* (poor) and *shoh* (sure). Among consonant changes from General American the *d* is often dropped after *n,* as in *wunner* (wonder); the participial *ing* is generally pronounced *in,* as in *sittin* (sitting); and the *n* is often dropped completely, as in *kawfuhdis* (confidence), being replaced with a distinctly nasalized *aw,* which one speech teacher calls among "the main reasons for the extreme nasality in Texas speech." There are, of course, many exceptions but both vowel and consonant pronunciations in Texian are more similar to those of Southern speech than any other.

The Southern *yawl* of *you-all* is just as popular in Texian as in Southern speech. *All,* in fact, is also used after the interrogative pronoun *what* ("What-all did you do yesterday?") and *who* ("Who-all is coming?"). *Is all,* a short form of *that's all,* is commonly added to the end of sentences, as in "He just wants some meat, is all." Sometimes unheard questions are replied to in Texian with *Says which?*, a practice similar to the Black English *Say what?* Other typical Texian usages are indicated in these sentences:

* ★ She's the hell-raisingist woman I know.
* ★ I'm about to rustle up some grub (prepare some food or a meal).
* ★ I reckon he's went (gone) to Houston.
* ★ He bought some blinky (sour) milk.
* ★ I might would (I may) do it.
* ★ She put a big pot in a little one (outdid herself entertaining).
* ★ He done went there.
* ★ Did you seed (see) that?
* ★ She give him the gate (divorced him).
* ★ I'll wait on (wait for) you.
* ★ He wouldn't go 'thout (contraction of *without* used in place of "unless") they took the train.
* ★ Don't pay him no nevermind (attention).
* ★ She's about to law (sue) him.
* ★ Ain't nary a one (nobody) coming.
* ★ I might could do that.

Sadly, a lot of Texans feel as embarrassed about their dialect as New Yorkers do about Brooklynese. An amusing article by *New York Times* Houston bureau chief Robert Reinhold, to which I owe several of these examples of Texian, reports Fred Tarpley, a language and literature professor at East Texas State University, as saying, "Unfortunately, Texans have a great inferiority complex about their language [though] this is an honorable dialect that we speak for historical reasons; I feel we need to extend the Texas pride to speech." As Jan Morris has noted, "One feels the pull of metropolitan life" in Texas, as one does all over the world, "like some massive unseen magnet over the horizon." While the rural areas are fighting a strong holding action, the big *innernational cities* in Texas are increasingly becoming merely international, losing a lot of their Texian flavor. Observers have reported that Houstonites, in particular, a breed of archetypal doers, are beginning to sound like everybody else, in both pronunciation and vocabulary, even eliminating such historic Texan redundancies as *cashmoney.* Few people shout *Yahoo!* in Houston anymore, but elsewhere there are still nice euphemisms, like *winter Texans* for senior citizens, places with names like *The Crazy Woman Hotel* at Mineral Falls, statues like the one to the cow called *MOO-LAH (42 gallons annually)* at Stephenville, and local football teams with names like the *Itasca Wampus Cats,* the *Mesquite Skeeters,* and the *Hutto Hippos.* The rural rearguard and others proud of their heritage are holding the Alamo and it will be a long time before they surrender, if ever. As a memorial to their valiant efforts, and a fitting end for *American Talk,* following is an All-American sampler of colorful ripsnortin' ripsniptious words and phrases that Texans and other Westerners have given to the English-speaking world.

Words from the Wild and Woolly West

★

DEADMAN'S HAND

James Butler ("Wild Bill") Hickok, only thirty-nine, had come to Deadwood, Dakota Territory, in 1876 to make a stake for the bride he had just taken, but lawless elements, fearing his appointment as town marshal, hired gunman Jack McCall to assassinate him, giving McCall three hundred dollars and all the cheap whiskey he needed for courage. Wild Bill was playing cards in the No. 10 saloon (his back to the open door for only the second time in his days of gunfighting) when McCall sneaked in and shot him in the back of the head, the bullet passing through his brain and striking the cardplayer across the table from him in the arm. Hickok's last hand, which he held tight in a death grip, was aces and eights, which has ever since been called the *deadman's hand.* McCall, freed by a packed miner's court, was later convicted by a federal court, his plea of "double jeopardy" disregarded on the ground that the miner's court had no jurisdiction. He was later hanged for his crime.

★

SON OF A BITCH STEW

You use "everything but the hair, horns, and holler," according to one recipe for *son of a bitch stew,* commonly made on chuck wagons in the old West. All the innards of a steer, including hearts, brains, and kidneys, had to be included in the stew, but the most indispensable ingredient was guts (tripe). This inspired the old saying "A son of a bitch might not have any brains and no heart, but if he ain't got guts he ain't a son of a bitch."

★

CASH ON THE BARRELHEAD

The origins of this expression are most likely in the makeshift saloons on the American frontier more than a century ago, which were often no more than a room in a log cabin with a barrel serving as both booze container and counter. Any customer who wanted a smack of tarantula juice, or any rotgut likely to make him brave enough not to pay, was required to put down *cash on the barrelhead,* or counter. No credit was extended. The coffin varnish might embalm a customer.

★

HAIRY MONEY

Hairy money? Money with hair on it? Yes. Hairy money was a term for beaver pelts in the American fur trade out West, the skins worth a lot of money and even used as a medium of exchange.

★

BETWEEN A ROCK AND A HARD PLACE

In days past, if one was badly in need of money, almost bankrupt, he or she was said to be *between a rock and a hard place.* This expression was probably born in Arizona during a financial panic early in this century, but over the years its meaning changed. It came to mean being in a very tight spot, on the horns of a dilemma in making a hard decision. The words do lend themselves best to this last definition, for wherever one turns in making the decision there is rock or something as hard or harder than rock.

★

CATWAGON

Cat was slang for a prostitute as far back as 1401, when a poem of the day warned men to "beware of cats' tails." Though this term associating the cat and commercial sex is obsolete, the connotation hangs on in the word *cathouse* for a bordello, crib, fancy house, whorehouse, or sporting house. A *cathouse* is usually a cheap bordello and even cheaper *cat wagons* pulled by horses brought harlots thataway when the West was being won.

★

CHICKEN RANCH

Unlike most sexual euphemisms, this synonym for a brothel takes its name from a real place. The original Chicken Ranch was a bordello in Gilbet, Texas, early in this century, so named because poor farmer clients often paid for their visits with chickens.

★

CHICKEN FEED

Chickens were fed grain too poor for any other use by American pioneers and these pieces of poor-quality grain had to be

218 ★ American Talk

small so the chickens could swallow them. This obviously suggested the contemptuous term *chicken feed* for small change (pennies, nickels, and dimes) to riverboat gamblers fleecing small-town suckers. The first mention of the expression is in *Colonel (Davy) Crockett's Exploits* (1836): "I stood looking on, seeing him pick up chicken feed from the green horns." By extension *chicken feed* has come to mean any small or insignificant amount of money, and even (rarely today) misleading information deliberately supplied or leaked by a government to spies employed by another government.

★

MAN FOR BREAKFAST

Lawlessness often went unpunished in the American West, and people reading their morning newspapers had their *man for breakfast,* or murder, every day. The expression persisted from the late nineteenth well into the twentieth century. Though the phrase isn't used today, we, too, have our man (or woman, or child, or all three) daily for breakfast.

★

DOING A LAND-OFFICE BUSINESS

Before the Civil War, the U.S. government established "land offices" out West for the allotment of government-owned land in territories just opened to settlers. These offices registered applicants, and the rush of citizens lining up mornings long before the office opened made the expression *doing a land-office business* (a tremendous amount of business) part of the language by at least 1853. Adding to the queues were prospectors filing mining claims, which were also handled by land offices. After several decades the phrase was applied figuratively to a great business in something other than land, even, in one case I remember, to a land-office business in fish.

★

FROZEN WORDS

An old story from the Texas Panhandle tells of a winter so cold that spoken words froze in the air, fell entangled on the ground, and had to be fried up in a skillet before the letters would re-form and any sense could be made of them. The idea is an ancient one, though, used by Rabelais and familiar to the Greek dramatist Antiphanes, who is said to have used it in praising the work of Plato: "As the cold of certain cities is so intense that it freezes the very words we utter, which remain congealed till the heat of summer thaws them, so the mind of youth is so thoughtless that the wisdom of Plato lies there frozen, as it were, till it is thawed by the refined judgment of mature age."

★

TEXAS

Texas takes its name from a Caddo Indian word meaning "friends or allies" (written variously *texas, texias, tejas, teyas*) and applied to the Caddos by the Spanish in eastern Texas, who regarded them as friends and allies against the Apaches.

★

TEXAS LEAGUER

A cheap hit that falls between the infield and the outfield in baseball is called a Texas leaguer because back in 1886 three players who had been traded up to the majors from a Texas league team enabled Toledo to beat Syracuse by repeatedly getting such hits. After the game, the disgusted Syracuse pitcher described the hits as just "little old dinky Texas leaguers" and the name stuck.

★

WEARING CALLUSES ON HIS ELBOWS

Western Words (1961) by Ramon F. Adams defines *wearing calluses on his elbows* as "spending time in a saloon." Similarly, an *elbow bender,* another Westernism, means a "drinking man."

★

MAVERICK

Texas lawyer Samuel Augustus Maverick (1803–70) reluctantly became a rancher in 1845 when he acquired a herd of cattle in payment for a debt. Maverick, a hero who was imprisoned twice in the war for independence from Mexico, eventually moved his cattle to the Conquistar Ranch on the Matagorda Peninsula, fifty miles from San Antonio. But he was too involved in other activities to prove much of a rancher. When in 1855 he sold out to A. Toutant de Beauregard, their contract included all the unbranded cattle on the ranch. Since careless hired hands had failed to brand many of Maverick's calves, Beauregard's cowboys claimed every unbranded animal they came upon as a *Maverick*. So, apparently, did some of Maverick's neighbors. Though Sam Maverick never owned another cow, his name soon meant any unbranded stock, and, later, any person who holds himself apart from the herd, a nonconformist, like his grandson, Maury Maverick, who coined the word *gobbledygook,* following.

★

GOBBLEDYGOOK

Gobbledygook means obscure, verbose, bureaucratic language characterized by circumlocution and jargon, and usually refers to the meaningless officialese turned out by government agencies. The late Representative Maury Maverick coined the word in 1944, when he was chairman of the Smaller War Plant Committee in Congress. Maverick had just attended a meeting of the committee, at which phrases such as "cause an investigation to be made with a view to ascertaining" were rife. He wrote a memo condemning such officialese and labeled it *gobbledygook,* later explaining that he was thinking of the gobbling of turkeys while they strutted pompously. *Bafflegab, jargantuan, pudder,* and *pentagonese* are all synonyms. George Orwell's "translation" of Lord Nelson's immortal phrase "England expects every man to do his duty" is a good example of gobbledygook: "England anticipates that, as regards the current emergency, personnel will face up to the issues, and exercise appropriately the functions allocated to their respective occupational groups."

★

A SEVEN-SIDED SON OF A BITCH

A one-eyed man or woman: "each having a right side and a left side, a fore side and a back side, an inside and an outside, and a blind side." The Western expression originated in the late seventeenth century and lasted until the early twentieth century.

★

THE WILD AND WOOLLY WEST

First came the *wild West,* recorded in 1851 and so called because the American West was relatively lawless compared to the "civilized" East. Some thirty years passed before the more alliterative *wild and woolly West* was invented by some unknown poet, the *woolly* in the phrase perhaps referring to uncurried wild horses, or the sheepskin chaps some cowboys wore, or perhaps to the bragging of those hippies on horseback in a popular song:

> *I'm a woolly wolf and full of fleas,*
> *I never be curried below the knees—*
> *And this is my night to howl!*

COWPOKE, COWPUNCHER

Cowpokes and *cowpunchers* were originally cowboys who poked cattle onto railroad cars with long poles. The terms, first recorded in 1880, were soon applied to all cowboys.

★

BUCKAROO

While some scholars derive *buckaroo* (cowboy) from the Pidgin English *buckra* (white man), it is more likely a corruption of the Spanish *vaquero,* meaning the same. The Americanism is first recorded in 1827.

★

HORSE SENSE

Horse sense (good plain sense) comes from the American West, about 1850, inspired by the cowboy's trusting, intelligent little cow pony, trained even to do a good deal of cattle-herding work without directions from its rider.

★

GIT ALONG, LITTLE DOGIE

The American cowboy has been shouting and singing *Git along, little dogie* for more than a century, but no one knows where the word *dogie* for a motherless calf comes from. Maybe it derives from "dough-guts," referring to the bloated bellies of such calves; perhaps *dogie* is a clipped form of the Spanish *adobe* (mud); possibly the cows were so small that they were playfully called *doggies* and the pronunciation changed. Since some American cowboys were black there is also the possibility that the Bambara *dogo* (small, short) is the source, or the

Afro-Creole *dogi dogi,* which means the same. Your guess is as good as any etymologist's.

★

TO KNOW ONE'S CANS

Cowboys on the range in the nineteenth century were usually starved for reading matter and often read the labels on the cook's tin cans, learning them by heart. A tenderfoot could always be distinguished because he didn't *know his cans.* The expression isn't recorded in the *Dictionary of Americanisms* but is given in Ray Allen Billington's *America's Frontier Culture* (1977). One wonders how the cowboy would have handled modern ingredients like "monosodium glutamate," etc., included among label ingredients.

★

BELLY CHEATER, BELLY ROBBER, BELLY BURGLAR

Belly cheater is an old American cowboy term for a cook, which may date back to the nineteenth century, but is first recorded as U.S. Navy slang in the form of *belly robber,* specifically referring to a commissary steward. The term has also been used for an Army mess sargeant. Another, later variant is *belly burglar.*

★

HIGH-TAIL IT

Mustangs, rabbits, and other animals raise their tails high and flee quickly when they sense danger. Trappers in the American West noticed this, over a century ago, probably when hunting wild horses, and invented the expression *to high-tail it,* to make a fast getaway on foot, on a horse, or in a vehicle.

★

BULLDOGGING

"One of the men . . . reached well over the animal's back to get a slack of the loose hide next to the belly, lifted strongly, and tripped. This is called 'bulldogging.' " So did an early writer describe the way cowboys wrestled steers to the ground in the American West. They often, however, leaped from their horses and twisted the cow's neck, flipping it over. Neither method suggests the way bulldogs fought bulls when such cruel contests were held in England—for the bulldog seized the bull's nose in its mouth. Esse F. O'Brien's *The First Bulldogger* (1961) therefore suggests that a black cowboy named Bill Pickett is responsible for the word—Pickett would sink his teeth into a bull's nose while wrestling it to the ground, his method responsible for the name of the more conventional method!

★

SNUFFING THE CANDLE

I've never seen the practice depicted in a Western film, but *snuffing the candle* was a genuine entertainment on the American frontier. The term is recorded as early as 1838 and referred to a frontier amusement in which incredibly accurate riflemen snuffed candles with bullets as a test of marksmanship. Some (using either rifles or pistols) were so good that they could shoot through the flames without putting the candle out.

★

SPIZORINKUM

Born on the American frontier, *spizorinkum* was originally used during the 1850s as the term for "good" hard money, as opposed to greenbacks or paper currency, but soon came to have many diverse meanings, including "tireless energy." It was possibly used so much just because people liked the sound of the word! In any case, *spizorinkum* is "an impossible combination" of the Latin *specie* (kind) and *rectum* (right)— that is, "the right kind."

★

A MIKE FINK

In days past, *a Mike Fink* was used to mean a rough-and-ready hero given to exaggeration about his exploits. Mike Fink was a real American frontier hero (c. 1770–1822), a river boatman and Indian fighter whose tall tales contributed greatly to the American folklore of exaggeration, a fact attested by the twelve or more different accounts of his death. According to one tale, he "once set his wife on fire in a pyre of leaves because she winked at another man."

★

SNOLLYGOSTER

One very rarely hears this word today, but in the nineteenth century it was a common Western Americanism, meaning a pretentious boaster. The word is probably a fanciful formation coined by some folk poet who liked its appropriate sound; it is first recorded in 1862. One early editor defined a *snollygoster* as "a fellow who wants office regardless of party, platform, or principles, and who, whenever he wins, gets there by the sheer force of monumental talknophical assumnacy." The type is still common, even if the word isn't.

★

THE GREAT AMERICAN DESERT

The idea of a Great American Desert in the West discouraged many people from settling in the region, which they thought was uninhabitable. The term *Great American Desert* was used in newspapers and geographies as early as 1834. Before this, the area, which is actually part of the fertile Great Plains, was called the Great Desert, this term recorded fifty years earlier.

★

TUCSON BED

A humorous expression from the western range that probably dates back to the late nineteenth century, a *Tucson bed*, after Tucson, Arizona, means 'Lying on your stomach and covering that with your back." Early cowboys apparently didn't think much of Tucson accomodations.

★

ARIZONA STRAWBERRIES

American cowboys and lumberjacks used this term as a humorous synonym for beans, also employing the variations *Arkansas strawberries, Mexican strawberries,* and *prairie strawberries*. Dried beans *were* pink in color, like strawberries. One wit noted that the only way these beans could be digested was for the consumer to break wild horses.

★

TO RUB OUT

To kill. George Frederick Ruxton mentioned this expression in *Life in the Far West* (1849). He claimed that the Mountain Men translated the term directly from various Indian languages. From the Mountain Men it passed on to cattlemen, who passed it along to the cities and the hoodlums it is most often associated with today.

★

GUNNYSACKER

This colorful name describes cattlemen who warred on sheepherders in the late-nineteenth-century American West. The cowmen often disguised themselves by wearing gunnysacks over their heads.

★

TONGUE OIL

In my continuing quest for synonyms for whiskey and other strong drink I've come upon *tongue oil* several times. It's a western U.S. expression dating back perhaps to the mid-nineteenth century and obviously refers to the way spirits loosen one's tongue.

★

WALKAHEAP; HEAP-WALK-MAN

American Indians of various tribes out West used these colorful names for Army infantrymen in the latter part of the nineteenth century.

★

NO-SEE-UM

Northwestern loggers still use this term, which comes from Chinook jargon or a pidgin English once spoken between loggers and Indians in the area. The *no-see-um*, also called the *punkie*, is a minute, almost invisible fly or midge of the family Chironomedae that has a terrific bie.

★

THE GRAND TETONS, MAMELLE

French voyagers early named these mountains in northwestern Wyoming the *Grand Tetons,* the "big breasts" or "big tits," because of their resemblance to a woman's breasts. For the same reason the rounded hillocks or mounds west of the Mississippi are called *mamelle,* from the French for a woman's breast.

★

CHISHOLM TRAIL

In the spring of 1866 Jesse Chisholm (c. 1806–68), a half-breed Cherokee Indian trader and government agent, drove his wagon loaded with buffalo hides through the Oklahoma Territory to Wichita, Kansas. The wheels cut deep into the prairie, providing rut marks for a route that was to become the most important and most famous of all Western cattle trails, extending from San Antonio, Texas, to Abilene and other Kansas railheads. The trail was used for more than twenty years after the Civil War, 450,000 Texas longhorns having been driven up it in 1872 alone. Remnants of the trail, celebrated in folklore and cowboy ballads like "The Old Chisholm Trail," still remain along the Santa Fe railroad line.

★

UP GREEN RIVER

When American mountain men killed a man a century ago they sent him *up Green River,* this referring not to Wyoming's

Green River but to the common Green River knives used in many a fight, so called because they were made at the Green River works on the river and stamped with that designation.

★

MESMERIZER CREEK, TEXAS

Over a century ago, a settler on the banks of this Texas waterway domesticated American bison by hypnosis, his colorful ways inspiring the colorful place name *Mesmerizer Creek.*

★

A WIDE PLACE IN THE ROAD

Truckers popularized this synonym for a very small town. But the phrase was born more than a century ago in the American West, where there were many towns so small they were not even on the map.

★

ACID TEST

Acid test dates to frontier days in America, when peddlers determined the gold content of objects by scratching them and applying nitric acid. Since gold, which is chemically inactive, resists acids that corrode other metals, the (nitric) *acid test* distinguished it from copper, iron, or similar substances someone might be trying to palm off on the peddlers. People were so dishonest, or peddlers so paranoid, that the term quickly became part of the language, coming to mean a severe test of reliability.

★

LEVI'S

The word *Levi's* has become more popular in the Eastern United States recently as a synonym for jeans, denims, or dungarees—probably due to the bright-colored styles that Levi Strauss and Company are manufacturing today. The trademarked name has been around since the gold rush days, though, when a pioneer San Francisco overall manufacturer began making them. Levi Strauss reinforced his heavy blue denims with copper rivets at strain points such as the corners of pockets, this innovation making his product especially valuable to miners, who often loaded their pockets with ore samples. Within a few years the pants were widely known throughout the West, where the name *Levi's* has always been more common than any other for tight-fitting, heavy blue denims.

★

GO WEST, YOUNG MAN, GO WEST

In America *Go west* came to stand for new life and hope instead of death with the expansion of the frontier westward. There is some controversy about who first said "Go west, young man." Horace Greeley used the expression in an editorial in his *New York Tribune:* "Go west, young man, and grow with the country." Later, as the phrase grew in popularity, Greeley said that his inspiration was John Babsone Soule, who wrote "Go West, young man" in an 1851 article in the *Terre Haute Express.* Greeley even reprinted Soule's article from the Indiana newspaper to give credit where it was due, but several writers insisted that Greeley had given them identical advice before Soule had written the words. William S. Verity said that the great editor had coined the expression a full year before Soule.

★

L' ENVOI

I hear the sound I love, the sound of the human voice,
I hear all sounds running together, combined, fused or following,
Sounds of the city and sounds out of the city, sounds of day and
night . . .
I hear the chorus, it is a grand opera,
Ah this indeed is music—this suits me.

—Walt Whitman, "Song of Myself"